Also by Christopher Russo and Allen St. John

The Mad Dog 100: The Greatest Sports Arguments of All Time

Also by Allen St. John

Clapton's Guitar: Watching Wayne Henderson Build the Perfect Instrument

THE MAD DOG

HALL OF FAME

THE ULTIMATE TOP-TEN RANKINGS OF THE BEST IN SPORTS

CHRISTOPHER RUSSO

AND ALLEN ST. JOHN

ADDITIONAL REPORTING BY MATTHEW SHEPATIN

DOUBLEDAY

NEW YORK LONDON TORONTO SYDNEY AUCKLAND

PUBLISHED BY DOUBLEDAY
a division of Random House, Inc.

DOUBLEDAY and the portrayal of an anchor with a dolphin
are registered trademarks of Random House, Inc.

The cataloging-in-publication data is on file at the Library of Congress.

ISBN-13: 978-0-385-51746-1
ISBN-10: 0-385-51746-7

PRINTED IN THE UNITED STATES OF AMERICA

10 9 8 7 6 5 4 3 2 1

FIRST EDITION

To the people who keep me on my toes: my children, Timothy, Kiera, Colin, and Patrick; and in loving memory of their grandfather, the late James Lavelle, aka "The Chief."

—CR

To Wayne Henderson, who let me watch while he reversed the curse

—ASJ

CONTENTS

ACKNOWLEDGMENTS

Christopher Russo's Acknowledgments

The ground work for *The Mad Dog Hall of Fame* was laid over more than two decades of sports talk radio. So every listener, every caller, and everyone I ever argued with about sports from Jacksonville to New York deserves some of the credit for this book.

First and foremost, a great big thank-you to Don Imus, who was the catalyst for the creation of the *Mike and the Mad Dog* show. Big thanks also to Mike Francesa, my radio partner of 17 years, and still counting, who's not only a great broadcaster but a great student of the game.

My thanks to everyone in the WFAN family: my producers, Bob Gelb, Chris Carlin, Mark Malusis, and Eddie Scozzare; program directors Mark Chernoff and Eric Spitz. Hats off to Joe Benigno—a greater Jet fan there isn't, and my buddy Eddie Coleman, who finally got to see the Red Sox win the World Series. I'm forever indebted to Joel Hollander, CEO of CBS radio, who has been a supporter and a visionary from the very beginning.

And while thousands of guests and callers on the *Mike and the Mad Dog* show helped to provide the stories and shape the opinions you'll find in this book, I'd like to give special thanks to Ernie Accorsi, Lee Corso, Dan Jenkins, Beano Cook, and Billy Packer, who gave generously of their time and expertise.

My longtime agent Sandy Montag always has my back and Patrick Cosgrove has been a loyal friend and supporter since the WMCA days. And my pal Steve Torre has always been there when I needed him.

Thanks to my father, Anthony, who taught me to love baseball, and my mother, Molly, who did the same for tennis. And last but never least, all my love and gratitude to my wife of 11 years, Jeanne.

Allen St. John's Acknowledgments

Writing a book is a team sport and I'm lucky enough to have the 1970 Knicks on my side. My editor and friend Jason Kaufman is Doubleday's unselfish superstar—think Walt Frazier without the floor-length white mink. On every great team there's a player who simply sees what needs to be done and does it. On Team Mad Dog, that's the indispensable Jenny Choi.

Matthew Shepatin, who provided the reporting for the Dogbites and bio boxes, is the reason I said, "Wow, I didn't know that" a hundred times while writing this book. And thanks to John Schweibacher, for his smart and painstaking research. The indomitable Emily Sklar and the unsinkable Karen Brown transcribed the tapes that were the foundation for this book. Intern Brian Lawshe was my go-to guy at crunch time. Thanks also to copy editor Scott Gray, who's a fine writer in his own right. When you're done with this book, read his insightful bio of one of my heroes, stat guru Bill James. And thanks to everyone at WFAN for making me feel like a member of the family at the best sports talk station in the country.

Thanks to my agent, Mark Reiter, who, as Yogi Berra might have said, made this book necessary. And finally, thanks to all of my editors, past and present, but especially my friends at *The Wall Street Journal*: Paul Steiger, Amy Stevens, Jeff Grocott, Bart Ziegler, Steve Barnes, and Sam Walker.

And finally, my wife, Sally, and my children, Ethan and Emma, are a constant source of inspiration and much, much more.

THE MAD DOG
HALL OF FAME

Introduction

What's the ultimate debate in the world of sports?

Who's great?

And who's merely good?

Who's a Hall of Famer?

And who's merely an All-Star?

Who's better?

Who's best?

These are the questions that every self-respecting sports fan comes back to again and again, the all-time classics in the world of sports. It's the argument that Mike Francesa and I debate continually on our show on WFAN in New York, and one that our callers and listeners can't ever seem to get enough of.

Why is he in and why is he not in? Would you take this guy over that guy? Which people, places and events are unimpeachably great, worthy of being spoken of in hushed tones, remembered for generations? And which ones are more like the flavor of the month?

And that's where the idea for this book came from, that one classic enduring topic of discussion. Wing by wing, I created my own personal Hall of Fame. I started out with the best athletes in each of the major sports. And I made it tough on myself by limiting each list to ten. Which means that while the Baseball Writers may have to decide whether or not Bruce Sutter is a Hall of Famer, my job was much harder. I had to decide between Ty Cobb and Lou Gehrig. Between Roger Clemens and Christy Mathewson. Between Hank Aaron and Joe DiMaggio.

It was the same in the other sports. Dan Marino or Johnny Unitas in pro football? Elgin Baylor or Shaquille O'Neal in the NBA? The choices weren't easy. There are guys I've left out who are all-time greats. Just not quite great enough. In this book I wrestled with the big questions that every sports fan has to come to grips with.

Then it was on to the great places in the world of sports. Ranking the tenth best baseball park—or the tenth best college football stadium—didn't have much juice. So I upped the ante and rolled every sport together into one giant list. Which comes first, Fenway Park or Augusta National? Can I leave out the place where my favorite team plays? (A hint: yes.) I took the same approaches for coaches—Phil Jackson or Paul Brown? Movers and shakers—Avery Brundage or Al Davis? And sports moments—Carlton Fisk's Reaction Shot or The Catch by Dwight Clark? It was fun. But it wasn't easy.

I didn't just come up with these lists off the top of my head. I thought long and hard about each list. I bounced my ideas off lots of people, got ideas from smart sports fans, former coaches and GMs, experts of every stripe. And then I did a lot of research, as I made the case for each player.

Now I know that if you're a good sports fan you've got your own lists in your head. You've got your own ideas about what constitutes greatness. And you're not going to agree with my list. You'll have your own favorites, and your own pet peeves. That, my friend, is where the fun begins. Think about each category. Write down your list. Gather your own evidence. Build your own argument. And then call your best buddy and have it out. You take Wilt? I'll take Russell.

That's what I love about sports. It gives you thrills, it gives you goosebumps, and it gives you memories. But most of all it gives you arguments. This guy is better than that guy, that guy is better than someone else. That's what this book is about. And to me, that's part of what sports is all about. Memories. Competition.

Chapter 1

The Top-Ten NBA Players of All Time

Basketball, especially pro basketball, is the ultimate individualist's game. One guy can and does make a huge difference for a team. Look at who wins championships. It's usually the team with the best player. Magic. Bird. Jordan. Hakeem. Shaq. Tim Duncan. They're all legendary players, and when a team like the Pistons sneaks in there and wins a championship, it's the exception rather than the rule. So I'm taking that into account in my rankings. Over the long term in the NBA, a team's success and the individual's success are intertwined. Everyone in this Top Ten won at least one championship, and most of the guys on the list have multiple titles. With that in mind, don't be surprised to see a lot of Lakers and Celtics on this list. In fact, there are only two guys who didn't play for one of those storied franchises at some point in their careers. So you can rant all you want about Karl Malone, Charles Barkley, and Patrick Ewing. I'm not buying it. They're not going to crack this kind of a list without at least one championship ring.

The other thing is sort of an intangible factor. The history of professional basketball is full of giants, literally and figuratively, and I think every player on this list qualifies. Call it star power. Charisma. The ability to transcend the game. Some guys were more demonstrative, some were a little more laid-back. But every one of these guys had it.

10. Diesel Powered

Want to understand Shaquille O'Neal's greatness?
Just turn on the television.

Shaquille O'Neal is a rarity in this book. You want to see most of the other athletes in this book, you'll have to go to the Hall of Fame on induction day, or maybe to some memorabilia show, where they're signing autographs and talking about the old days. The only thing they're playing these days is golf. Shaq? You can just flip on the Trinitron and catch a Miami Heat game. He's still playing, and though injured a lot, very close to the top of his game, and that's what separates him.

Now, I don't think Shaquille is as good, just from an athletic standpoint, as the three centers who are going to be ahead of him on this list—Kareem, Wilt, and Russell. Physically, obviously, he's bigger and stronger than any of them, except maybe Wilt. But I don't think he's as good an athlete. Shaq gets by with his strength. And his greatness, his dominance, is all about brute force more than basketball delicacy. He just overpowers the other guys. He's a bull in a china shop.

And he's been able to get away with that for one reason: He's really the only great center of his era. Sure, when he was young he played a little against Hakeem Olajuwon and David Robinson and Patrick Ewing. But look who he's gone up against to win his championships. Rik Smits. Dikembe Mutombo. Jason Collins. Todd MacCulloch. This is not Wilt against Russell, Willis Reed, and Nate Thurmond.

By any stretch of the imagination, I don't think he's as good as Wilt, who is the easiest comparison as far as size is concerned. Wilt had power and grace. Shaq just has power. And if I were starting a team tomorrow I might think long and hard about taking Hakeem "The Dream" Olajuwon over Shaq, but I can't put Hakeem on this list, because he lacks some other elements that Shaq has.

Here's the biggest reason why Shaq cracks my Top Ten. For every game that he has played in his career since he came out of LSU, he has been the most dominant presence in that game. Every single one. For three different franchises. Every team he played on—the Magic, the Lakers, or the Heat—he immediately made them title contenders. If you can contain Shaq, you've got a shot at winning the game. If not, no chance. That's greatness. And while you can chalk a little bit of that up to the lack of competition, you can't really blame Shaq for it.

And while his free-throw shooting is awful, it's not like it was with Wilt, where you simply can't give him the ball at the end of the game. O'Neal has quietly improved his free-throw shooting enough that the Hack-a-Shaq doesn't really work anymore. It's funny in a way, his free-throw shooting actually adds to his legend. It's kind of fun to watch an all-time great, knowing that if you were hanging out after a barbecue you could probably hit more free throws on the hoop in the driveway than he could. But name me a huge game where Shaq's free-throw shooting—or lack thereof—cost his team the game. I can't think of one.

SHAQUILLE O'NEAL

- Three-time NBA Finals MVP after leading the Lakers to back-to-back-to-back NBA titles (2000, 2001, 2002)
- Fifth all-time in playoff scoring and rebounds and third in block shots, as of April 2006
- Selected in 1996 as one of the 50 Greatest Players in NBA History
- All-time NBA leader in free throws attempted in the playoffs with 1,889
- Sixth all-time in free throws made in the playoffs, one spot ahead of Larry Bird

And Shaq is the center of attention off the court, too. He has personality. He's larger than life in more ways than one. He's funny—pretending to break down in tears when he hears that Steve Nash won the MVP instead of him. He'll make the classy gesture, like offering to pay for George Mikan's funeral. He knows that he's a little bit of a cartoon character and he has fun with that. Plus he's a real, live sheriff. When you think of NBA basketball at the turn of the millennium, you're going to think of one player, Shaquille O'Neal. That's why he makes the Mad Dog Hall of Fame.

BOUND FOR THE HALL?

Are there any other active players who could have a shot at cracking this list? To show you how tricky it is to judge a player in the middle of his career, a few years ago, you would have thought that Kobe Bryant would be the guy. He was young, he was charismatic, and he had a bunch of championships under his belt. On an age-for-age basis, he was way ahead of Michael Jordan. But then there were the legal problems he had in Colorado, and even though the charges were dropped, that had to tarnish his image. On the court, the Lakers lost a Final to the Pistons, which tarnished his legacy a little bit more. He took more shots than Dominique Wilkins ever would have. And Wilkins never had a teammate like Shaq. And worst of all, he basically ran Shaq out of town. (A) It's a dumb move—when you're playing with an all-time great player you have to learn to co-exist. (B) Shaq's had the last laugh. He took the Heat to the conference finals. As for the Lakers, they didn't make the playoffs for the first time in a million years, and Kobe looks like just another really good player on a pretty bad team even though he scored 81 points. Now maybe he bounces back with Phil Jackson . . . or maybe not.

That's why I'm not ready to go crazy about LeBron James just yet. He's an incredible athlete and he does some things on the basketball court you've never seen before. But he's 21 years old and in his first couple of seasons he never played a playoff game, much less won a championship. He's got a long, long way to go. Or to put a more positive spin on it: He's got the physical tools to be one of the game's all-time greats; let's see what he can do with them.

The other guy you've got to consider? Tim Duncan. He's not flashy, and he doesn't transcend the game the way most of these other guys do. And he's not really electric, the way a lot of other players are, the one player on the floor you can't take your eyes off of. But he won back-to-back MVP awards and he's got three championships and there's no reason to think he couldn't get a couple more.

9. Mr. Clutch

Game's on the line?
Jerry West's the guy you want to take the shot.

It's 98-97 in Game 7 of the NBA Finals. Down by a point. Three point six seconds on the clock. The next shot wins it—or loses it. Who do you want to take that shot? If I'm drawing up a play for the jumper to win the game, I'm going to try to get the ball to Jerry West.

In my opinion, he is the greatest clutch shooter of all time. And as far as my Hall of Fame is concerned, he is kind of representing all the pure shooters out there, the guy who did his damage from the perimeter, who could shoot that perfect, elegant 25-footer with the game on the line and a hand in his face. Reggie Miller. Rick Barry. Glen Rice. Maybe Ray Allen. But, of course, West is far better than any of those guys.

Why isn't Jerry West higher on this list? Simple. He's only got one ring. Even Wilt's got two rings. A couple of good bounces and the Lakers would have beaten the Celtics a time or two, like 1962 when Frank Selvy missed that wide-open jump shot at the end of regulation in Game 7 in Boston. Jerry West's Lakers would have won the title. But Selvy didn't and West only won one title.

Who's the other guy I considered for this spot? West's teammate Elgin Baylor. Baylor was a tremendous player, but he's been forgotten a little bit, and part of that is about how his front office career has gone. As a GM, West went on to build the Lakers and win all of those championships, mentoring Hall of Fame players like Magic and Worthy and Shaq and Kobe. Elgin? The only time you see him anymore is when the Clippers are in the draft lottery and he's picking some 17-year-old high school kid with his fingers crossed behind his back.

Baylor was in a lot of ways the prototype of the modern NBA player, the guy who could go flying down the lane, playing the game above the rim. Before there was Dr. J or Air Jordan, there was Elgin Baylor. Amazing player, fun to watch.

JERRY WEST

- Second all-time only to Michael Jordan in career scoring average in the playoffs, and second to Kareem Abdul-Jabbar in total playoff points
- Named to the NBA All-Defensive First Team four times and the All-NBA First Team ten times
- When he retired in 1974, West was the only player in NBA history selected as an All-Star in each season of his career, a total of 14 times.
- His 31.2 ppg in 1969–70 was the highest average ever for a player over 30 as of the start of the 2005–2006 season.

And Baylor has better statistics than West. They both averaged 27 points a game for their careers, but Elgin pulled down a ton of rebounds, 13 a night. He once scored 71 points in a game. He scored 61 points in a playoff game, all in regulation. But if you've got to put West down a notch for only winning one championship, then what do you say about Baylor not winning any?

The Lakers never could get over the hump and win a championship when Baylor was there. They just couldn't beat Russell and the Celtics. You can say the same things about West, but he did win that one title in 1972 with a team that won 69 games—including 33 straight—and might be the best team of all time. It doesn't help Baylor's case that the year that the Lakers did win the title, Elgin had gotten hurt and Jimmy McMillian was playing. Jimmy Mac wasn't anywhere near the player that Elgin was, but he was kind of a poor man's Bill Bradley, a guy who'd get you 13, 15 points a night, and help move the ball around. Maybe it's a chemistry thing, who knows?

As far as West is concerned, you've got to give him a lot of credit for his ability to mesh with another great player, first Elgin and then Wilt. We all think of him as a shooter—he was third in career scoring when he retired—but did you know that he was fifth on the all-time assists list?

The biggest thing that puts West here ahead of Baylor is the clutch aspect. His nickname was Mr. Clutch, and it wasn't because he hated automatic transmissions. West hit as many big shots down the stretch as anyone in the history of the league. Remember that 60-foot Hail Mary with no time left on the clock against the Knicks in the NBA Finals to send the game into overtime? And old Zeke from Cabin Creek was a tough son of a gun himself—he broke his nose nine times during his career. West was a tremendous, tremendous shooter, and that's the kind of thing that can decide big games. It's just the nature of the sport. Baylor flew through the air and made you go ooh and ah, but you can't fly through the air at the end of games to win in big spots. You're gonna get fouled, you're gonna get hacked, you're gonna fall down. The 360-jam, that's something that happens in the first half. You don't win a game with a highlight-reel dunk, but you can win a game with a 25-foot jump shot. Jerry West made a ton of them during his career and that's why he's on our list.

DOGBITE: THE LOGO

You know the red, white, and blue NBA logo that you find on every jersey and basketball and press release from the league? You know who's handling the ball? Jerry West. Probably.

A reporter from LA asked the NBA to confirm this and the league played coy, telling him it's "sort of an urban myth." Who else could it be? Frank Selvy, who was West's teammate, posed in a picture once that looks a lot like the NBA logo. And a few folks believe it's Pete Maravich. As for Kevin Modesti, the reporter who asked the NBA, he has no doubt that it's Mr. Clutch who is pictured on the logo. "Put it this way: It sure doesn't look like Kareem Abdul-Jabbar."

8. Triple Player

Shoot, pass, and rebound, Oscar Robertson could do it all.

I love Oscar Robertson, but I'm going to spend more time telling you why he isn't higher on this list. There's no doubt in my mind that Robertson is the second-best shooting guard in basketball history. Jordan one. Oscar two.

Today we all go crazy about Jason Kidd or LeBron James scoring a triple-double in a game a few times a year. Oscar *averaged* a triple-double for a whole season in 1962. And he did it scoring 30.8 points a game. Here's what Red Auerbach had to say about Oscar: "He is so great he scares me." At his best Oscar was unstoppable. He was so big and strong and he'd just back you in, put his big fanny in front of you, and then he'd turn around and make that jump shot—bump, swish, score the basket. Here's what Dick Barnett of the Knicks, who spent a lot of time guarding Oscar, had to say about him: "If you give him a 12-foot shot, he'll work on you until he's got a 10-foot shot. Give him 6, he wants 4. Give him 2 feet and you know what he wants? That's right, man, a layup." Oscar was a guy who drove defenders crazy.

One of the knocks on Oscar is the same as the knock on West: not a lot of championships. But while West was in the Finals every year, losing to the Celtics, Oscar was sitting home watching the games on TV. Oscar put up phenomenal numbers but he put up those numbers for some pretty bad teams. He played for the Cincinnati Royals, and he helped make them decent, but not really, really good. They were pretty much a 40-win team during the time he was there. They'd make the playoffs some of the time, and even win a series now and again, but they were never really serious contenders for the championship, even though there were some pretty decent players on the team—Jerry Lucas, Wayne Embry, Bob Love, Happy Hairston, Jack Twyman. The NBA was an eight-team league when Oscar broke in and you had teams that were completely stacked with talent. The

Lakers had West, a Top-Ten-all-time player, and Elgin Baylor, who would be in my all-time Top 15. And then they added Wilt Chamberlain to that mix. Jerry Lucas may have been a college Hall of Famer, but he wasn't Wilt.

Oscar was the kind of guy who dominated the game for better or for worse. He'd pass you the ball, but if you missed a shot, Oscar would be wondering why he didn't take the shot himself and he'd let you know it. You'd see it in his body language. That scowl. That anger. He'd get frustrated, downright ticked off. If you were his teammate, you'd be on pins and needles a little bit trying to live up to Robertson's expectations. In that way, he was a lot more like Michael Jordan than Magic Johnson.

One thing that you like about Robertson is the way that he capped off his career. Bob Cousy became the coach of the Royals, and he tried to get Oscar to pass more. They hated each other, Oscar held out and the team finally traded him to the Milwaukee Bucks. This was the best thing that could have happened to him because he ended up playing with a young Kareem. He blended in perfectly with Abdul-Jabbar. Finally he had a teammate who was as good as he was. He wasn't going to get mad at Kareem and yell at him. And this was a pretty good team overall. You know, with Larry Costello as the coach, and Bobby Dandridge and Greg Smith playing supporting roles, they had a very nice team. That first season they won 66 games, and they won the title, sweeping the Bullets in the Finals. And the next two years they won 60 games in the regular season, and played that great Laker team really tough in the conference finals, which was probably the only time in his life Wilt was the underdog. By this time Oscar had changed his game a little. He

OSCAR ROBERTSON

- Arguably the most complete NBA player in history, the Big O averaged a triple-double for an entire season: 30.8 points, 12.5 rebounds, and 11.4 assists per game, a feat that has never been duplicated.
- Fourth all-time in NBA assists (9,887), eighth in scoring (26,710), and second in free throws made (7,694)
- Voted Player of the Century by the National Association of Basketball Coaches
- As president of the players union, his 1970 suit against the NBA resulted in free agency for NBA players, a first in professional sports.

was 32, 33 years old and he had been in the league for 11 years. He went from being a 25-point-a-game scorer to a 20-point-a-game scorer and he actually gets credit for that. He was taking fewer shots, and taking tougher shots, because he let Kareem score in the paint. You've got to give Oscar a lot of credit for this and you'd have to wonder what his résumé would look like if he'd had one other great player on his team during the early years of his career, instead of a bunch of pretty good ones.

The other reason why Oscar isn't higher on this list is that he doesn't really transcend the sport the way these other guys do. All of the other guys ahead of him played on truly legendary teams or had a larger-than-life personality. You don't have to be a big basketball fan to know who Larry Bird was, or who Wilt Chamberlain was. Oscar is a player who's most appreciated by the basketball purist, but boy could he play.

DOGBITE: WHEN IS A STAT NOT A STAT?

When Oscar Robertson averaged a triple-double for a whole season, it was front page news, right? Wrong. No headlines. No press conferences. Nothing. Even Robertson didn't notice.

In 1962 the term triple-double didn't really exist. It was what Robertson called "a bunch of numbers that nobody had bothered to crunch." Only when Magic Johnson started putting up triple-doubles in the early 1980s did reporters begin to wonder how many people had pulled off this feat and how many times.

Robertson ended his Hall of Fame career with 181 triple-doubles to Magic's 138. And if you ask the Big O, he had a harder time getting them. He said, "Magic Johnson could look right or left and see James Worthy on one side, Byron Scott on the other side. I looked to my left, and there was a guy who couldn't hit free throws. I looked to my right, and there was a guy who couldn't go to the basket." But who ever raised the level of their game playing with Oscar?

7. Old School Style, New School Hoops

If you think of Bob Cousy as a throwback,
you probably never saw him play.

If you're playing a one-on-one tournament, Bob Cousy isn't going to be your guy. He's just little bit over 6 feet tall, and he doesn't have that Allen Iverson one-step-and-he's-gone kind of quickness. He's not built like a fire plug and he can't jump.

But what he can do—and what he did do—is make other players better. Cousy was really the NBA's first great point guard, the guy who defined that all-important position. His main objective was to get the ball and set up a teammate for a basket. And he did that better than anyone ever had. He led the league in assists eight times in a row. Think about that. And if you're not blown away by his 7.5 assists per game—career-wise that ranks him just behind Mark Jackson and Muggsy Bogues and just ahead of Rod Strickland and Johnny Moore—remember, he played most of his career without the shot clock, and official scorers were much, much stingier about handing out assists back then.

And, of course, Cousy was a winner. He was really the one who got Boston's dynasty rolling. He made them a good team until Russell got there. In his seventh year, the Celtics won his first championship—their first championship—and from there, the Celtics won five more titles in a row. Aside from Bill Russell, you could argue that Bob Cousy is the greatest winner in the history of the league.

But the thing that earns Bob Cousy a place in the Mad Dog Hall of Fame is the way that professional basketball changed when Cousy became a star in the NBA.

I think that a lot of younger fans, people who didn't see him play, still kind of lump Cousy with the George Mikan–style of basketball. White guys in crew cuts and canvas high tops. Plodding basketball. 55-53 games. Not very athletic. Too long ago to count. George Mikan and the Minneapolis Lakers may have been great, but they were not fun to watch. That's what the game was like when Cousy broke into the league in 1950–51. Cousy, he was fun to watch. He was flashy, with the no-look passes, spin moves, behind-the-back assists. Cousy was amazing running the fast break. That's why he was called the Houdini of the Hardwood. His college coach, Alvin Julian at Holy Cross, thought Cousy was too flashy a lot of the time, a guy who was a little bit out of control, making the crowd-pleasing showboat move when the coach thought he should have just thrown a bounce pass. It got so bad that he thought about transferring. That ended when Holy Cross was losing badly to Loyola at the Boston Garden and the crowd started chanting "We Want Cousy." When Julian brought him in Cousy scored 12 points in five minutes, including the game win-ner—a behind-the-back dribble that set up a left-handed hook shot.

Even Red Auerbach wasn't impressed with Cousy at first. He drafted a center, Chuck Share, ahead of him, saying "Lit-tle men are a dime a dozen. I'm supposed to win, not go after local yokels."

But Cousy, who came to the Celtics in an expansion draft, kept right on playing the game his way, and basketball was very different by the time he left. A lot more athletic, a lot more fast breaks, a lot more showmanship. And Cousy was one of those guys who was able to be successful in two eras. Sure he had early success against the George Mikans and Dolph Schayeses. But he also won an MVP late in his career, in 1957. And in 1960–61, Cousy was first-team All-NBA with Wilt Cham-berlain, Bob Pettit, Elgin Baylor, and Oscar Robertson. To show you how he spans the generations, Cousy played with John Havlicek, who played against Julius Erving at the end of his career. One degree of separation from Bob Cousy to Dr. J, that's it.

You can sum up Bob Cousy's legacy in four words: He changed the game. More than just about any player on this list, he changed the way basketball was played. And that's the mark of a truly great player. When Babe Ruth broke in, baseball was a dead-ball game with everybody bunting all over the place. When he retired, players were scoring runs left and right. When Bob Cousy got to the NBA, guys like George Mikan were glued to the floor. When he left, guys like Elgin Baylor were flying above the rim. And as much as anyone, Cousy was responsible for that change. The ultimate tribute to Cousy's lasting influence? In 2005, the NBA MVP Award went not to a 7-foot-tall center, or some 6'8'' small forward whose hang time you can measure with a calendar. It went to Steve Nash, a point guard, who hit some tough shots, ran the fast break superbly, and made his teammates better. In short, a guy who played a lot like Bob Cousy.

DOGBITE: COUSY'S CLOSE CALL

Bob Cousy was at the station last year and we talked about the old-time days and everything. What does he remember most? All those championships, right? No. What he remembers most of all is that Frank Selvy was his man in Game 7 of the 1962 Finals. In Cousy's eyes, it drives him nuts to think of his career if in fact that shot had gone in. He won NBA championships, was the MVP, all-NBA, won a college championship at Holy Cross. He won championships with Russell and played against Wilt. But the fact that he doubled the wrong guy, got there late, and left his guy open, that's what he remembers. Selvy was a great shooter, a guy who scored 100 points in a game in college, and he had a great look. The ball hit the rim, bounced up, and the Lakers blew a golden opportunity. And 45 years later the great Bob Cousy still remembers that. I don't think he would have ever been able to forgive himself if Selvy had made that wide-open shot.

6. Free as a Bird

*Larry Legend was the NBA's greatest forward . . .
and the best player I ever saw.*

L et me say two things about Larry Bird. At his very best, he was the best basketball player I've ever seen. And I couldn't stand him. I always rooted against the Celtics. And I always rooted against him. But it was futile, like rooting against Derek Jeter. You could boo all you want but he always seemed to find a way to win.

Bird's got all the things you need to make this list. First off, he played for a legendary franchise. Boston is the most historic franchise in the NBA, and Bird is the player who restored the team to its former glory. As far as I'm concerned, Bird is the second-best Celtic of all time, behind Bill Russell, and up in Boston they'd probably put him number one. That tells you something, too. There's no doubt that part of Bird's mystique is the fact that he was a kind of Great White Hope at a time when a lot of fans were losing interest in the league. I hate to say it, but the fact that Bird was white was a big part of his appeal to a lot of people, especially in New England.

In a lot of ways, I think of Joe DiMaggio when I think of Larry Bird. Joe D went out there with this work-ethic mentality, giving his best every day. He said "I want to make sure that if you've never seen me play before, I give you your money's worth." You get that same impression with Bird. He was kind of a

LARRY BIRD

- Led the Celtics to five NBA Finals in the 1980s and three championships (1981, 1984, 1986)
- He was a 12-time All-Star, a two-time NBA Finals MVP, and a nine-time member of the All-NBA First Team.
- By the time Bird retired in 1992, he held or shared 27 Celtics records.
- First player in NBA history to shoot 50 percent from the field and 90 percent from the line in the same season, and the only player to do it twice

throwback, a blue-collar, lunch-pail kind of guy. He was a great shooter, a great passer, and he could rebound. He wasn't a great defender, he didn't have the quickness or the physicality you need for that. But who's the best forward of all time? It's Bird, ahead of Elgin Baylor.

There's no doubt that Bird had a lot to do with creating the NBA as we know it today. When he came into the league, the NBA was in the absolute doldrums. There was the perception that the league had a drug problem. The games were too much about playground ball. And the game didn't have the kind of star who really captured the imagination of the casual sports fan. The championship games were tape-delayed, the NBA Finals aired at midnight. At *midnight*. Wanna watch Philly and the Lakers, Game 6? It's not over until after two in the morning on the East Coast.

The four people who get credit for making the NBA ready for prime time again are, in ascending order: Michael Jordan, David Stern, Bird, and Magic. Magic and Bird. It's hard to separate the two of them. You couldn't have custom ordered two better guys to rejuvenate the sport. They were pretty evenly matched in terms of ability. They had a rivalry that started in college. They each ended up on teams with good players and great traditions. And there was the contrast in styles. At some level, it was a race thing. Bird represented Middle America, that brand of shooting–in–your–driveway, Hoosiers kind of basketball. White basketball, in a way. Magic's game had more playground in it, but he still had that big smile and the way he passed the ball, he was an appealing figure. This was a rivalry but

---

ALMOST A WARRIOR

Think about how the NBA might have been different if Red Auerbach didn't find a loophole in the draft rules. Bird could have easily ended up as a Golden State Warrior or something. Back in 1978, a team could draft an undergraduate and let him finish his senior year in school. So with the sixth pick in the 1978 draft, Auerbach drafted Bird after guys like Purvis Short were already picked. Bird stayed in college for his senior year, almost won a title, and Red had the first building block of a championship team. Two years later Auerbach traded the rights to Joe Barry Carroll for Robert Parish and Kevin McHale and away they went.

there really wasn't a good guy and a bad guy. To have them squaring off, year after year, that put some juice back in the league.

When I say that Bird was the best player I ever saw live with my own two eyes, here's what I mean. In his heyday, at his absolute peak, I think that Bird was better than Magic. They only met a couple of times at their very best, but that 1984 Final was the decisive matchup, and Magic collapsed in that series and Bird did not. On the other hand, Magic has a better résumé. He played longer, won more championships. And he had much more of an impact on the way the game was played than Bird. We'll discuss that in a little while.

Bird just had a moxie—a nerve, an incredible appetite to win—that is just impossible to not reflect on with admiration. And I'm not a Celtics fan. Remember that Game 5 against Indiana where he got knocked out, came back, and willed his team to victory? Or that Game 7 shootout with Dominique Wilkins? Kevin McHale said, "When I'm an old man lying in bed at night thinking about Larry Bird, I'll remember that game." One time Bird shows up at the three-point-shooting contest at the All-Star Game and while they're warming up he asks, "So who's going to finish second?" You knew it wasn't going to be Larry Bird.

5. Believe in Magic

A Hall of Famer at five positions?
Magic Johnson could have done it.

Magic and Bird. Bird and Magic. History threw them together and they'll always be linked in the minds of every sports fan. Me, I think it's Magic and Bird in that order. Close. But Magic has the slight edge. In my mind, it's a little like Mantle and Mays. In the mid 1950s, Mantle was a better hitter, winning triple crowns, and the Yankees were in the World Series just about every year. But Mays had a longer and better career, and that's why I would rank him just ahead.

It's the same thing with Bird and Magic. Just like Mickey, I think that Bird, at his very best, was better than Magic. Take that 1984 championship series, the one time when they were both at their peak. The Celtics won in seven and Magic collapsed. So why do you put Magic ahead of Bird? The ring factor. Magic won five championships and Bird only won three. Plus he beat Bird two out of three times they met in the Finals, and that counts for something, not to mention the fact that Michigan State beat Indiana State in the NCAA Finals. In terms of the supporting casts I'd say they were pretty even. The Celtics had Kevin McHale and Robert Parish, two Hall of Fame–type players, and a bunch of very good supporting players like Dennis Johnson (who I think belongs in the Hall of Fame), Danny Ainge, and even Bill Walton for a while. The Lakers had Kareem, who, at his best, was better than anyone that Boston had, but

MAGIC JOHNSON

- Led the Lakers to five NBA championships (1980, 1982, 1985, 1987, 1988)
- Holds the record for playoff assists (2,346) and steals (358)
- All-NBA First Team nine times (1983–91)
- Magic was the first rookie NBA Finals MVP, in 1980, playing all five positions and scoring 42 points in the championship-clinching sixth game.

he was somewhat past his prime when he paired up with Magic. Worthy was a really good player, maybe a notch below McHale, and the other guys—Jamaal Wilkes, Norm Nixon, Byron Scott—were pretty much comparable to the guys on the Celtics. So I think it's a fair comparison.

The other big factor is the way that Magic changed the game. Larry Bird was kind of a Rick Barry on steroids, so to speak. He could pass, hit the outside shot, do all the little things. We'd seen it all before, maybe never quite as good as Bird, but it wasn't new. Bird just took old-school basketball and kicked it up a notch. On the other hand, you can't compare Magic to anyone before him or since. He was a 6'9" point guard, a pure pass-first point guard. In a strange way, he was probably most like Bob Cousy, but with so much more physical presence. The closest guy you've got to Magic today is Jason Kidd, and he's not really anywhere near that level. Magic was a guy who could dominate a game on a night when he didn't shoot a lot. He'd score 8 points but dish out 15 assists and grab a dozen rebounds. Bird couldn't do that.

Think about the advantage that Magic Johnson gave the Los Angeles Lakers. Either the other team was going to have to try and guard him with a point guard—a guy who was giving up seven inches and 50 pounds. Or, if they switched, that meant that Byron Scott or Worthy was going to get that mismatch, and you knew that Magic was going to find them when they got open for the jumper or the alley oop. That ability to find the open man made him a great leader. His teammates would run through a wall for him because he made them better. The Laker players didn't call him Magic, you know; they called him Buck, and that was kind of fitting. For them he was about being tough, and solid, and dependable, one of the guys. And while Magic wasn't a great shooter, certainly not as good a shooter as Bird, he did have an uncanny ability to hit the big shot.

And then there's the way it ended for Magic. Bird's career played out in a conventional way. He hurt his back, he got old, and he ultimately retired. With Magic, you had the whole AIDS scenario. We were on the air during the news conference, and it was a very dramatic moment. At that point, nobody knew as much about AIDS as they do today, and it was really thought to be a death sentence. He retired, came back for the Olympics, did a lot to raise awareness about the disease. It was one of those stories that transcended the sports page. Magic has said that if he knew then what he knows now about AIDS he never would have retired in the first place. When he came back for good, he wasn't really the same player, and coming back as a coach, that was pretty much a disaster. But Magic is a singular talent in the history of basketball.

Try this one on for size: He's the only guy who could have been an All-Star, and probably a Hall of Famer, at all five positions. Point guard, he did it. Shooting guard, he could have been an Oscar Robertson type, backing in and posting up. Could have dominated either of the forward positions, as he did for a little bit later in his career. If he bulked up a little, he could have played center and been great there. Remember how he took Kareem's place in the last game of the 1980 finals? The baby hook might have become his trademark instead of the no-look pass. Five positions. You know Bird couldn't have done that, and I don't think there's another player in history who could have done that, and that makes Earvin Johnson Hall of Fame material.

DOGBITE: WASHING AWAY THE HURT

That '84 NBA final was one of the classic NBA Finals of all time. Celtics-Lakers, seven games, back and forth, a lot like the '61–'62 finals. In Game 7, Magic did not play well. He was hoisting up jumpers. Played very badly in the game. And he was so disappointed that he and Michael Cooper just sat in the shower inconsolable. I had Magic on in 2005, and he said, "You know what? You're 100 percent right. I sat in that shower with Cooper for literally two hours, as upset as I've ever been on the basketball court, realizing I cost my team the championship." But a lesser player might not have gotten over it. Magic, however, vowed that it would never happen again, and it didn't. They came back the next year and they beat them in six games. Remember that they had never beaten Boston in a playoff series in the finals, never—and Magic believes that those next two titles stemmed from him sitting in the shower and thinking about how he blew the seventh game of that whole series against Boston.

4. The Game's Greatest Shot

Kareem Abdul-Jabbar's sky hook was utterly unstoppable.

There's one thing that you can say about Kareem Abdul-Jabbar: There probably wasn't a game in his entire career, from the time he played at Power Memorial High School, through his days at UCLA, and then in the NBA with the Bucks and the Lakers, where he wasn't the first option. And these were great teams he played on.

And whether it was Game 6 when he made a sky hook over Hank Finkel in the 1974 Finals against the Celtics, or whether it was the two free throws he made when he got fouled by Detroit in Game 6 of the 1988 Finals, Kareem always answered in the big spots. Find me a game in a big scenario where Kareem came up small. Didn't happen too often. Remember the 1985 Finals, Kareem's Lakers against the Celtics? It started out with the Memorial Day Massacre, and Kareem played badly in that first game. And he was 38 years old and everyone was saying he was through. And remember, at that point, the ghosts were very much alive for the Lakers. While LA did manage to win the title against the Sixers, that old can't-beat-Boston monkey was still very much on their backs. They had gotten beaten by the Celtics the year before, and they had lost to Boston a hundred times in the 1960s. So what did Kareem do in Game 2 of that series against Boston at Boston

KAREEM ABDUL-JABBAR

- Holds the NBA career records for most minutes played (57,446), most points (38,387), most field goals made (15,837), and most field goals attempted (28,307)
- Six-time league MVP and two-time NBA Finals MVP
- Played in 18 NBA All-Star Games
- All-time leader in personal fouls in the playoffs with 797, over 100 more than the man in second place, Dennis Rodman

Garden? He scored 30 points and grabbed 17 rebounds. He dominated the game. He single-handedly turned that series around.

And the other thing you remember is that Kareem came into the league and won the championship in his second season with the Bucks. That's huge. Even the great Oscar Robertson deferred to his obvious talent. Kareem's sky hook was simply the most unblockable shot in the history of the game. Of all the signature shots in the history of pro basketball—West's jumpers, Dr. J's slam dunks, Wilt's dipsy-do—Kareem's sky hook was not only the most beautiful, it was also the most unstoppable. He could get that shot off under any circumstances. You just could not defend it. He was a portrait of grace and agility. He was a 7'2" ballerina. Now, he wasn't the great rebounder that you would have expected given his size. With that wingspan and leaping ability and those great hands, you would have expected that he could have put up some Wilt-like numbers, averaging 20 rebounds a game. He never did that. To be a ferocious rebounder you have to get under the basket and throw an elbow and be willing to catch some, too. That wasn't Kareem's style. And while he was a good defender, it was more about him changing the trajectory of a guy's shot than swatting it into the third row. He wasn't a physical player on offense or defense, and at times guys like Moses

---

DOGBITE: LOOK AT MR. LEE

You know why Kareem wore the number 33? In honor of Bruce Lee, the martial arts star, who would have been 33 the year he died. Lee, who was only 5'7", was good friends with Kareem and taught him the keet june style of fighting. "He liked sparring with me because of my height and reach," said Kareem. "That gave me enough of an advantage to make him work a little bit."

The two became friends, and Abdul-Jabbar even had a pivotal role in *The Game of Death,* Lee's final movie. In a climactic scene, he says, "Little fellow, you must have given up the hope of living." Abdul-Jabbar, who started working with Lee when he came to Los Angeles, credits the martial arts legend with helping his strength and toughness late in his career. Think they made an odd couple? Abdul-Jabbar didn't think so: "He had a lot of the same principles as John Wooden."

Malone would bang on him and grab him and that would frustrate him. Kareem wasn't a trench warfare guy. He was an artist.

That said, it was kind of hard to root for Kareem. You respected him more than you loved him. It was even hard to root *against* him. It wasn't like the nobody-roots-for-Goliath thing with Wilt. It wasn't Kareem's size so much as his personality. He kind of kept fans at a distance and was happy to keep it that way. Wilt was a fun-loving guy—he liked fast cars and fancy houses and lots of women. Wilt was a guy's guy, so to speak. Kareem wasn't. Kareem, you got the feeling, was just as happy curled up in a chair reading a book. But when he got on the court, it was another story. Kareem owned the most unstoppable shot in the history of basketball. And that's why he's number four on our list.

3. Giant Steps

Where there's a Wilt, there's a way.

A lot of people would put Wilt Chamberlain number one on a list like this. And it's really hard to argue with the numbers. Just look at his 1962 season. He averaged 50.4 points per game, 25.7 rebounds. In any era 25 points and 12 rebounds puts you on the All-NBA team, and Wilt had those numbers by halftime. Halftime. And his career numbers—30.1 points and 22.9 rebounds—are as good as any player in history. He had 118 games of 50 points or more—that's almost a season and half. He had 65 games in a row scoring more than 30 points. Sixty-five games. When asked if Wilt was the greatest ever, Oscar Robertson said, "The books don't lie."

But despite those incredible, unbelievable numbers, I can't put Wilt any higher than third. The reasons are pretty simple. He disappeared too many times in the huge spotlight game. In Game 7 against the Knicks in 1970—this is Wilt Chamberlain, now, and he's looking around in the pre-game shoot-around and asking everybody, "Is Willis playing tonight?" This is a guy who had 45 points and 27 rebounds in Game 6. And he's looking around to see if Willis Reed is playing tonight. What is he worrying about

Willis Reed for? Willis was a great warrior, but even on his best day he was never Wilt Chamberlain. And because Wilt wasn't willing to take over the game—he shot 2 for 9 from the field—the Lakers got destroyed, with Willis hobbling around on one leg.

The previous year, in Bill Russell's last game, Game 7 at the Forum, Wilt took himself out of the game in the fourth quarter. I know he said he was hurt, but you don't take yourself out of the fourth quarter of a deciding game under any circumstances. You just don't. Forget about the Laker fans, and forget about his teammates. This angered *Russell* for a long time—"Wilt's leaving was like a misspelled word at the end of a cherished book," Russell would write. They've had this epic rivalry and it's Russell's last game ever, the seventh game of the Finals. It was almost disrespectful to back away from that one last confrontation. How do you do that if you're Wilt Chamberlain? Did Russell ever take himself out of a Game 7, fourth quarter? Did Michael Jordan ever say to Phil Jackson, "Coach, you know what—I need a blow. Give me seven minutes off"? Did he do that? No, he did not.

The year before that, in the Eastern Conference finals, Game 7 against Boston in Philly, the 76ers were the defending champs and had home court. This was the year after that epic, epic team. And Wilt, in the fourth quarter of a tight game, did not take a shot. A guy who once scored 100 points in a game did not take one single shot. Why? Wilt had never fouled out of a game in his career, and he didn't want to foul out. So he played passively, stood around watching. Now, let me get this straight. This was Game 7 of an NBA Eastern Conference final, essentially playing for the championship, against the Celtics, in your building, and you're worried about some kind of silly streak of not fouling out? Seems to me that that's actually a negative; if you don't foul out once in a while, you're not really playing defense

---

WILT CHAMBERLAIN

- Second all-time in regular-season scoring average (30.1 ppg) and first in rebounding (22.9 rpg)
- Four-time NBA MVP
- Only player in history to score over 4,000 points in a season. Michael Jordan is second, almost 1,000 points behind.
- Once made 35 consecutive shots (February 17–28, 1967)

as tough as you should. The streak Wilt should be thinking about there is winning his second title in a row. But instead Wilt was worried about his sixth foul. I say let the ref foul you out. Do you think the ref wants to be remembered as the first guy to foul Wilt Chamberlain out of a game? Absolutely not. So those three or four things in Wilt's career bother me a lot.

And then there's his free throw shooting. It wasn't just bad, like Shaq. It was abysmal, below 50 percent a lot of the time. And it got worse over time. He started out as a 60 percent free throw shooter, and by 1967 he shot 38 percent from the line. Wilt's free throw shooting was so bad that his team had the greatest offensive player of all time, but they were afraid to give him the ball in the fourth quarter because they knew the other team would foul him and Wilt would miss two free throws for every one he made. That's what happened in 1965, Game 7, Eastern Conference Finals. The inbounds pass went to Hal Greer, not to Wilt.

We've got the negatives out of the way, now it's on to the positives. The biggest one is that Wilt played on the two best teams in the history of the NBA, the 1966–67 Sixers and the 1971–72 Lakers that won 69 games, 33 straight. That's huge. And he was simply the most physically dominating

---

DOGBITE: WILT'S IMPROBABLE CENTURY

The game wasn't televised, and there's no film or videotape of it, and there were only 4,124 people at the Hershey Arena in Pennsylvania where it was played, but Wilt Chamberlain was forever meeting people who remember his historic 100-point performance against the Knicks. "I never correct them," he said. "I always let them feel like they saw it. I just say, 'So you saw it? Hey, well good. I was there too.'" Wilt had 69 points by the end of the third quarter, and soon passed his own record of 73 points in a regulation game, and the 78 points he scored three months earlier in a triple overtime loss. He scored his 100th point with 46 seconds left, and later admitted while listening to a tape of the radio broadcast, "I don't remember a single thing about this." And while Wilt credited his teammates—"It would have been impossible to score that many if they hadn't kept feeding me"—he said goodbye to his Philadelphia-bound teammates in Hershey. After dropping 100 on New York, Wilt caught a ride back to his Central Park West apartment with the Knicks.

player in the history of the game. He was huge, he was strong, he was agile. And he could handle the ball. He led the league in assists for goodness sake. That was one of those weird things—do you want a 7'4", 300-pound center leading the league in assists? Of course not. You want him to take shots and pass the ball every now and then to keep the defense honest. But it showed you what Wilt could do.

But what keeps him from being the best player in the history of the game was a lack of toughness. The greatest players all have a mean streak in them, and Wilt didn't. Russell was tougher mentally than Wilt. And no, Wilt didn't have the best supporting cast all the time—Russell's Celtics were better—but he did play with some very good players: Hal Greer and Jerry West and Gail Goodrich and Elgin Baylor and Billy Cunningham and Chet Walker. Those were guys who could play. But Wilt played for 14 years and only won two championships. Hakeem Olajuwon won that many. Shaq has already won three. Kareem won six. And that hurts him a lot on a list like this. Two or three more championships, especially if they came at the expense of Russell's Celtics, could have put him in the number one slot. But instead, Wilt's legacy will be this: He's the most fascinating figure in the history of the NBA, a giant with amazing skills and equally amazing flaws.

2. Bill of Might

Russell was a great player . . . and the greatest winner.

Bill Russell is the greatest winner in the history of the NBA, maybe even in the history of sports. He never lost a Game 7 that he played in. Ten-and-oh. Think about that.

And remember that Russell played most of his career against Wilt. And while they were both centers, there was really no comparison sizewise. Wilt was 7'4", 300 pounds. He was big enough and strong enough that he could have pushed Shaq around. Russell was much smaller—6'9", 250—and he didn't have incredible leaping ability, which would make him a kind of undersized power forward in today's NBA, a Ben Wallace type, or maybe a smaller Tim Duncan. Russell was a skinny kid from Oakland—he went to high school with Frank Robinson—and he really worked to make himself a legendary player. So Russell worked every angle. He compared himself to Wilt, and he knew that it was going to take more than strength and speed to overcome his opponent. Tom Heinsohn told me this story about the beginning of their rivalry. One of the first times Wilt ever played Russell in a game, he killed him. Destroyed him. He had 55 rebounds, breaking Russell's NBA record. Russell had dominated the NBA from the mid-fifties until the early sixties, and in comes Wilt, who just dominated him physically.

This came at a part of his career when maybe Russell's getting a little stagnant. He'd won so many titles already. He could have just rolled over and said, "The good Lord didn't make me seven feet tall and three hundred pounds. What can you do?" But he didn't. Heinsohn said that that motivated Russell to play better. It gave Russell an opportunity to use his mind, which was his great strength anyway, to combat Wilt. Here are Russell's three rules: (1) You must make the other player do what you want him to do; (2) Remember that basketball is a game of habit; and (3) You've got to have the killer instinct. With those tenets in mind, Russell went after Wilt.

Russell loved to get into people's heads. So he made friends with Wilt. They'd have dinner at Wilt's house before games. Wilt was a nice guy, almost too nice, and Russell used that to his advantage. Obviously sitting down over a steak with his rival didn't keep Russell from playing his hardest. But it did affect Wilt. So Wilt became his foil, the guy that he could play mind games with and the guy who inspired him to become a better player. Russell measured himself against Wilt in every way possible. When Wilt signed a three-year $100,000 contract, Russell threatened to retire if he didn't get paid more, so the Celtics gave him a contract for $100,001. In a lot of ways, Russell's not Russell without Wilt.

When Heinsohn ranks the centers, here's what he says. Imagine a map of the United States. Russell would be in Los Angeles—LA being the best spot. Wilt is back in Chicago. Kareem's off in Buffalo, and Shaq's in the Atlantic Ocean. That's Heinsohn, a Hall of Famer in his own right. Now, Russell never transcended the sport like some other guys—even guys behind him on the list, like Wilt and Bird and Magic. Russell was not the most famous athlete of his era. Mickey Mantle and Willie Mays were much bigger celebrities than Bill Russell.

And he didn't dominate statistically. Russell wasn't one of those guys who scored 25, 28 points a game. He averaged 15 points a game. But Russell was the ultimate winner. He's just about the smartest player in the history of the game. He'd do everything that he had to do to win that game, whether that'd be blocking a shot to a teammate or whether that would be setting up a fast break with a rebound and an outlet pass. Russell had had a tremendous supporting cast. He had Hall of Fame teammates—Bill Sharman and Bob Cousy and Sam Jones and John Havlicek and Tom Heinsohn. He had a tremendous system and the greatest coach

DOGBITE: RUSSO AND RUSSELL

Bill Russell has an interesting aura about him. About six or seven years ago I went to the Imus Teed-Off Challenge out in New Jersey. And I'm playing golf with Mike Francesa, a little three-hole thing for charity. I don't know why Russell was there, but he was. And there's Russell for three holes following us around on that golf course, watching Chris Russo hit tee shots in the woods, chips 50 feet past the cup. Bill Russell, just standing there with his big grey beard. And I found it amazing that he was there for 40 minutes, with a lot of people around, big sports fans, and nobody took advantage of this opportunity to talk to Bill Russell. Not even me. I'm so wrapped up in my little stupid golf game that I don't go up and talk to Russell.

in Red Auerbach. We understand that. But Russell had the great ability to blend in, to do what he needed to do that particular year, that particular season, that particular playoff series, that particular game, to give his team that edge. If he needed to score 25 points he could do it. If he needed to grab 25 rebounds, he'd do it. He went about his job quietly, but he was the leader of the greatest dynasty the sport had ever known. Go ask all the Celtic players if they would have won 11 championships if Wilt was on their team. The answer? No. Wilt was about stats, individual achievement. Russell was about winning.

1. Jordan Rules

Want to be the perfect basketball player?
Just be like Mike.

Be like Mike. That's what every basketball player wants to do. That's what every fan wants the guys on their team to do. Michael Jordan is really the perfect basketball player in a way, the ultimate combination of body and mind. In terms of physical skills, he had more than anyone. He could drive inside, he could nail the 20-foot jumper, he could penetrate and pass. He could rebound. He was a son of a gun when it came to playing defense. In a game of one-on-one there isn't a player ever who was going to beat Michael Jordan.

He combined those physical skills with a real killer instinct. He was like Bird and Russell, he wanted to win more than anything. But he had even better skills than either of those guys, and that was a deadly combination.

He won 10 scoring titles in his first 10 full years. He's the all-time leader in scoring average—and he stopped only a handful of games before he would have slipped below Wilt in that category. All-defensive team nine straight years that he played. There really isn't a flaw in his game on either end of the court. He was Picasso with a basketball.

Jordan's legacy was winning. Jordan won six titles, essentially in a row, and I don't think there's really any doubt that he would have found a way to beat the Rockets during those two years he was off playing baseball. Could have been eight in a row.

But it was also the way he won. He was theatrical. A kind of a hush came over the arena every time he touched the ball toward the end of the game. We all remember the way that he faked Bryon Russell out of his shorts at the end of Game 6 in Utah. Well, he did that a million times. And he had that in him from the beginning of his career. In a series against the Cavaliers, he missed two free throws in Game 4 to force a Game 5 in Cleveland. What did he do the next game? Made the game-winning shot over Craig Ehlo to win that series. Next. He had no fear whatsoever.

Now, from what we've read in a couple of books, Jordan's no saint. If you're not on his level, or he thinks that you're not hustling, he can be a bully. And you'd find him doing things you didn't like. Going out to a casino in Atlantic City between games of a playoff series.

MICHAEL JORDAN

- Five-time NBA Most Valuable Player (1987–88, 1990–91, 1991–92, 1995–96, 1997–98)
- Six-time NBA Finals Most Valuable Player
- Led the league in scoring 10 times, an NBA record; third all time in points scored
- Holds the NBA record for most consecutive games scoring in double-digits (842)
- His 63 points against the Boston Celtics on April 20, 1986, is an NBA playoff game record.
- As a member of the Birmingham Barons in 1994, it took him 354 games to hit a home run. He finished with a .202 batting average.

Losing huge amounts of money on the golf course. And his comeback with the Wizards was just a bad idea all around. But that doesn't tarnish what he accomplished, because his record was truly exemplary.

A lot of people—me included—say that Jordan's Bulls teams really weren't that good. Jordan, Pippen, maybe Dennis Rodman, and then who—John Paxson? Toni Kukoc? Luc Longley? I think that the Celtics of the mid-1980s would have destroyed them. And they didn't have to play any all-time great teams to win their titles. You don't see Charles Barkley, or Karl Malone, or Gary Payton on anyone's all-time Top-Ten list. And all that's true. But you play the teams that are in front of you. And that's what the Bulls did. He won six titles. Two three-peats. A streak of 25 out of 26 playoff series. That speaks for itself.

How intense is Michael Jordan? Here's a story from Bennett Salvatore, the great NBA ref who has officiated forever. It's a playoff game in Chicago, Game 5 against Utah, and a call goes against the Bulls. Jordan's peeved about it and he's jawing at Salvatore. Finally, Bennett has had enough. "Just keep quiet about the call. And by the way, I went to your golf store, and those balls I bought, they stink. I kept slicing them off into the woods." Jordan was getting a little entrepreneurial, and had opened a couple of high-end golf shops in the area, and Salvatore is just cracking a little joke, and Jordan gets all serious and comes back over to him and says, "So Bennett, which balls were they? The Titleist or the Wilsons?" Salvatore just cracks up. Michael Jordan will never let you have the last word.

And if you're talking about a guy who changed the game, Jordan is it. Jordan didn't save the game—you've got to give credit to Magic and Bird, as well as to David Stern, for that. But he did help bring the league to a new level from a marketing point of view. He was the biggest, most recognizable athlete of his time, and even in the years since he's retired, no one has surpassed him. He was on every magazine cover. He and Spike Lee helped Nike sell a million sneakers at a hundred bucks a pop. He sold McDonalds french fries. He sold Gatorade. Even now, ten years

---

DOGBITE: AIR APPARENT

"I was supposed to be the new Dr. J." That's what Michael Jordan said when he came into the league. Know what happened the first time they played? Jordan stunk it up. He went 4-for-17 from the field. But November 17, 1984 was the start of something bigger. It was the first night that Michael wore his Air Jordans. The new red and black sneakers violated the league's color policy so they started fining him up to $5,000 a game—which Nike gladly paid. Nike ended up selling $130 million worth of shoes the next year, and $2.6 billion in Air Jordan product all told. Like Spike Lee said in the commercial, "Must be the shoes."

later, when you say "Be Like Mike," everyone knows who you're talking about.

Bottom line, statswise Jordan compares favorably to Wilt. Winning-wise, he compares favorably to Russell. And he's a much bigger star than any of them. That, sports fans, is why Michael Jordan earns the top spot in the Mad Dog Hall of Fame as the greatest basketball player of all time.

Chapter 2

The Top-Ten Movers and Shakers of All Time

Which commish is top dog? And which owner more than gets his money's worth?

Not everybody who made a difference in the world of sports wore a uniform. You can argue, in fact, that the people who had the largest and most lasting influence on the world of sports were guys who wore suits and ties.

In this list, we're including everyone who's not on the field or the sidelines. Coaches are a separate category. In this section, we're honoring owners, commissioners, general managers, and anyone else who really made a difference in the world of sports. The movers and shakers.

And when it comes to the criteria, it's about the amount of moving and shaking as much as it is the direction. The thing these ten guys have in common is the amount they've changed the game, the indelible stamp they put on the world of sports. Almost all of them did some things you don't like. A few of them even did mostly things you don't like. But while you might disagree with some of their actions, you can't deny their impact.

10. Hey, Bud

Selig gets no respect, but he reshaped October baseball.

Bud Selig? *Bud Selig?* Yes, Bud Selig. Maybe it's just the forces of history, but there probably isn't a baseball commissioner in history who's had more things happen on his watch—both positive and negative—than Bud Selig. Think about the last 10, 12 years in Major League Baseball. A tremendous amount has happened while he's been in office. If you want to draw an analogy to a U.S. president, Bud Selig is hardly Abraham Lincoln. He's a little like Harry Truman, a guy who was there at a decisive moment, had a little bit of greatness thrust upon him.

The rap on Selig is that he's a former owner. Whereas previous baseball commissioners have at least maintained the appearance of independence—that they're only concerned about the best interest of the game—Selig is an owner's guy and that's that. When someone wants to criticize something that Bud's done, they remind you of this. The fact that he made his fortune as a used-car salesman doesn't help his reputation either.

In a sport that moves at a snail's pace when it comes to breaking with tradition, Selig has been able to get a lot done. Probably the most immediate thing is the wild card playoff system. It's been a huge deal. Huge. A lot of traditionalists, like my friend Bob Costas, thought it was a terrible idea, that it would dilute the importance of the regular season, but it's done exactly the opposite. The wild card put a lot of juice back in the pennant races. A team like the Florida Marlins can get off to a bad start, drop 10 games behind in their division, but with that wild card out there, they keep plugging because they've still got something to play for in September. And you've had really good playoff baseball in these early rounds, from the Yankees and the Mariners to the Giants and the Marlins. And let's not forget that you've had four wild card teams win the World Series, including three in a row. The wild card has been a great thing for baseball, and Bud Selig has to get credit for that.

Same thing with creating and enhancing rivalries. It started with inter-league play in the mid-1990s. All of a sudden you had the Dodgers and the Angels playing in June. Yankees-Mets. Cubs–White Sox. You had Barry Bonds playing in Yankee Stadium, every NL star getting a chance to play in every AL park, and vice versa. These games added some juice to the regular season. If people complain that interleague play is no longer a novelty, all you have to tell them is that there's never been an empty seat for a Yankees-Mets game.

And baseball's taken that concept to the next level with the unbalanced schedule. Now instead of the Yankees playing the Royals 13 times and the Red Sox 13 times, the Yankees play the Red Sox 19 times, and those kinds of rivalries are great for the game. That's all good.

The labor road has been rocky, because the Players' Association is following the example of their longtime leader Marvin Miller and won't budge an inch. But Selig has done a great job in building a consensus on the owners' side of the table. The New York Yankees and the Kansas City Royals have very different agendas, and Selig has been able to get George Steinbrenner to give up some of his cable TV money and share it with the small market clubs through revenue sharing. In the last labor negotiations, there was a little of that "we'll hang together" mentality that the players have always shown, and the owners finally got a little bit of what they wanted. The luxury tax has slowed the incredible spiraling of salaries. Now teams, at least in their own heads, have a salary cap to think about, and that's around $117 million. Only the Yankees and maybe the Red Sox spend more. There's a sense of unity among the owners that never existed before.

> **BUD SELIG**
>
> - Before he was named the ninth commissioner of baseball in 1998, Selig was the owner of the Milwaukee Brewers and a car dealer.
> - As commissioner he ushered in interleague play, the wild card playoff format, increased revenue sharing, and a luxury tax.
> - In 1969 Selig tried to buy the White Sox. Had he been successful he would have moved the team to Milwaukee.
> - Senator Herb Kohl of Wisconsin was Selig's roommate in college.

DOGBITE: COMMISSIONER BUSH?

For all the impact Bud Selig has had on baseball, he might have had a bigger impact on American history. In his book *The Last Commissioner*, Fay Vincent wrote that after he got his vote of no confidence and was forced to step down, there was one man who wanted nothing more than to be his replacement: George W. Bush. Bush was considering running for governor of Texas, but he didn't think he could beat Ann Richards. Vincent claims that Bush was under the impression that Selig would get him the votes to become baseball commissioner. Suspecting that Selig wanted the job for himself, Vincent told Bush, "George, I don't think he's going to deliver for you." "It was only when he finally realized that Bud wasn't going to step aside that he decided to try [running for office]." Vincent recalls, "The last time I talked to George W. about it, I said, 'Do you believe me now?' And he said, 'Yes, I'm beginning to understand.' "

I think that what hurts Selig in the minds of many fans is his lack of that "commissioner's presence." He's not a leader of men. A perfect example of that is the All-Star game when he threw his hands up in the air and decided to let the game end in a tie. Could you see Kenesaw Landis doing that? I don't kill him for that so much. One big negative in my mind for Selig is the steroid scenario. He saw the incredible increase in home runs. He had to hear some of the whispers. And then you had Ken Caminiti, a former MVP, on the cover of *Sports Illustrated* admitting he used steroids. Then the 2002 labor agreement produced a plan that was toothless. Ironically the minor league policy had some teeth to it, but he wasn't ready to go to the mattresses with the union on this even though there was no way they'd strike a year after 9/11. It finally took Congress getting involved before they did something and that only happened after Jose Canseco's book came out. The steroid controversy has clouded the game for the last four years. It has put baseball in a terrible position. Baseball is about records and history, and now we've got to deal with guys who broke them being steroid users. A major problem. And as the commissioner, Selig should have understood and not buried his head in the sand. Donald Fehr doesn't have to understand. He's all about protecting his players. But Selig should have seen the big picture.

If Bud Selig has one strength, it's this. He's a guy who's a real baseball fan, a guy who loved Henry Aaron and watched his team win the World Series in 1957. You can say what you will about Bud Selig, but he really does have the best interests of the game at heart. And when he's had the chances—and he's had plenty—he's tried in earnest to do the right thing.

9. The Dodger Way

Walter O'Malley always did the right thing—except once.

The Dodger Way. That's Walter O'Malley's legacy. Everything—well just about everything—he did as owner of the Dodgers was all about class. In a lot of ways, the Dodgers were—and are—the model of how to run a sports franchise; and for that matter, how to run a business.

There's a plan, and everything is run according to that plan, from the way they teach pitchers to cover first base to the corporate vacations in Hawaii that include everyone from the GM to the secretaries. This is an organization that not only has the best broadcaster in the business—Vin Scully—but has kept him for 60 years. Sixty years. Even Chavez Ravine is a part of that legacy. Of all the stadiums that were built during that period—early sixties to mid-seventies—Dodger Stadium is one of the few places you'd actually still want to see a game. Is Shea Stadium a beautiful place? No, it's a dump. And a lot of the rest of the stadiums from that time—Veterans Stadium, for example—have been torn down and it's pretty much good riddance to them.

But Chavez Ravine, it's still beautiful, a great pitcher's park, and they've still got the same ushers. The place is so clean you can eat popcorn off the floor.

On the field, it's the same story. During O'Malley's tenure, he hired two managers: Chuck Dressen and Walter Alston. They didn't trade guys just to trade them, bring in ten new free agents every year. Bad season? Nobody's going to get fired. In a lot of ways, O'Malley is the anti-Steinbrenner.

But I can hear it now. All those old Brooklyn Dodger fans are screaming. They would rank Walter O'Malley below Pete Rose and Jose Canseco and probably Richard Nixon, too. Sure, O'Malley made a mistake. A huge one. When you own a sports franchise, it's not just a business, it's a public trust.

But before you hang this all on O'Malley, consider the circumstances. The 1957 Dodgers were a good team, but they couldn't draw flies in Brooklyn. They drew just over a million fans, making them fifth out of eight teams in the National League. The franchise was losing money. And Robert Moses and the Brooklyn politicians were stonewalling him on the subject of building a new stadium. Moses had no interest in helping out O'Malley and the land O'Malley wanted was a wasteland. He had been talking with Moses about building a new ballpark on abandoned property near the Long Island Railroad since the early 1950s. It's not like he sprung it on them in 1956–57. Basically, the New York politicians called his bluff and they got burned. Remember that in 1958 moving a team was pretty much uncharted waters. In 1953 the Braves moved from Boston to Milwaukee and no one even noticed they were gone. But I don't think O'Malley could have really anticipated the reaction from the Brooklyn fans.

I know that Dodger fans are going to kill me for saying this, but you do have to give O'Malley credit for bringing baseball—for bringing big-time professional sports—to the West Coast. You've got to remember that in 1958, major league baseball stopped at Kansas City. And you've got to give O'Malley credit for orchestrating the move brilliantly. He found a huge new market, and found a partner in Horace Stoneham and the Giants to make the move viable. Purely as a business decision, it was a master stroke.

In retrospect, I think O'Malley was a little bit too focused on this manifest destiny thing, focusing all his attention on this great new opportunity on the West Coast, and not enough on the fans he was leaving behind in Brooklyn.

What O'Malley did may not have been the right thing, but it was a very powerful example. Think about all the stadiums that rightly or wrongly got built because an owner threatened to move the franchise out of town. And because of Walter O'Malley and the Dodgers, that wasn't an empty threat anymore. No one was going to call anyone's bluff anymore. But the guys who followed O'Malley's example and actually abandoned their fans weren't a credit to their sports. Robert Irsay didn't create anything by backing up the trucks in the middle of the night and moving the Colts out of Baltimore. And Art Modell moving the Browns out of Cleveland? Disgraceful. They should have learned from O'Malley's example, and yes, Walter O'Malley's mistake.

8. The Mouth that Roared

Howard Cosell made the broadcast booth the center of attention.

Normally you would not think of a broadcaster as a mover and shaker, but I think you have to put Cosell on this list. Two reasons: *Monday Night Football* and Muhammad Ali. First let's talk about Ali. In a lot of ways, Cosell and Ali were joined at the hip, part of a team. And while Ali is one of the most charismatic athletes of all time, he couldn't have done it alone. Ali needed a foil, and Cosell, who was every bit as brash and outspoken as Ali, was the perfect foil. Think about if some conventional announcer, a guy like Chris Schenkel, had done those Ali fights. It wouldn't have worked. Ali turned the ring into theater, whether it was the weigh-in or the post-fight interview, and Cosell was smart enough to play along.

Ali was a controversial figure, and Cosell supported him at a time when he needed support in the worst way. He was key in helping to shape public opinion about Ali. I think Cosell from the bottom of his heart agreed with Ali that what he was doing was right when it came to refusing to fight in the Vietnam War.

And then there was *Monday Night Football. Monday Night Football* may not have survived without Cosell's presence. It's easy to forget how revolutionary *Monday Night Football* was. Up until then, big time sports were something that was played during the day. World Series games were all day games. NFL playoff games and the Super Bowl were all Sunday afternoon affairs.

When you turned on the television to ABC at nine o'clock, you expected to see *Baretta* or *Streets of San Francisco*. This was a whole new concept, the idea of a game in prime time. And it needed someone who was a little bit different, someone who could keep you from turning the channel when the lead stretched out to 21-3. That someone was Howard Cosell. He had the personality, the charisma, the magnetism, the presence to pull that off, to cut through. Just with the way he did the halftime highlights, he managed to make *Monday Night Football* must-see TV.

I know Cosell could be abrasive; he could be pompous. I wasn't a huge fan of his, personally. Toward the end of his career, the whole thing wore a little thin. And he was awful when it came to baseball. But he was the first television announcer with a larger than life personality. He had the tremendous ability to give an event presence. You knew it was a big event if Howard was there. You knew you had to watch.

Howard Cosell wasn't afraid to speak his mind. He didn't care if his opinions were controversial, if he might rub some people the wrong way. He liked taking on the establishment. He brought to the airwaves what columnists like Dick Young had been doing for years. Before Cosell, television sports was a place where blandness ruled, where you let the game unfold and as an announcer you stayed out of the way.

Howard Cosell was really among the first to realize that sports was entertainment, that you had to do more than just do the play-by-play and tell people who made the tackle. Now, Cosell's crossover appeal went only so far. That variety show he did on Saturday night was a tremendous flop, and I'm sure his colossal ego took a huge hit with that one.

He made people realize that what went on in the broadcast booth was every bit as important as what went on

HOWARD COSELL

- Rose to prominence as a boxing reporter, covering the biggest fights of the sixties and seventies. His public relationship with Muhammad Ali furthered both men's fame.
- An original announcer on *Monday Night Football*, the first time football was broadcast in prime time. He held the post from 1970–83.
- A mid-1970s poll called him both the most hated and the most liked sportscaster in America.
- In his early thirties, Cosell was a lawyer who served clients like Willie Mays and the Little League of New York.

on the field. I know it's a cliché but everyone who picks up a microphone today and talks about sports owes a debt to Howard Cosell. And that's what made him a tremendously influential figure, and worthy of a place in the Mad Dog Hall of Fame.

DOGBITE: WHATEVER GETS YOU THROUGH MONDAY NIGHT

Perhaps Howard Cosell's biggest moment had nothing to do with sports. On December 8, 1980, it was Cosell who announced the news to millions of *Monday Night Football* viewers that John Lennon had been shot dead in New York City. "My heart aches and a drowsy numbness pains my sense," Cosell said, quoting Keats' "Ode to a Nightingale." Later he would say of the telecast, "I knew I was the right one to tell America that John Lennon had been assassinated. I had a very special relationship with him. I thought John Lennon was a genius. I knew of his impact upon the civilization of my time."

Six years earlier Lennon was the first celebrity to appear in the booth, Cosell interviewing him during halftime of a 1974 *Monday Night* game between the Redskins and the Rams at Memorial Coliseum in LA. Lennon appeared with, of all people, Ronald Reagan, who gave the bearded Beatle a quick tutorial on the game. A year later, according to Cosell, John Lennon and Yoko Ono were considering an appearance on *Saturday Night Live* (Cosell's show, not the one with John Belushi), and Lennon went so far as to suggest that the show would be the perfect vehicle for a Beatles reunion.

---

7. Just Win, Baby

Oakland's Al Davis is the NFL's most controversial owner.

In a lot of ways, he's a guy you love to hate, but for more than 40 years Al Davis has been one of the dominant figures in the NFL. The Oakland Raiders are one of the top two or three franchises in professional football. And Al Davis made the Oakland Raiders in his image.

AL DAVIS

- At 33 he became coach and general manager of the Oakland Raiders. In 1963 he was named AFL Coach of the Year after leading his team to a 10-4 record.
- As AFL commissioner in 1966, Davis encouraged raids on NFL rosters by AFL owners, which helped lead to a merger between the two leagues.
- Under Davis the Raiders have won three Super Bowls (1977, 1981, 1984) and 15 division titles. He was inducted into the Hall of Fame in 1992.
- Davis hired the first Latino coach, Tom Flores, and the first African-American coach, Art Shell.

This is a team that takes its image seriously. When you wear the Silver and Black, it means something. Davis sees himself as a swashbuckling pirate, a guy who'll thumb his nose at the NFL establishment. He likes guys who are rebels, and he's always willing to take a chance on a guy like Randy Moss or Bo Jackson or Jim Plunkett. He collects trophies, loves having the big star on his team. And he's had success with them. After all, the Raiders won three Super Bowls in eight years: 1977, 1981, and 1984. The Raiders always played exciting football, always ready to throw the 70-yard bomb to Cliff Branch. But recently the team has been a joke. Davis really needed that Super Bowl against Tampa Bay to prove the game hasn't passed him by.

Unlike most owners, he really did know football. He coached the team for a while and he did a pretty good job. He was one of the first coaches to use the no-huddle offense. When you talk about the owners who try to get involved in the day-to-day operations of their franchises, guys like Jerry Jones and Daniel Snyder, they're pretty much emulating Al Davis. And they usually pale by comparison. Davis was smart enough to make a young assistant named John Madden his head coach and stay with him.

Now, I'll be the first to tell you that Davis took things too far. He pushed his players to cross the line, to go from being tough and intimidating to actual thugs. He loved saying "Let's go to war." Look at the nicknames these guys had. Jack Tatum was the Assassin, George Atkinson was The Hitman, and Skip Thomas was Dr. Death. And that all kind of came to a head when Tatum paralyzed Daryl Stingley in an exhibition game. Now,

I'm sure Tatum didn't mean to put Stingley in a wheelchair, but this kind of hard hitting, send-a-message play is what Al Davis preached.

Davis is an interesting figure in the history of the league. He was the commissioner of the old AFL and he was one of the driving forces behind the merger with the NFL. But once he got his team into the league, it was all about pushing the boundaries. He was the anti–Pete Rozelle, and he fought the league establishment tooth and nail. He was always filing lawsuits, tweaking his fellow owners. He's an NFL owner, yet he testified on behalf of the USFL in an antitrust suit. When the Raiders won the Super Bowl, he designed championship rings for the team that were so elaborate and so expensive that the league, which paid for them, had to put a price limit on rings from then on.

He can turn on his own, too. He's been downright spiteful to Marcus Allen, who for some reason he doesn't like. And he holds grudges. Just ask Mike Shanahan.

He did a terrible job with the city of Oakland. He's burned that city to no end. He ruined a good thing by moving the franchise. He had a loyal fan base, and when the team left Oakland to go to LA, it was one of the worst things you ever could do. Since coming back, they've never really recaptured that early seventies Oakland magic in that city again. It's like the city's just waiting for him to leave again, and the underachieving teams haven't helped either.

So while there's a lot to admire about Al Davis, one of the great individualists in the world of sports, there's also a lot not to like. And as far as Davis is concerned, that wouldn't bother him one single bit.

DOGBITE: BEANING THE BOSS

How much does Al Davis rub people the wrong way? Former coach Mike Shanahan reportedly told quarterback Elvis Grbac to throw a football at the head of the Raiders owner. Davis managed to duck out of the way. When he spun and spotted Shanahan, Davis flipped him the bird. Asked to confirm Grbac's story, Shanahan said, "He must be confusing me with another coach. Would I do something like that?"

6. The Mountain Man

Kenesaw Landis wasn't a saint, but he did save baseball.

When you're making up a list like this, you have to ask yourself: How do you weight things? How do you weight one huge mistake in the middle of an otherwise distinguished career? That was the question with Walter O'Malley. How do you weight one great accomplishment against a whole lot of things that you don't like? That's the issue with baseball's first commissioner, Kenesaw Mountain Landis.

You can sum up his accomplishments in three words: He saved baseball. Saved baseball. At a time when there was a chance that the game would topple under a cloud of corruption, when the public would completely lose faith in the integrity of the game, he came in and he did something about it. Sure, Ruth had a tremendous influence in helping people get excited about baseball again, but all those home runs wouldn't have amounted to a hill of beans if people didn't think the game was honest.

He took control of the 1919 Black Sox scandal with an iron fist. He banned the Black Sox players for life, regardless of the fact that they were acquitted in a court of law—which is interesting because he was a big-time judge before he became commissioner. He presided over a big antitrust case against Standard Oil. Was this fair? In retrospect, it's easy to second-guess him. But the bottom line is that it worked. He came in and cleaned house, made the American public believe

KENESAW LANDIS

- From 1920 until his death in 1944, he served as baseball's first commissioner, banishing 15 players from the game early in his reign, including the eight Black Sox for life.
- Landis suspended Babe Ruth for 39 days in 1922 after the slugger ignored a ban on barnstorming in the offseason.
- He was inducted into the Hall of Fame in 1939.

that baseball was headed by a man who was above the fray, someone who would act solely in the best interests of the game.

Phil Rizzuto once told me he was scared to death of the judge. Scared to death. Landis had an aura about him. He wasn't some kind of a yes-man for the owners. You got the sense that if you crossed the line, you were going to have to pay for it.

Now, the reality was a little bit different. In the years after the Black Sox scandal, he let other players get away with murder. Ty Cobb and Tris Speaker were implicated in a conspiracy to fix a game in 1926, and they pretty much got off scot-free.

The biggest knock on Landis is on the question of the color barrier. He dismissed the notion of Negro League players by just saying that they weren't good enough, although anyone with two eyes knew that they were. He was a bigot. This was a man who was born in 1866, right after the Civil War, a nineteenth-century man still living, and wielding immense power in, a twentieth-century world. He was from a different time. It's no coincidence that baseball's color line came down only a few years after Landis died.

There were plenty of other things that Landis did that make you scratch your head. He opposed the minor league system with a passion. Hated it, and at one point ruled to set a whole bunch of farm system players free. When a minor league team in Chattanooga signed a female pitcher, Jackie Mitchell, who struck out Babe Ruth and Lou Gehrig in an exhibition, he voided her contract. For 24 years Landis pretty much did whatever he darn well pleased, and didn't care what anyone else thought of it. He was able to wield his power arbitrarily at times because he had so much of it. The owners were desperate in 1919, and they gave Landis anything he wanted. American League president Ban Johnson called him a "wild-eyed nut," and that was probably true.

So while his image isn't as squeaky clean as you might think, Landis did a couple of important things. He established this idea of the independent sports commissioner, a guy who would act solely in the best interest of the game. Now, we know that when push comes to shove, this is mostly fiction, but it does allow commissioners to do some things that they wouldn't be able to do otherwise. And when baseball needed a strong figure to take charge and, even more importantly, to let everyone know he was in charge, Landis was there.

You have to wonder how baseball history might have been different if they had chosen a different guy or not created the commissioner's job at all. Had Landis not acted decisively, Major League Baseball might not even exist today. Landis handled the crisis, and that's why he's earned a place in the Mad Dog Hall of Fame.

DOGBITE: THE OTHER RULING

It's very likely that the Black Sox scandal was even deeper than anyone thought. On December 30, 1926, Swede Risberg, one of the original eight Black Sox, came forward with a shocking claim. He said that the Sox had thrown two games in the 1919 regular season in a quid pro quo arrangement with Detroit players who had thrown two games against the White Sox during a pennant race in 1917. He also alleged that Chicago players paid Detroit pitchers $45 for winning the last series against the Boston Red Sox. Judge Landis held a three-day public hearing on January 5, 1927, and after Risberg and all the accused players testified, Landis ruled there was a lack of evidence, and the Detroit players, including Ty Cobb, were in the clear. The incident led Landis to establish the first publicly stated guidelines for player conduct and punishment, and in a move to bury baseball's sordid past once and for all, he declared a statute of limitations on any wrongdoing that had occurred before 1920.

---

5. Who's The Boss?

Love him or hate him, George Steinbrenner spares no expense.

Try this with your buddies sometime. Ask them who they would want to be the owner of their favorite team. Tell them, "This is going to be the guy who's ultimately going to decide whether your team is in the playoffs every year and contending for a championship, or struggling along in the standings but making good profit margins in parking and concessions."

Who do you want? I just might hand my favorite team over to George Steinbrenner. There are a lot of things you don't like about Steinbrenner. He's hard to defend. He fired a thousand different managers and a million pitching coaches. He fired Yogi Berra 16 games into the season. And sometimes he just can't control himself. From the crazy stuff with punching the marshmallow salesman in the elevator to these ridiculous apologies when the Yankees lose the World Series. Remember the 1996 World Series celebration. Steinbrenner insisted that only the players could ride on the floats. This didn't sit well with Jim Leyritz's wife, who wanted to be with her husband. Lo and behold, a month later Leyritz gets traded. The Game 4 hero, no less. And let's not even get into the Howie Spira thing, spying on Dave Winfield.

But there are two reasons you've got to like George Steinbrenner. First, he respects the tradition of the team. George has been the face of the most important franchise in sports for 33 years. He brings guys like Whitey Ford and Phil Rizzuto back to the Stadium, and DiMaggio and Mantle when they were still alive. He put his ego aside and made up with Yogi, and Reggie Jackson, and Dave Winfield. (Although, truth be told, he needed Yogi—he was running out of old-time Yankees.) And he made the deal to keep the Yankees in the Bronx where they belong. He gets a little bit crazy sometimes, but at the end of the day he remembers that these are the New York Yankees we're talking about.

> ## GEORGE STEINBRENNER
>
> - In 1973 Steinbrenner became principal owner of the Yankees. During his tenure, the Yankees have won 10 pennants and 6 World Series (1977, 1978, 1996, 1998–2000).
> - Signed the first free agent, paying Catfish Hunter a then-staggering $3.75 million for five years
> - Changed managers 20 times and GMs 11 times in 31 years, including firing Billy Martin four times
> - Suspended from baseball in 1974 after pleading guilty to making illegal contributions to Richard Nixon's re-election campaign and to obstruction of justice; granted clemency in 1989 by Ronald Reagan, who made this one of his final acts in office

The second and even more important reason to like Steinbrenner is, George wants to win. He cares more about winning than he does about making money. He'll spend, spend, spend to get the players he wants. The ends justify the means. It just drives him crazy when his team loses. Whether it's a Subway Series in June against the Mets or even losing a couple of games to the Devil Rays in spring training, he just cannot stand losing. If the Yankees are in last place for a couple of days in April, he takes it as a personal affront. That's what drives the guy. And that has resulted in plenty of bad decisions—from Dave Collins to Dave LaPoint. He says things that he shouldn't say, from calling Dave Winfield Mr. May to calling Hideki Irabu a "fat, pussy toad." And the less said about George and Billy Martin the better. You can certainly say that George Steinbrenner wants to win for the wrong reasons. He wants to win to feed his own ego, and he thinks that if the team does badly it's a reflection on him.

But to his credit, he never says, "No, we can't afford this guy." If a guy like Roger Clemens or Jason Giambi or Hideki Matsui or Johnny Damon becomes available, he hands his baseball guys a blank check and says, "Go get him." Can't say that about too many other owners. It all started with that dramatic December 31 signing of Catfish Hunter. All that said, if we were writing this chapter ten years ago, George Steinbrenner doesn't make the list. These last four championships and six pennants are huge in his legacy. If the Yankees continued the way they were in the 1980s, spending crazy money, trading away good young players for washed-up veterans and finishing second or third every year, he doesn't make this list.

And I think he might have gotten a bit lucky with this team. A lot of the guys who were the heart and soul of this organization—Jeter, Bernie Williams, Andy Pettitte, Mariano, and even Posada—were developed during a time when he was suspended from baseball. He couldn't trade these guys away for some washed up pitcher or send them back to Columbus. And he lucked out with Joe Torre. Everyone said that he was nuts when he essentially fired Buck Showalter, who got the team back into the playoffs for the first time in more than a decade. I said it, I admit. But Torre has been just the right guy, the kind of guy who can serve as a buffer between the clubhouse and the craziness that goes on in the front office.

The bottom line is that if you look at Steinbrenner's record, it's darn good. Six championships. O'Malley's Dodgers won six, but it took them 20 years longer. The Reds didn't win six. The A's didn't win six. He's really had more success than any owner of the last 40 years. I'm sure that you wouldn't want to work for the guy. You'd be answering the phone at three o'clock in the morning and coming into work wondering if you're going to still have a job by the end of the day. But if you're a fan, and you're looking for the guy who's not going to let anything get in the way of a championship, you could do a lot worse than having George Steinbrenner as your team's owner.

DOGBITE: THE BOSS OF BASKETBALL

Before baseball, there was basketball. In 1961 Steinbrenner was owner of the Cleveland Pipers of the American Basketball League, a rival to the National Basketball Association, and by all accounts, Steinbrenner was Mark Cuban before Mark Cuban was. He would join team huddles, suggest strategy, criticize players, coaches, and officials, once even ripping the whistle off of a ref. "He was the nicest person in the world when you won," recalled Pipers coach Bill Sharman. "He'd take us all out to dinner after games. But when we lost, he would be pretty upset."

The Pipers ended up winning the ABL title in the league's lone season of existence, but Steinbrenner ran out of money. He had trouble paying his players, but that didn't stop him from luring top college prospect Jerry Lucas to play for the Pipers. Later, Steinbrenner became part owner of the Chicago Bulls, but, against Jerry Reinsdorf's advice, sold his stake before Michael Jordan arrived.

4. Little Big Man

NBA commissioner David Stern had the savvy to market Michael and Co.

Sports in the late twentieth century and early twenty-first century is all about marketing, and there's no one who's been more astute about that than NBA commissioner David Stern.

He didn't build a league up from nothing like Pete Rozelle, so he doesn't get credit for that. Remember that when he took over in 1984, Magic Johnson and Larry Bird were already in the league, and the game was already on its way back from that bad time in the late 1970s when basketball was becoming irrelevant to the average sports fan. No, David Stern didn't save basketball, but he did take it to the next level. Stern made the NBA a personality league. In much the same way that a great basketball coach has to form a partnership with a great player in order to be successful—think of Red Auerbach and Bill Russell, or Phil Jackson and Michael Jordan—Stern did that on a larger scale. He does a magnificent job of finding a player that he can market, and then takes advantage of that. And that's not a small thing. In baseball, there's such animosity and distrust between the players and the owners, you see the owners trying to market the game without marketing the players. The reasoning is that if the players become too huge as stars, then you're going to have to pay them too much. Stern said to heck with all that. He understood that Nike and Adidas were his partners, and that if you could make the players larger than life, it's good for the game. You saw it with Magic and Bird. You saw it with Michael Jordan. You saw it with Shaq, and you're seeing it with LeBron James. And he's done a good job of keeping these guys involved in the league after they retire. Jordan, Magic, Isiah, and Bird all had at least one high-profile gig as a coach or in management after they hung up their sneakers. You like that.

We all know that Stern is a great marketer. But people forget what a good job he's done with the NBA's labor situation. His biggest legacy might be as the inventor of the salary cap. The NBA was the first league with a salary cap, and the soft cap has worked very, very well, allowing small market teams like San Antonio and Sacramento to compete for a championship, while still allowing teams to keep their big stars. Under the NBA's system, how many times did you see a really top free agent bolt some small market team to go for the bright lights in the big city? Once, Shaq to the Lakers. And from a fan's point of view, you can't ask for more than that, competitive balance on the one hand and keeping teams together on the other. The NBA's system forces a team to have visionary management—you pay big-time for your mistakes—but isn't that the way sports is supposed to be? Ask Isiah Thomas.

And maybe part of it is his personality—he's a funny, likeable guy—but Stern has been able to drive a hard bargain in negotiations without rubbing the players' faces in it. The owners, who pay his salary, after all, got a great deal, and the players are still talking to him. Sure, they had a lockout a few years ago, but that was nothing compared to the nuclear winters you had in baseball and hockey, where you lost a whole post-season and poisoned the well between the players and the owners for years to come. Even the NFL had to resort to using replacement players back in the 1980s.

Stern moved the game toward the idea of a partnership between the players and the owners, linking revenue and salaries. By taking the pie and slicing it up, and saying to the players, "Here's our revenue, and 55 percent of it goes to salaries," it removes the animosity factor.

Stern has done a huge amount to internationalize the game. The first part of that was the Dream Team. It was the biggest story of the 1992 Olympics. The games themselves were a joke—beating

DAVID STERN

- Elected fourth NBA commissioner on February 1, 1984
- The NBA's revenue has increased by 500 percent over the past 20 years under Stern's guidance. The league has also added six teams.
- Brought the game to a global audience: 175 countries now televise NBA games and 11 international offices have been opened.
- His other accomplishments include the creation of the draft lottery, the WNBA, and the National Basketball Development League, and the 1999 launch of NBA.com TV, a 24-hour digital network.

Angola 116-48—but the idea of having Bird, Magic, Jordan, Barkley, Ewing, Malone together on the same team really captivated people. You had this funny sight of a player being lit up by Charles Barkley and then asking for his autograph. Chuck Daly said it was like traveling with Elvis and the Beatles all at once. Sure, the novelty has worn off, but it was a great idea then, and it's had a lasting impact.

Since then, you've had a tremendous number of foreign-born players come into the league: Dirk Nowitzki, Yao Ming, Peja Stojakovic. Tony Parker and Manu Ginobili.

These guys are very very good players and the Europeans are very well schooled in the fundamentals. And they create tremendous interest in pro basketball in their home countries, and that has made the NBA a truly international league. They don't care about baseball in Europe. They don't care about hockey in Latin America or Asia. But there's some interest in the NBA on every other continent but Antarctica, and that has helped the game immensely. Stern also realized that it's a problem having high school kids playing in the league—for every LeBron James there's a bunch of Kwame Browns, Leon Smiths, and Korleone Youngs—and he did a good job getting the players to agree to a 20-year-old minimum age.

Now, a lot of fans will complain that the NBA has lost its connection with its old fan base, the older white guys in middle America. These guys don't relate to players with cornrows and tattoos. And that's true to a point—the ratings aren't what they were when Magic and Bird and Jordan were playing. More than any other commissioner, Stern's in a tough spot. His players are mostly 23-year-old guys from the inner city who listen to rap, and his audience is the 38- to 50-year-old guy who has a house

---

DOGBITE: NO BULLS IN CHINA

What was David Stern's agenda as commissioner? "Are you kidding?" he told a reporter. "The world!" In the early 1990s on a trip to China, Stern mentioned to his tour guide at the imperial burial grounds in Xi'an that he was with the NBA. "Ah!" said the guide, who spoke only a little English. "The Red Oxen!" Stern scratched his head. Was this the name of a Chinese club team? The interpreter explained to Stern that Red Oxen was the Chinese nickname for the Chicago Bulls.

in the suburbs. Stern's got to bridge that gap, and he does it about as well as anyone could.

And he's a classy guy. I was a young radio-talk-show host, doing a show in Phoenix, when the NBA was talking about expanding to Orlando. It was a small station. No producer. Stern didn't know me from Adam. But he agreed to do it, sat there next to me, waiting patiently through some technical delays and treated the interview seriously. That says something about the guy. My bigger problem with Stern is this. He'll chase every nickel as hard as he can, and he does that at the expense of the game. Stern made a very bad decision with the last television deal. He blew off the league's relationship with NBC and now you've got the all-star game and the conference finals on cable TV. You also end up with this ridiculous playoff schedule in which it takes two weeks to play an opening-round series, just to cater to TV. And in that way, Stern has become a slave to TV.

But just think about where the league was 20 years ago when Stern took over—Michael Jordan was just a kid who made a big jumper in an NCAA tournament game—and think about it now. And you've got to give David Stern huge credit for that.

3. The State of the Union

Marvin Miller shifted the balance of power between players and owners.

Marvin Miller should be in the Hall of Fame. No doubt about it. It would chafe the owners no end, but he should have a bronze plaque in Cooperstown right next to Kenesaw Landis and Ban Johnson. For the time being he'll have to settle for a place in *my* Hall of Fame.

Let's look at the history of labor in baseball. Rewind, if you will, to the 1919 season. Charles Comiskey, the guy they named the park after, owns the best team in baseball, the Chicago White Sox. His best pitcher, Eddie Cicotte, is this close to earning his bonus for winning 30 games. Comiskey doesn't want to pay, so he tells the manager to sit Cicotte. And remember

MARVIN MILLER

- Before he was elected head of the MLB Players Association in 1966, Miller was chief economist and assistant to the president of the Steelworkers Union Association.
- From 1966 to 1982, the average player salary increased from $19,000 to $241,497.
- As the players' union head, Miller helped secure free agency, salary arbitration, and pension rights. He also achieved official recognition of the union, the right to bargain collectively, and the use of agents to negotiate individual contracts.
- *The Sporting News* named him the fifth most powerful person in sports in the twentieth century, but Miller has never come close to being elected to the Baseball Hall of Fame.

that Cicotte and the rest of these players weren't making big money. They had to work second jobs in the off-season. So Cicotte got ticked off at Comiskey—and started looking for another way to make some money—and that was the beginning of the Black Sox scandal. And the owners didn't learn a thing from that. They hung these guys out to dry as an example, they barred these kinds of performance incentives in contracts, and they kept right on squeezing the players. After the season, they handed you a contract and said sign it. Don't like it? Go dig a ditch. And the ironclad reserve clause meant that players had absolutely no say in where they played, and if none of this seemed fair, the owners had a congressional antitrust exemption protecting them.

Then in 1966 along came Marvin Miller, a West Virginia steelworker's union executive hired by Jim Bunning and Robin Roberts. He saw how one-sided the deal was between the players and the owners, and he set out to do something about it. Miller understood the magnitude of the struggle the players faced, and he knew that the only way to face down the owners was to have some economic strength. So he built up a union war chest by getting the licensing money from baseball cards and funneling it back to the union. He got the owners to cave on small incremental issues. The owners were not smart enough to realize that these small gains would add up and become big gains. "Aw, let them have licensing. Who cares? Not a big deal." Per diem increases. A day off after a certain number of games in a row. But those little things started the pendulum swinging back the other way.

Simply, Miller was smarter than the owners. And he was tougher than they were. He understood the competitiveness, the toughness of the professional athlete. They wanted to win, and they just needed someone to lay out the rules of the game for them and show them that the owners were the real enemy. And that was Miller. And he counted on their respect for the team concept. Everyone was on the same page, whether it was Reggie Jackson and Mike Schmidt or Oscar Gamble and Don Hahn. You and your fellow players, you're a team, and you back up your teammates. That complete unified front is the thing that has allowed the players to stay together through nasty, prolonged strikes. Solidarity, that's what Miller preached and that's what he got. Miller galvanized the players, steeled their resolve, and turned them from pushovers into maybe the toughest labor association in America.

Even the owners knew this. In the 1994–95 strike, the owners trotted out replacement players by offering big league jobs to borderline minor leaguers. But the real prospects, the Derek Jeters, were nowhere near this strike, because the owners knew that these guys would be branded as

---

DOGBITE: SAYING NO TO NIXON

In a meeting with baseball player representatives in New York in 1965, Marvin Miller was told if he took the job of union spokesman he would have to work alongside the man they wanted as their legal counsel: Richard Nixon. Miller's reaction? He walked out of the meeting. Who knows if he was bluffing, but, according to Miller, he came back to Pittsburgh and told his wife that he had blown it.

The liberal Democrat felt that "hiring two incompatible people as the only two professionals in the organization" spelled disaster for the union. "Nixon wouldn't know a pension plan from the Empire State Building," he added. Two weeks after the meeting, Miller got a call. He was in, Nixon was out. This was his first successful negotiation in baseball, but hardly his last. If Miller had refused this post, he could have ended up representing a very different group: the Playboy Bunnies. They wanted to unionize and asked Miller to be their labor advisor, but he declined.

scabs for the rest of their careers. If the players in the other sports stuck together the way that baseball players do, it'd be a different world.

And Miller dropped the bomb on the owners by dismantling the reserve clause. We all remember Curt Flood, the slick-fielding outfielder who got traded from the Cardinals to the Phillies. He didn't want to go, and he took the case all the way to the Supreme Court. How many of you remember that Flood lost that case? Miller told him that it was a hopeless cause. He knew that the justices on the Supreme Court were fat cats who would back up the status quo. He also knew that it would take so long that Flood's career—and remember, he was only 31 and was an All-Star center fielder in 1968—would be over by the time the case was heard. He told Flood this and Flood said, "Let's fight." Just trying to attack the reserve clause cracked the door a little, but Miller found the side entrance, with the Andy Messersmith–Dave McNally case going to an independent arbitrator who wasn't beholden to the precedent set by the Supreme Court. And that was the beginning of free agency as we know it.

And that's Marvin Miller's legacy. He's the guy who brought players from near slavery to the position of power they enjoy today. Huge impact. Now, if you ask me, the pendulum has swung back too far in the other direction. The players have beaten up the owners at just about every negotiation for the last 30 years, to the detriment of the game. And three-quarters of them have probably never heard of Curt Flood. Bottom line: Marvin Miller is the Babe Ruth of sports union leaders—the first and the best.

2. The Integrator

Branch Rickey did far more than demolish baseball's color barrier.

If the only thing that Branch Rickey did was break baseball's color barrier by signing and playing Jackie Robinson, you'd have to consider him for a list like this. But while that's the most important line on his résumé, it's hardly the only one. Rickey put together the whole concept of a dedicated minor league system that funnels into your major league team. Commissioner Landis fought him tooth and nail on this, but boy did it work. At one point, there were 65 products of Rickey's Cardinal farm system playing in the major leagues. And before too long, the rest of baseball stopped trying to fight Rickey and they joined him, with every major league team getting its own minor league system.

Think about that for a second. How different would baseball be right now if every minor league team was independent, and all the players were available to the highest bidder? The whole game would be different, and frankly it would be impossible for teams like the Marlins and the A's, which do a good job of drafting and developing players, to compete with the Yankees and the Dodgers and the Red Sox.

Rickey was one of the first guys to look at statistics in a serious way. He saw that batting average wasn't everything and, along with Allan Roth, he came up with on-base percentage, which gives credit to guys who draw walks, and every year the Cardinals were right at the top of the league in on-base percentage, walks, and runs scored. It took 60, 70 years, but the rest of baseball has come around on this. He was a pioneer when it came to all kinds of innovations, from the batting helmet to the mechanical pitching machine.

Rickey was the architect of not one but two of the greatest teams in the sport. He put together those great Cardinal teams of the late 1920s and until the early 1940s. Between 1926 and 1946 the Cardinals were in the World Series nine times and won six, and while Rickey left for Brooklyn in 1943, you've still got to give him credit for building that team in St. Louis. All in all, that's the best run ever for a National League team. Rickey brought in all kinds of great players— Dizzy Dean, Johnny Mize, Enos Slaughter, Grover Cleveland Alexander, Frankie

BRANCH RICKEY

- Invented the modern farm system that brought the Cardinals nine pennants and six World Series through the 1940s
- Became the first executive to defy baseball's segregation policy when in 1945 he signed Jackie Robinson to the Brooklyn Dodgers
- His attempt to develop a third major league, the Continental League, spurred expansion in 1961–62.
- In 1967 he was elected to the Hall of Fame.

Frisch, Ducky Medwick, Stan Musial. And they beat some all-time great teams. They beat the 1926 Yankees with Ruth and Gehrig. And they beat that great A's team in 1931, with all those Hall of Famers—Lefty Grove, Jimmy Foxx, and Al Simmons—stopping them from a three-peat. They won the title again in 1934 with the Gashouse Gang, and beat the DiMaggio Yankees in 1942. All those great St. Louis teams had Mahatma's stamp on them.

And then we get to his work with the Dodgers. The Dodgers had started to become a pretty good team by the time he got there, headed in the right direction. But he really put his stamp on the history of baseball. The idea of breaking the color barrier was in the air, but it was all about the execution. He had to find a guy who just could not fail, because the stakes were so high. Rickey found the right guy in Jackie Robinson. First off, Jackie Robinson was a great ballplayer, a guy who was kind of a cross between Joe Morgan and Rickey Henderson. Robinson was a good enough player that he would have ended up in the Hall of Fame even if he had been the third black ballplayer in the majors. There had to be no doubt that he would be able to hit, run, and field.

But Rickey also knew he needed a guy who had the character to stand

---

DOGBITE: HOMERS OVER HAVANA

It took a lot of finesse on Branch Rickey's part to bring Jackie Robinson to the big leagues. In spring training, for example, Rickey worried Robinson would face a hostile atmosphere in Daytona Beach, so the Dodgers moved their spring training to Havana, Cuba. Rickey figured that playing in a country accustomed to integrated baseball would let Robinson keep his focus on the field. He also made him a non-roster player and let him practice and play with the minor league team to keep the pressure off. However, even in Cuba he wasn't allowed to stay with the rest of the team at the American-owned Hotel Nacionale. And Dixie Walker and a few other southern players circulated a petition stating they wouldn't play if Robinson made the cut. But Rickey stayed calm, and toward the end of spring training said of Robinson's teammates, "First they'll endure Robinson, then pity him, then embrace him." He was right.

up to all kinds of abuse—from fans, from opponents, and even from his own teammates—and who had the self-discipline to turn the other cheek no matter how bad it got, at least at the beginning. Rickey was smart enough to understand this side of the issue, and he found just the right man in Jackie Robinson.

And Rickey followed up Robinson with Roy Campanella and Don Newcombe. He had a falling out with Walter O'Malley, but the guys that he brought in were the heart and soul of those great Brooklyn Dodger teams of the 1950s. He left for Pittsburgh, where he was pretty much known for two things—helping to make the batting helmet standard equipment, and telling Ralph Kiner, "We finished last with you, we can finish last without you." Boy, was he a cheapskate. And in his last incarnation, Rickey started the Continental League. It wasn't successful per se—it folded without playing a game—but it forced the major leagues in 1961 to approve the first of what would be many rounds of expansion, after keeping the status quo for almost a whole century.

Branch Rickey was one of the game's great minds, an innovative thinker and a guy who could spot a ballplayer a mile away. The fact that he found a place in baseball for Jackie Robinson only enhances his legend.

1. The Father of Super Bowl Sunday

Pete Rozelle helped make the NFL the biggest show on the sports landscape.

What's the biggest event on the sports calendar every year? Hands down, it's got to be Super Bowl Sunday. Not even close. It's become a national holiday, practically. It's the one day where everyone, whether you're a big sports fan or not, sits down in front of the TV, gets a big bowl of nachos and guacamole, and watches the game. In terms of eyeballs to sets, there's no contest, and that's why advertisers spend hundreds of millions of dollars on commercials during the game.

The guy who came up with the idea? NFL commissioner Pete Rozelle.

If that was the only thing he did, if he spent the rest of his term sitting on his fanny in his office, playing tiddledywinks on a big old mahogany desk, he would still deserve a place at the top of this list. But that's just the tip of the iceberg with Pete Rozelle.

When Rozelle came to the league in 1960, the NFL was a mom-and-pop organization. Pro football was at best the fourth most popular sport behind baseball, boxing, and college football. Sure, you can talk about the 1958 championship game as a turning point for the league, but the reality is that the ratings in 1959 were not good. Without Pete Rozelle that great game between the Giants and Colts could have been a little blip, the same way that professional soccer in the U.S. had its moment in the sun in the mid-1970s.

But Pete Rozelle had a vision for professional football. He started out as the PR guy for the Rams in the 1950s. He moved the league offices from Philadelphia to New York, where the action is. He understood that television was the future of sports, and did everything he could to make football a TV-friendly sport. He ushered in the idea that for the sports fan, Sunday was the day that you sit in front of the television and watch NFL games. Every football widow in America has Pete Rozelle to thank.

He took that one step further with the *Monday Night Football* concept, making the game prime-time entertainment. Howard Cosell and Dandy Don Meredith were just as important a part of the formula as the players were. Think about it. How many shows have run as long as *Monday Night Football*? *60 Minutes*? Well we all know that they pre-empt the beginning of *60 Minutes* on Sunday for the end of a football game. Under Rozelle, each of the three networks had a piece of the pro football pie. CBS had the NFC, NBC had the AFC, and ABC had Monday night. That in itself is pretty amazing, being able to work with each of these three fierce competitors.

NFL Films started under Rozelle's watch, and that really helped to romanticize the game, those beautiful slow motion images and John Facenda's booming baritone doing the voice over: "As the gladiators march onto the field of battle on the frozen tundra of Lambeau Field." Fans got to hear the players talking on the sideline, got these cameos of the guys on the bench, great clouds of frozen breath, shivering in the cold, the coaches barking orders. That was really our first look at this kind of behind the scenes, inside stuff, and now sports coverage in every sport is all about that.

And to that end, Rozelle marketed the personalities in the league in a unique and subtle way. It started with Vince Lombardi, who is about as clean cut as you can get. And then he was able to turn around and market Joe Namath as a sex symbol and a rebel. It takes some skill to be able to create a league that's diverse enough that both of these guys can represent it.

But the thing that I like best about Rozelle is that he wasn't just a suit, a guy who would be as happy to sell washing machines. He was a real football guy. He really loved the NFL and went to a million football games, and you like that about him.

But a great commissioner is more than a salesman. Sometimes you've got to be judge and jury, and sometimes you've got to be a backroom dealmaker. Pete Rozelle was all of that and more. He put his foot down when Paul Hornung and Alex Karras got involved with gamblers. He brokered the merger deal with the AFL, which was huge. One thing that everyone points to as a big mistake early in Rozelle's tenure is playing the games only three days after President Kennedy was killed. Looking back it seems kind of unthinkable. But let's not forget, the fans had a choice of staying home, and it wasn't as if they played the games in empty stadiums. I've talked about this with Frank Gifford, who was playing for the Giants back then, and he told me that they had 60,000 fans at Yankee Stadium. And he also said that, honestly, he never really considered *not* playing the game. Now, it was a quiet stadium, and it got quieter after Jack Ruby shot Lee Harvey Oswald that morning, but even though Pierre Salinger suggested after the fact that this was a national disgrace, it's hard to really slam Rozelle too hard on this one. Rozelle did

PETE ROZELLE

- Served as NFL commissioner for almost 30 years, 1960 to 1989
- After helping to get a bill passed in Congress that allowed single-network television contracts, he signed with CBS to televise all the league's regular-season games for the first time.
- The AFL and NFL merged on June 8, 1966, under his leadership, and he guided the league through expansion from 12 to 28 teams and through two player strikes in 1982 and 1987.

have some trouble with labor negotiations. There were two strikes on his watch, one with replacement players.

Here's the point. If you were to look at the second half of the twentieth century and try to identify the one person—athlete, coach, agent, owner, or anything else—who changed the world of sports more than anyone, who would you name? I would name Pete Rozelle, and it wouldn't even be close. Football is the number one sport in America no matter how you look at it, and he is the man, over the course of 28, 29 years, who made it what it is today. That's why he's the number one mover and shaker in the Mad Dog Hall of Fame.

DOGBITE: NOT SO SUPER

If it was up to Pete Rozelle, it wouldn't be called Super Bowl Sunday. Rozelle felt the term Super Bowl was "a corny cliché." He wanted something classy like "World Series." "Do not call it the Super Bowl," he said prior to the game. "This is the AFL-NFL world championship game." Turns out that the name Super Bowl was actually inspired by a little boy's toy. Chiefs owner Lamar Hunt had watched his son Lamar Jr. play with a Super Ball and the rest is history. But if you kept your ticket stub from that first title game, you would see that Rozelle had AFL-NFL WORLD CHAMPIONSHIP GAME printed on the tickets. By Super Bowl III, Rozelle came around, and by Super Bowl IV, the game drew bigger ratings than Neil Armstrong's moon walk. "It took on a life of its own," Rozelle admitted.

Chapter 3

The Top-Ten College Football Players of All Time

Which rising star cracked the Top Ten with a breath-taking performance?
Which old-time back is the ultimate immortal?

I think college football is by far the toughest category to analyze. First off, so many college greats in football are from 50, 60, 75 years ago, when college football was the second biggest team sport, behind only baseball. The NFL, basketball, and hockey were not a factor in those days.

And when you're going back that far, so many of these players played two ways. They played offense and defense, and usually special teams, too, and that's got to be a consideration. You're talking about kids who played 57 or 58 minutes a game. Players from 1955 on, they only play half the game.

And the other stipulation I'm going to make is that I'm going to focus on what the guy did in college. Lawrence Taylor was great at North Carolina, and he turned out to be an awesome NFL player. But he played in a lousy football conference and the team he played for didn't do a darn thing, so he doesn't make the list.

And college football is such a big sport, so many teams, so many conferences, and so much history, that more than any of the other lists in this book, I consulted with other experts. So, right off the top, I'd like to especially thank Lee Corso, Beano Cook, and Dan Jenkins for their insight and opinions about the greatest college football players of all time.

10. Young and Fearless

One spectacular performance vaulted Vince Young into college football's pantheon.

Prior to the 2005 Rose Bowl, I would never, ever have even considered Vince Young to be among the top college football players of the decade, much less of all time. This is a guy who had not won a championship. He did not win a Heisman trophy. He didn't even have a great game against Oklahoma. Texas lost to Oklahoma 12-0 in his sophomore year and Young did nothing in the game.

The Rose Bowl against Michigan opened my eyes, though. How could you not be impressed by the way he played. In that game he accounted for five touchdowns, 373 yards of offense, rushed for 192 yards on 21 carries, completed 16 of 28 passes for 180 yards, and was by far and away the star of the game. That was sort of his coming out party. But the Michigan team they played was only so-so, and it was hard for me to take a team coached by Mack Brown all that seriously.

Over the course of the 2005–06 season, I began to take notice a little bit. On September 10 in Columbus against an Ohio State team that has a lot of future NFL players on defense, including linebacker A.J. Hawk, Vince Young kind of picked up where he left off in Pasadena. He went 18 for 29, 270 yards, two touchdowns, and 76 yards rushing and sealed this big road win against one of the top teams in the country with a game-winning touchdown pass. He cruised

---

VINCE YOUNG

- In 2005–06, he led the Longhorns to a perfect 13-0 record and the national championship. They currently hold a 20-game win streak.
- Young became the only player in NCAA history to rush for 1,000 yards (1,150) and pass for 3,000 yards in a season (3,036).
- Over his college career as a starter, he owns a record of 30-2—the best in Texas history.

through the rest of the season—although he didn't play great against A&M—and Texas went undefeated.

And you saw a few signs. We all knew he was a great, great runner, kind of a super-sized Michael Vick. But in the fall of 2005, he showed that he was a very, very good passer. He led the nation in passing efficiency, put up better numbers than Matt Leinart of USC, the reigning Heisman Trophy winner.

But still, Vince Young didn't belong on a lofty plateau with the greatest players in the history of the game. Until the 2006 Rose Bowl. Vince Young turned in simply the greatest performance I've ever seen in 35 years of watching college football. I'm not alone. Lee Corso said it was the greatest game he had ever seen. Roger Staubach, too. You can start out with the numbers. He accounted for 467 yards of offense, 200 on the ground, 267 passing, and three touchdowns. But the amazing thing is the circumstances. This was the most hyped game since the Oklahoma-Nebraska regular season game in 1971. It was a national championship game, between two undefeated teams.

And let's look for a moment at the team that Texas knocked off. That USC team was gunning for its third consecutive national championship. They had won 34 consecutive games, the most impressive collegiate streak since those Bud Wilkinson Oklahoma teams of the early 1950s. USC had a million future pros. For the first time ever, they had two Heisman trophy winners in the same backfield, Matt Leinart and Reggie Bush. This is simply one of the greatest college football teams of all time. And Pete Carroll, a former NFL head coach and defensive coordinator had a month to prepare for Vince Young.

What did Vince Young do? All he did was score two touchdowns in the last six minutes of the game to lead Texas back from 12 points down in the fourth quarter. He was in total control of this contest. Mighty USC just couldn't stop him. He won this game single-handedly against one of the best college football teams ever. He was cruising around out there like Joe DiMaggio. He was playing at his own speed. On the last play of the game, he scores on fourth and five like it was no big deal. He was fresh as a daisy at the end of this game, like he could have played another game. As my partner Mike pointed out, the Rose Bowl is the granddaddy of all bowl games, and no one ever had back-to-back Rose Bowls that compared to those two performances by Vince Young. Especially that second one. This, sports fans, was a game for the ages, and no question that Vince Young was the hero.

Yes, I'm putting Vince Young on this list based on one game. But in college football one game can make a career. It's not like the pros where you have to do it week-in and week-out for ten years.

Many of the greatest players of all time—Tom Harmon, even Red Grange—cemented their legacies with just a couple of amazing performances, and Vince Young's amazing game vaults him into that elite company. If I had to sum up his performance in one word, here it is: un-freaking-believable.

DOGBITE: VINCE YOUNG'S BIG PAPA

Vince Young's father, a career criminal who's serving a 16-year prison sentence, walked out on him when he was four, so it wasn't surprising that Young got himself caught up in local gangs. But a huge turning point in his life was when his older cousin, Ivory Young, who played basketball at Alcorn State, introduced him to his old college pal, Tennessee Titans quarterback Steve McNair. The summer before his junior year in high school, Young attended McNair's football camp in Mississippi, where he was MVP. "He was a young kid at the time, but he was the team leader on this team of older kids," McNair said. Young calls McNair "Big Papa" and talks to his mentor two or three times a week. "Vince is becoming a man," McNair said. "It's great to see how much he's matured, not just as a player but more importantly as a person."

---

9. Two-Way Tommy

On offense and defense, Nobis led the way for Texas.

Here's a guy who I would not have thought about. My pal Dan Jenkins made a case for Nobis and then I started finding out more about him. Nobis was a legendary two-way player for Texas in the early 1960s. He won the Outland Trophy and got some consideration for the Heisman despite the fact that linemen never win it. Darrell Royal said he was the greatest two-way player he ever coached. Played guard on offense, linebacker on defense. He averaged 20 tackles per game during his career. That's five a quarter. And that's despite the fact that teams tended to run away from him. Not to mention the fact that he's an offensive guard. And all Texas did was run the football, and when they did, it was Tommy Nobis opening holes and moving guys out of the way.

Texas is one of the legendary programs in college football—Hook 'em Horns. And in the Texas pantheon Nobis is right at the very top. In 1963 he helped lead them to their first national championship, and he was the only sophomore starter on that great team. They went undefeated in the regular season. In the Cotton Bowl they held Navy, with Roger Staubach at quarterback, to just six points. The defense, led by Nobis—completely stymied Roger the Dodger, and

TOMMY NOBIS

- Two time All-American at linebacker, sophomore Nobis helped lead the Longhorns to a perfect 11-0 season and the National Championship in 1963.
- He won the Knute Rockne Award, given to the best lineman, the Outland Trophy, awarded to the best interior lineman, and the Maxwell Award, given to the college football's best player.
- A two-way player during his career at Texas, Nobis averaged nearly 20 tackles per game while also distinguishing himself as one of the nation's best guards.

the Longhorns won 28-6. And in '65 they beat number-one Alabama. That's a big-time impact, folks; two consecutive years, Tommy Nobis's teams are right in the thick of deciding the national championship. In three years, Texas went 27-5. Each of those teams was ranked number one in the nation at some point in the season. That's as good a run as you can ask of a modern college football team. And despite their great tradition, Texas has won only four national titles, and Tommy Nobis won the first. Go back and ask any fan of Texas football about the glory days of that program, and they're going to start telling you about Tommy Nobis.

He was a two-way player at a time when that was being phased out, so you give him an amazing amount of credit for that. Not only was he an All-American linebacker, but while the other guys were sitting on the bench, he was on the field, being a better offensive lineman than guys who specialized at that position.

If you want to distill Nobis's greatness into a single moment, let's try this one. In the '65 Orange Bowl, Texas is clinging to a 21-17 lead. They're playing Alabama, an excellent team, number one in the nation, with Joe Namath at quarterback. It's fourth down and inches, and Alabama is about to score. Nobis makes a huge, game-saving play.

DOGBITE: A MESSAGE FROM ABOVE

After leading Texas to a national championship in his sophomore season and averaging 20 tackles per game as a senior, Nobis was a hot commodity in the spring of 1966. He was drafted number one in two different leagues—by the Atlanta Falcons of the NFL and the Houston Oilers of the AFL. With both sides desperately trying to sway the All-American linebacker, he got some advice via a long-distance message. "Tell Nobis to sign with the Oilers," said astronaut Frank Borman, in orbit aboard Gemini 7. Despite playing very well during an 11-year pro career, Nobis played on mostly mediocre teams. He said, "Donny Anderson. The running back. You remember him? When he was at Texas Tech, I used to kick [him] all over the field. Then I get drafted by Atlanta, a new expansion team, and Donny goes to the Green Bay Packers. They go to the first two Super Bowls and win the whole thing. We never even made the playoffs." Maybe he should have listened to Borman.

Now, Nobis didn't go on to have the same kind of pro career that a lot of guys on this list did. He was drafted by the Atlanta Falcons, and even now a lot of Atlanta fans consider him Mr. Falcon. During his career, he was a very, very good player—he played in five Pro Bowls. And he's a good guy. He started the Tommy Nobis Foundation, which helps people with disabilities, and he's been with the Atlanta organization pretty much forever. But at the same time he had problems with injuries, played on lousy teams, and was pretty much overshadowed by Dick Butkus. That's one of the reasons why Nobis has been forgotten a little. But in college he was a great player for a legendary program. And that's why Tommy Nobis is in the Mad Dog Hall of Fame.

8. Roger the Dodger

Staubach single-handedly made a small school big time.

Who's the best quarterback in college football over the last 50 years? I think it's got to be Roger Staubach. Look at the recent history of college football. Name me a really dominant quarterback. On the one hand, you can pick a guy who wins, like a Jason White or a Carson Palmer, and I'll tell you that they're winning because of the system. If White or Palmer got hurt in a game in September and had to miss the rest of the season, Oklahoma or USC would have got the second-string guy in there and the team would have found a way to win.

Then you've got these guys at small schools like BYU or Boise State who pile up a million yards against bad teams in a lousy conference. The team doesn't make an impact on a national level. And I find it pretty hard to get excited about that.

Roger Staubach did both, and that's what you love about him. Put up huge numbers, which is important. But he also led Navy to a level where they were contending for a national title. Probably the best analogy among recent players is Doug Flutie, a guy who took a program that was nowhere, just took it on his back, and raised it to national prominence. And excuse the expression, but Staubach was kind of like Flutie on steroids. Staubach was tremendously athletic, a guy who created things by scrambling around in the backfield—Roger the Dodger—and then had the tremendous arm to get the ball there. To coin a phrase, he was a guy who scared both benches.

Staubach won the Heisman his junior year, by a huge margin, and he was only the fourth player to do that. He got injured his senior year, and that's why his numbers were down and the team lost five games.

Staubach has plenty of intangibles that you like. President Kennedy came to watch Navy football—or, more to the point, to watch Roger Staubach. Staubach also had great leadership ability. When he won the Heisman he was quick to give credit to his teammates. He said "I promised that I'd cut it up in pieces and give it to them. They're still waiting for that."

And, of course, Staubach went on to have a stellar NFL career, coming to the Cowboys after serving out his hitch in the Navy.

When you're rating quarterbacks in college football, it's not like the NFL, where everyone plays the same teams, the same level of competition, and you can compare pass completions and touchdowns and interceptions. In college football, you can't do that. You've got to depend a little more on gut reaction. Which guy got it done in the big spot. Go ask Lee Corso, who's been around for 50 years, who's the greatest college quarterback he ever saw. He'll say Roger Staubach. That's good enough for me, and that's good enough for a place in the Mad Dog Hall of Fame.

After that amazing college career, Roger Staubach was a 10th-round draft pick. That's right, a 10th-round pick. That's because Staubach went right from the Naval Academy to the service and was one of only three NFL players to see action in Vietnam. Even Dallas wasn't overly confident. "I never thought we would see this Heisman Trophy winner in a Cowboys uniform," remarked head coach Tom Landry. He was drafted in 1964 but didn't end up in Dallas until 1969 as a 27-year-old rookie and didn't get the starting job until 1971. But while serving in the armed forces, Staubach attended the Cowboys' training camps every year during his annual leave from the Navy. He kept a copy of the Cowboys' playbook with him and studied it whenever he had the chance.

7. Johnny Be Good

Lujack was the greatest player on Notre Dame's greatest teams.

Here's the signature play of Johnny Lujack's career. Yankee Stadium. 1946. Notre Dame against Army. Huge game. Titanic defensive struggle. Scoreless tie late in the fourth quarter. Doc Blanchard, who was Mr. Inside along with Glenn Davis's Mr. Outside, gets through the line, and there's nothing between him and the goal line. Except Lujack, who makes the tackle. Huge, enormous hit. Took Blanchard off the field on a stretcher. That play saved the game for Notre Dame and allowed them to go on and win the National Championship.

It's one of the greatest games in the history of college football, and Johnny Lujack made the decisive play. And one other detail—Johnny Lujack was the quarterback. Here's a Heisman-winning quarterback, and 60 years later the thing he's best remembered for is a defensive play. What does Lujack remember about that day? He threw three interceptions—all picked off by Arnold Tucker. "He was the only man open, Coach," he told

- In 1947 he won the Heisman and was AP Male Athlete of the Year.
- Led Notre Dame to three national titles (1943,1946,1947) and two undefeated seasons (1946 and 1947). Three years elapsed between his national titles because he was serving in the navy.
- As quarterback he was 144 of 280 for 2,908 yards and 19 touchdowns. He also ran for 438 yards and two touchdowns.

Frank Leahy. It was a lot funnier because he made that legendary play.

Lujack was also a huge star. He piled up accolades left and right. In addition to winning the Heisman in 1947, he was named Athlete of the Year by the Associated Press and was on the cover of *Life* magazine in 1947.

He was also an amazing all-around athlete. He was a letterman in baseball, basketball, and track during his sophomore year, the only four-letter man in Notre Dame history. One time he went three-for-four in a baseball game while winning the high jump and javelin throw in a track meet the same afternoon.

But here's Johnny Lujack's legacy. He was the star of what might have been the greatest college football team of all time. In 1946 and 1947, Notre Dame went 17-0-1 and outscored the oppostion 562-76. That's a 27-point margin of victory. This team not only never lost, they hardly even trailed. During Johnny Lujack's career, the Irish lost one game. And Lujack was a huge part of that, a guy who was playing 57 minutes a game. So when you want to talk about legendary college football programs, Notre Dame's got to be right at the top of any list you want to make. And if you sit a bunch of Notre Dame fans down and ask them "Who's the greatest Notre Dame player of all time," the consensus might very well be Johnny Lujack. That makes him worthy of a spot in the Mad Dog Hall of Fame.

6. Walker, Texas Runner

The House That Doak Built? It's also called the Cotton Bowl.

How big a star was Doak Walker in the 1940s? Kyle Rote, who was one of the biggest stars in college football himself, was at a newsstand and saw someone buying a football magazine. He said, "Hey, don't buy that one. It's not official." Not official? "No. It doesn't have a picture of Doak Walker on the cover." Walker, by all accounts, appeared on 47 magazine covers, and not just sports magazines. He was on the cover of the big glossy magazines that were usually reserved for presidents and movie stars, like *Life*, *Look*, and *Collier's*. Doak Walker was sort of the Brad Pitt of his day. The stores in Texas sold so many of his jerseys, one coach gave up and called his team the 37s because that's what all the kids were wearing anyway. They named a racehorse after him, for gosh sakes.

But Walker wasn't just famous, he was great. Back in 1948, he was only the second junior to win the Heisman. Dan Jenkins told me that if you do a list of the greatest college football players and you don't put Doak Walker on it, you're nuts. Nuts. Walker is the best player in the history of the Southwest Conference, which is one of the big-time conferences in college football.

Doak was another one of these multiple-threat players. He played both ways, ran, threw, kicked field goals, punted. He averaged 40 yards a punt. He did everything but mow the field between games. He was an All-American three times. And his SMU teams weren't just good, they were great. Over two seasons they went 18-1-3, and they went to the Cotton Bowl two years in a row. The Cotton Bowl itself became known as the House That Doak Built, because SMU had to move their games from Ownby Stadium due to the huge crowds that Walker drew.

One of the best Doak Walker stories comes from a game that ended in a tie. He gained 471 yards against TCU, but SMU was still down 19-13 in the fourth quarter. TCU tackle Harold Kilman turned to Walker and said, "What are you going to do now, Doak?" Bad idea. Walker returned the kickoff 56 yards, and made a circus catch on the nine-yard line. Then he was the decoy on the tying touchdown. To prove he was human—just barely—he missed the extra point and TCU had to settle for a tie.

And even now he's remembered. Every year the Doak Walker Award is given to the best running back in college football. And when Walker died, Ricky Williams put a decal with Walker's number 37 on his helmet in tribute. That, my friends, is a legacy.

5. In Harmon's Way

This Michigan great was a star on and off the field.

How's this for a football game? Tom Harmon ran for three touchdowns, passed for two more, kicked four extra points, and punted three times for an average of 50 yards all in a heavy rain. He led Michigan to a 40-0 win over Ohio State. And when he left that 1940 game with 15 seconds left, the Ohio State fans gave him a standing ovation and tried to tear off pieces of his uniform as souvenirs.

How about this one? In a game against California, Harmon scored four touchdowns—a 94-yard kickoff return, a 72-yard punt return, and an 86-yard run from scrimmage.

Michigan is one of the all-time great programs in college football, and Harmon is simply the best player they ever had. A tremendous elusive runner. He could kick and punt. He could pass. He played both ways and he was a ball hawk on defense—in that Ohio State game he picked off three passes as well.

Harmon was also a colorful character. They called him Old 98, but did you ever wonder how a guy that good got a number that high? Because on the first day of high school practice in Gary, Indiana, he picked a jersey out of the pile. When the coach told him that the new jerseys were for upperclassmen, he picked out the raggediest jersey in the pile. That day he returned a punt for 95 yards. The coach told him he could take a new jersey, but he kept that old one, and his number 98.

Harmon had a really interesting life after he left college. Columbia Pictures made a movie about his life: *Harmon of Michigan!* in which he played himself. In fact, the tax bill that came from his proceeds of the movie convinced him to play pro football. Harmon was also a war hero. He survived three plane crashes including one in French Guiana where he was the only one of the six crewmen to survive. It took him seven days of hacking through the jungle and wading through swamps without food before he was rescued. When he married his wife, her wedding gown was made from the bullet-riddled silk of his parachute.

Harmon was one of the first athletes to make a successful transition to broadcasting. And Mark Harmon the actor is his son, and his daughter Kristin married Ricky Nelson. One time he was on a plane with Vin Scully and the stewardess asked Harmon if he was on television. Harmon said "No, but he is." And pointed at Scully. Scully looked at the stewardess and said "That's incredible. You don't know who he is?" Harmon looked back at her and said, "I'm Ricky Nelson's father-in-law."

And all that is fun, but it wouldn't matter if Harmon wasn't an amazing player. How good was Tom Harmon? He was a one-man gang for Michigan. He was a two-time All-American, running for 2,134 yards, scoring 33 touchdowns and throwing for 16 more, not to mention being one of the top punters in the country. If you don't believe me, con-

TOM HARMON

- In 1940 he won the Heisman Award, the Big Ten MVP, the Maxwell Award, and the Walter Camp Award.
- During three seasons at Michigan, the two-time All-American rushed for 2,134 yards and scored 33 touchdowns. In his career, he completed 100 passes and 16 touchdowns.
- Harmon led the nation in scoring in 1939 and 1940, finishing with 237 career points.

sider the opinion of the legendary Amos Alonzo Stagg, who said that Harmon was better than Red Grange. "I'll take Harmon on my team, and you can have all the rest."

DOGBITE: GET OFF THE FIELD

One of the all-time weirdest plays in college football history was the one where the band was on the field as Cal scored the winning touchdown. There's actually a precedent for this in a 1941 game against Michigan. The game began with Tom Harmon returning the kickoff 94 yards for a touchdown. Before the half was over, Harmon, who was celebrating his twenty-first birthday, would add a punt return of 72 yards for a touchdown and reach the end zone on an 86-yard run. On that run Harmon would have to swerve around desperate Cal fan Bud Brennan, who had rushed onto the field and tried to bring him down at the 3-yard line. Michigan won the game 41-0, and Harmon kicked four extra points and made a friend. After the game Harmon met Brennan and they kept in touch.

---

4. Many Happy Returns

Johnny Rodgers made every punt and kickoff an adventure.

For pure excitement, there isn't a play in football, maybe even in all of sports, that matches a long kickoff return or a punt return. And by that measure, Johnny Rodgers of Nebraska is probably the most exciting football player of all time. There's never been a better return man than Rodgers.

In a classic game against Oklahoma in 1971, which was billed the Game of the Century, Rodgers set the tone. He scored the game's first touchdown on a spectacular 72-yard punt return for a touchdown. In a 35-31 win that clinched the national championship for Nebraska, he was the difference-maker. In the Orange Bowl, he had a 77-yard touchdown return against Alabama as part of a 38-6 win which gave the Huskers their second national title in a row. All in all Johnny Rodgers returned eight punts for touchdowns, and scored on nine kick-offs, which are both NCAA records.

But he didn't just return kicks. He was a great receiver and an effective running back. His 5,586 all-purpose yards were an NCAA record, and he put up those numbers despite the fact that Bob Devaney played it conservatively and Rodgers spent most of his time as a receiver. He won the Heisman Trophy, and, of course, he's the biggest reason why Nebraska won back-to-back national championships and put together a 31-game winning streak. An amazing legendary team.

In his very last college game, the 1973 Orange Bowl against Notre Dame, you saw the greatness of Johnny Rodgers. In a 40-6 win, he ran for 81 yards from scrimmage on 15 carries. He caught three passes for 71 yards. He scored four touchdowns, three on the ground and one in the air. And for good measure, he threw a 52-yard touchdown pass. At only 5'9" and 165 pounds, Johnny Rodgers might have been, pound for pound, the best college player ever.

That punt return by Rodgers against Oklahoma is considered one of the greatest single plays in college football history. But it was almost over before it started. Most people thought he would fair catch it, because Greg Pruitt was right there and hit him just as he caught it, and Rodgers's hand actually hit the turf as he nearly went down. "I don't know what I did or what I was thinking about," Rodgers said later. "The return was set up to the right, but I saw a hole to the left and cut back. I do remember seeing Joe Blahak up ahead and thinking he would get a block for me."

Nebraska's radio announcer Lyell Bremser had a great call of the run. "Here's (Joe) Wylie's kick. It's high. It holds up there. Rodgers takes the ball at the thirty. He's hit and got away. Back upfield to the thirty-five. To the forty! He's to the forty-five! He's to the fifty! To the forty-five! To the forty! To the thirty-five! To the twenty! To the ten!! He's all the way home! Holy moly! Man, woman, and child, did that put 'em in the aisles! Johnny 'The Jet' Rodgers just tore 'em loose from their shoes." The word is that all these years later Joe Wylie is still remembered in Nebraska as the guy who punted the ball to Johnny Rodgers.

3. Passing Grades

A storm of circumstance helped Sammy Baugh become college football's first passing star.

How can a player who never finished better than a distant fourth in the Heisman Trophy voting make the Top Ten of all time? Well, you can when you're as far ahead of your time as Sammy Baugh was.

Baugh was really the first great quarterback in the history of college football, and the first one to really use the forward pass. Sammy was a great athlete, but he also came along at just the right time. In 1934, Baugh's first year at TCU, there was a Perfect Storm of rule changes that would change the game of football forever. The first rule allowed more than one forward pass during a series of downs. Before that, tossing the ball twice was a five-yard penalty.

Another rule that was abolished: Before 1934 an incomplete pass into the end zone resulted in a turnover.

But the biggest rule change was the result of a change in the football itself. The circumference of the ball around the laces was reduced from 23 inches to 21½ inches. The playing pressure was also reduced, from 13½ pounds to 12½ pounds. Simply, this streamlined football went from something that had to be carried to something that could be thrown. Huge difference. And the first guy to throw it was Sammy Baugh of TCU. In a day when throwing 10 passes in a game was unusual, Baugh would toss as many as 40.

Dutch Meyer, TCU's Hall of Fame coach, originally recruited Baugh to play baseball. When he became football coach, Meyer saw what Baugh could do with the ball and designed an offense to take advantage of his arm. He designed a double-wing formation called the Meyer spread, which moved the receivers toward the sideline and put them closer to their pass routes, a big move toward a modern offense. In his three varsity seasons, Baugh threw 597 passes and completed 285 for 3,471 yards and 39 touchdowns. And it worked. In 1935, Baugh's first year as a starter, TCU went 12-1 and their only loss came against eventual champion SMU when Baugh was out with an injury. The next year TCU went 9-2-2, beating the top team in the country, undefeated Santa Clara, with Baugh outclassing Santa Clara's star quarterback Nello Falaschi.

Baugh did lots of other things as well. He ran from scrimmage, he ran back kicks, he played defensive back, and he punted amazingly well. Over his career, he averaged 40.9 yards per kick on 198 punts, and one time he bombed one 85 yards. And you could see this in his two bowl game wins. In the 1935 Sugar Bowl, it was raining and blowing like the dickens. Baugh picked off two passes, punted 14 times for a 48-yard average, and ripped off a 44-yard run in a 3-2 win against LSU. In the very first Cotton

Bowl in 1937, Baugh faced off against one of the nation's best quarterbacks, Marquette's Buzz Buivid. The Frogs won 16-6 and Baugh played so well that head coach Dutch Meyer sat Baugh down for most of the fourth quarter because he didn't want to rub it in, until the crowd chanted so loudly that he put Baugh back in at the very end of the game for a curtain call. If you want to know about Baugh's amazing pro career, check out the chapter on the greatest NFL players. But suffice to say that while he didn't get as many Heisman votes as Larry Kelley of Yale or Sam Francis of Nebraska, Sammy Baugh's place in the history of college football is secure.

DOGBITE: IF AT THIRD . . .

How did Slingin' Sammy get his nickname? Not for his throws from the pocket but for that long throw from third to first. Baugh was originally recruited by TCU as a third baseman. "Everybody thought I was a better baseball player growing up," he said. "I thought I was going to be a big-league baseball player."

And he almost did. Branch Rickey signed Baugh in 1938 to play third base with the St. Louis Cardinals. After Baugh led Washington to the NFL title—he told the 'Skins he would play football for only one year—he reported to Cardinals camp. But a football injury convinced the team to move him from third to shortstop, which is where he played at Columbus and Rochester. Baugh was discouraged because of the top-rated shortstop ahead of him on the depth chart. "I watched Marty Marion and thought, 'I'll never play shortstop for the Cardinals,'" Baugh said. "That made it easy to stick with football." But if he had been left at third and the Redskins didn't win the title, football history might have been very different.

2. Juiced

Ever controversial, O.J. Simpson was also college football's perfect runner.

I know that it's hard to talk objectively about O.J. Simpson. What happened in his murder trial is going to forever overshadow what he did on the football field. But let's try to stick to Simpson's legacy on the field.

Orenthal James Simpson is the greatest pure runner in college football history. He had tremendous pure speed. He was timed at 9.4 for the 100-yard dash and was part of a world record in the 440 relay. And unlike the Johnny Lam Joneses of the world, he was football fast, incredibly elusive and powerful. He only played two seasons, because he started his career at a junior college, but boy, what seasons. In 18 games he rushed for 3,124 yards. That's 164 yards a game. He scored 36 touchdowns, two scores per game. And he averaged 23.7 yards per kick return.

In a huge game against UCLA with their great quarterback Gary Beban, a game that would decide not only a trip to the Rose Bowl, but probably the national championship, Simpson broke off one of the great runs in the history of college football. With USC down 20-14 in the fourth quarter, and USC in a third and eight, Toby Page, the USC quarterback, called Red-23 Blast. Simpson hit the line, cut left, cut back right, and rumbled for a 64-yard touchdown run. The ultimate highlight film as part of a 177-yard afternoon.

In his senior year he won the Heisman

O.J. SIMPSON

- Won the Heisman Award, Maxwell Award, and Walter Camp Award in 1968, and named AP and UPI College Athlete of the Year that year
- In 1968 Simpson set NCAA records for most yards rushing in the regular season (1,709) and most carries (355).
- As a member of USC's 440-yard relay team he helped set a world record.
- In 1985 Simpson became the first Heisman Trophy winner elected to the Pro Football Hall of Fame.

Trophy by the largest margin in the history of the award, 2,853 to 1,103, sweeping all five regions. It was a landslide. Simpson is also part of that great Tailback U. legacy at Southern Cal. Mike Garrett, Anthony Davis, Ricky Bell, and Marcus Allen were all great, but O.J. was the best of them by far. And he was a great, great runner in the NFL. That 2,003-yard season—in 14 games—is one of the great accomplishments in pro football history.

Of course, when you start talking about his legacy off the field, things get muddled. It's easy to forget what a huge pitchman he was, running through airports for Hertz, landing big parts in movies like *The Towering Inferno* and *The Naked Gun*. He was a likeable guy, didn't offend anyone. He was also probably a murderer. He got off, but that's more about the quality of the lawyers he hired than the weight of the evidence.

I know it's hard, but if you can stick to the things that happened on the field, O.J. Simpson had it all. Power, speed, quickness, and a sense of drama in the big game. If you were a college football quarterback, and you had a choice of anyone all time to hand the ball to, you'd be nuts if you didn't want to give it to O.J. Simpson.

CLOSE, BUT . . .

Reggie Bush has been phenomenal in three years for USC, but he doesn't deserve to crack this list. If you held the voting for the Heisman after the bowl games, I think there's no doubt that Vince Young of Texas would have won, especially after Bush's ridiculous showboat lateral. And even if USC did win its third national championship, Bush wasn't the main man on those great Trojan teams. Matt Leinart was really the guy for USC.

In 2003, when Bush was a freshman, Leinart led USC to a share of the national championship. In 2004, Leinart won the Heisman and was the best player on the team. And while Bush was great in 2005, Leinart was the guy who made the huge, season-changing plays. Against Notre Dame fourth and nine, late in the game, Leinart went to the line of scrimmage, saw that Charlie Weis made a mistake defensively and he had man-to-man coverage on his wide receiver, and he threw the bomb for a first down. And it was Leinart who clinched the game with the quarterback sneak. That's why Bush, as good as he was, doesn't crack this list.

1. The Ghost of Football Past

When the game was at its biggest, Red Grange was its best.

"He was three men and a horse rolled into one for football purposes. He is Jack Dempsey, Babe Ruth, Paavo Nurmi, and Man O'War." That's what the great sportswriter Grantland Rice said about Red Grange. It's a little hard to fathom now, but in the 1920s college football was a huge, huge game, as big as baseball or boxing, and Grange, the Galloping Ghost, was a massive star, a legend in his own time.

He created his legacy in the most amazing single quarter of football in the history of the game. In 1924, Illinois faced a Michigan team that everyone thought was unbeatable. They came into the game on a 20-game unbeaten streak. They had allowed only 32 points during that streak, and would allow only 24 points in their next 17 games. On the opening kickoff, Grange ran 95 yards for a touchdown. He then scored on runs of 67, 56, and 44 yards. All in the first quarter. He gained 262 yards in 12 minutes. Before the final whistle blew he scored five touchdowns, threw for another, and accounted for 402 yards of total offense in a 39-14 upset that shocked the nation.

Afterward, Grantland Rice dubbed Grange the Galloping Ghost and wrote this verse about his exploits:

A streak of fire, a breath of flame
Eluding all who reach and clutch;
A gray ghost thrown into the game
That rival hands may never touch;
A rubber bounding, blasting soul
Whose destination is the goal.

Wherever he went from then on, Grange attracted huge crowds and piled up huge numbers at a time when the games were pretty much defensive struggles. At Penn, 63,000 people showed up to see him and he didn't disappoint. He ran for 237 yards and three scores through ankle-deep mud, scoring on a 60-yard run on his first carry to set the tone for a 24-2 win.

And in a strange way, the greatest college football player of all time had a huge impact on the NFL. He again shocked the world when he signed a contract with the Bears. Nobody took pro football seriously then. The NFL was a ragamuffin league. At least until the great Galloping Ghost agreed to play for George Halas and the Bears. The deal was enormous—guaranteeing Grange $3,000 a game and a percentage of the gate. But it didn't sit well with the people in college. "I'd have been more popular with the colleges if I had joined Capone's mob in Chicago rather than the Bears," Grange said.

Why is Red Grange number one on this list? Because he was the dominant player in the game at the very peak of its popularity. Red Grange was the ultimate big man on campus, and totally worthy of the top spot in the college football wing of the Mad Dog Hall of Fame.

RED GRANGE

- Three-time All-American (1923–25) and Big Ten MVP (1924)
- In his 20-game career at Illinois, the 5-foot-11, 175-pound halfback averaged 5.3 yards per carry, compiling 2,071 yards on 388 carries.
- In his career, he also caught 14 passes for 253 yards and completed 40 of 82 passes for 575 yards.
- 16 of his 31 touchdowns were from at least 20 yards. Nine were from more than 50.

DOGBITE: THE BENCHING OF RED GRANGE

How great was Grange? His coach pulled him out of that game against Michigan because he was too good. In only the first 12 minutes, he scored every time he had his hands on the ball. Literally. Four touches, four scores. When his coach, Bob Zuppke, took him out, the crowd gave him an endless standing ovation. Zuppke later said, "I pulled him out and he asked me why. I told him, 'No Michigan man laid a hand on you and I want you to come out unsoiled.' " The coach decided in the second half to put him back in, and Grange ran for one more touchdown and passed for another. What does Grange recall about the legendary game? "When I got to the bench, Zuppke said, 'You should have had another touchdown. You didn't cut right on one play.' " A reporter once asked Grange if that game against Michigan in 1924 was the high point of his career, and he said no, his biggest college thrill was holding the ball for Earl Britton's game-winning field goal in the 1925 season opener against Nebraska.

Chapter 4

The Top-Ten Coaches of All Time

When you rank the greatest all-time coaches in the world of sports—and I mean *all* across the world of sports, pro and college, from hockey to football—there are a number of qualifications you have to consider. First and foremost is the number of championships the coach has won. Taking a champagne shower is every coach's goal at the beginning of the season. So you look at the coach's résumé. How many times did he win it all? Naturally all of the guys on this list are great winners. You just can't make this list if you haven't won multiple championships.

But I'm not basing this strictly on a list of titles. That's too easy. You'd just count up the rings and you'd be done. Can you put a guy with only two championships into this select group, and leave out a guy who's got nine? In other words, can you put Dean Smith in and leave Phil Jackson out? I think that you can, simply because you've got to look at factors like the level of competition. What kind of teams did this guy beat?

But if that's the case, what else do you take into consideration? I think you've got to measure a bunch of other things. Like longevity. Unlike players, coaches can stay around forever. So I think you have to give an edge to a guy who's around for 30 years, as opposed to a guy who's around for seven.

And then there's the legacy issue. A coach is a teacher, after all. What kind of players did this coach produce? Is his résumé filled with Hall of Famers? And what about his assistants? Did they go on to bigger and better things? That's a huge factor. In those ways, a coach can continue to influence the game long after he's retired.

And then you've got to look at a coach's impact on the game. Do we still remember him? Is it because of his personality? Or did he invent things that are still being used today? Could he still have been a winner today? You've got to take all of this into account. With those things in mind, let's look at the greatest coaches and managers of all time.

10. Dean's List

At North Carolina, Smith was the game's greatest teacher.

If you had your choice of one coach that you'd wanted to play for, it might very well have been Dean Smith. He'd have been a good pick for a lot of reasons. You knew the team would be good (he won at least 20 games for 27 straight years). You knew you'd be in the NCAA tournament (the Tar Heels made the big dance 23 years in a row). You knew you'd be in a system that would get you good shots (his teams shot better than 50 percent from the field 32 times in 36 years). You knew there wouldn't be any recruiting violations. You knew that your teammates wouldn't do anything to embarrass the program, and the coach wouldn't do anything to embarrass himself.

Most of all, you'd learn something about the game. Dean was an incredible Xs and Os guy. He's the guy who invented the run-and-jump defense, and all kinds of transition sets and screens on offense and defense, all plays that are still used today. He started saving time outs for the end of the game. He had his players huddle up before a free throw attempt. He popularized the four-corners offense as a way to protect a lead, but he also supported the shot clock, which made it obsolete.

And he'd treat you like an adult. He'd tell you that if you ever got tired in a game, you could signal to him by tugging on your uniform. And as long as you were honest, he'd pull you for a quick breather and get you right back in the game.

And you knew he'd win. His record was 879-254. Think about that. You'd have to win 20 games a year for 35 years and you'd still be almost nine years away from catching Dean. That's not just a record, that's a *record*.

And it was Smith who really created that Tar Heel tradition. Sure, Frank McGuire won in 1957, but one of the all-time great programs in sports blossomed under Smith. There's a legacy of great coaches who came from his system as players or assistants—Larry Brown, George Karl, Doug Moe, Roy Williams. And he's the reason why players feel a real bond with the school—once a Tar Heel always a Tar Heel—coming back to campus to play pickup games, wearing powder blue at press conferences, things like that. Michael Jordan says he thinks of Dean Smith as his second father.

And you've got to give Smith credit for winning with the 1976 Olympic team in Montreal. Given what happened in 1972 in Munich, that was a gold medal the U.S. had to have.

Remember that Dean Smith didn't step right up and succeed. His first five years he didn't make the tournament, and in 1965, after a brutal 22-point defeat to Wake Forest, Smith was riding home on the team bus staring out the window. The bus rolled into Chapel Hill, and the coach was greeted by a group of students holding an effigy of him with a rope around its neck, chanting, "We want Smith." Dean got madder and madder, and finally he said, "If they want me, they'll get me." He went out there and very calmly faced these kids, and the whole thing disbanded, just like that. That's character.

But still, there are some issues with Dean Smith that keep him from ranking higher on this list. First and foremost, he was there for 36 years, with all kinds of Hall of Famers, so many great pros, and

---

DEAN SMITH

- Winningest coach in college basketball history with 879 victories
- Under Smith, North Carolina won two national championships (1982, 1993), reached 11 Final Fours and won 13 ACC Tournament Championships.
- The only coach in history to lead his team to 20-win seasons for 27 straight years (30 out of 31). No team has even done it 20 consecutive years.*

* During his tenure, 96% of Smith's players graduated.

he won only two championships. I know that there's a certain Russian roulette aspect to the NCAA tournament. And through the mid-1970s, there were a couple of times where he had a pretty good team but didn't even get a tournament bid because he finished second or third in a very tough ACC. Still, he made it to 11 Final Fours, but won the championship only twice. It took him forever to get that first title—on his seventh trip to the Final Four, and I'll be the first to admit that Dean Smith had some terrible, terrible defeats. Florida State beat him in the Final Four back in 1972, and he should never have lost to Al McGuire in 1977. Instead of playing to win, he played not to lose and that cost him.

There's a half-empty, half-full aspect to Dean Smith. He produced more great players than just about any college coach. Jordan, for starters, was the greatest player ever, and Dean got him to play within the Tar Heel system. The old saying goes that the only guy who could stop Michael Jordan is Dean Smith. Then you've got James Worthy and Bob McAdoo, who was at Chapel Hill for a year, who are Hall of Famers. And then there's just a bunch of guys who were either All-Stars or solid pros—Vince Carter, Brad Daugherty, Jerry Stackhouse, Bobby Jones, Charlie Scott, Billy Cunningham, Sam Perkins, Antawn Jamison, Rasheed Wallace, Phil Ford, Kenny Smith, Walter Davis. It's a much better roster than you could put together from Bobby Knight's alumni. Isiah Thomas and then who else? And while Wooden had more absolute all-timers with the two great centers and Gail Goodrich, I think that North Carolina under Smith produced

DOGBITE: SIX MEN ON THE COURT

When he played at Kansas, Dean Smith didn't get to start the last game of his senior season, and that always stuck with him. So when he got to North Carolina, Dean started Senior Day. On the last home game of the season, he would start all the team's seniors, including the subs and the walk-ons, to give them their moment in the sun. Nowadays, of course, every school does this, but it was Dean Smith who started it. One year when he had six seniors, he put them all on the floor at the start of the game—and got a technical foul for it—rather than single out one player and leave him on the bench. That's class.

more quality players. On the one hand, you've got to give him immense credit for recruiting and developing these players—this isn't the NBA, where the GM found all these guys for him. But the question remains. With all that talent, why didn't Dean Smith win more?

9. Little Napoleon Dynamite

Gruff John McGraw was baseball's greatest innovator.

The day that John McGraw retired, Lou Gehrig hit four home runs. And who got top billing in the newspapers the next day? John McGraw. McGraw of the New York Giants was baseball's first legendary manager. Even his great rival Connie Mack admitted it, "There has been only one manager—and his name is McGraw." McGraw won ten pennants and three World Championships, but the real story is how he did it.

First off, he was just about the fieriest son of a gun you'd ever want to meet. One umpire said that he ate gunpowder every morning and washed it down with warm blood. He made Billy Martin and Earl Weaver seem mellow. He was ejected 131 times in his career. That's practically a full season's worth. He got tossed 13 times in one year. One time an umpire ejected him, and McGraw got so ticked off that he had him barred from the stadium the next day and tried to play the game with players behind the plate. And while nothing was ever proven, there were a lot of whispers about McGraw gambling on games. He co-owned a pool room with Arnold Rothstein, who fixed the 1919 World Series.

Unlike most other great managers, who were usually backup catchers and utility infielders, McGraw was a great player, too, a .334 career hitter, 436 stolen bases, walked a ton. In 1898 he scored 143 runs in 143 games. In 1899, he hit .391. And he took no prisoners. When he was a player, he tripped and kicked and grabbed so many players as they rounded third that they added an umpire down the line. After a brawl with Tommy Tucker in a game in Boston in 1894, a fire broke out in the stands that burned down the park and 170 buildings in the neighborhood. McGraw was one tough son of a gun, but he got along with Christy Mathewson, the refined, college-educated pitcher from Bucknell. But while there's no denying that McGraw was a tough customer, he wasn't all bad. He tried to break the color barrier back in 1901, bringing a second baseman named Charlie Grant into spring training, claiming that he was a Native American. When cranky old Charles Comiskey found out that Grant had played in the Negro Leagues the year before, that was the end of that. McGraw's Giants played—and lost to—a lot of Negro League teams in exhibition games during the early 1900s, and McGraw brought Rube Foster in on the sly to work with his pitchers. Some people think that Foster helped Christy Mathewson perfect his fadeaway pitch. McGraw had a tremendous eye for talent: Mathewson, Frankie Frisch, Rogers Hornsby, Bill Terry, Carl Hubbell, and Mel Ott—those are just some of the Hall of Famers that played for him.

Little Napoleon's real legacy is as a great innovator. He played at a time when the game was still kind of in its infancy, or at least its childhood. Next time you hear an announcer talk about an outfielder hitting—or missing—the cutoff man, tip your cap to John McGraw. He invented it. He was the first to use relief pitching extensively, and it was he, not Casey Stengel, who invented platooning. (And it was McGraw who taught it to Stengel, who was his protégé.) Mugsy, as they called him, was a huge innovator. The hit-and-run? The squeeze play? The Baltimore chop? He invented all of them.

McGraw wasn't perfect. One day he held a tryout in the early 1920s, and this big guy wallops the ball all over the Polo Grounds. But when McGraw puts him at first, he's a little clumsy. McGraw doesn't

---

JOHN MCGRAW

- Coached the Giants to three World Series titles (1905, 1921, 1922)
- Led the Giants to 10 National League pennants and finished first or second 21 times
- His 2,840 wins rank second all-time behind Connie Mack.
- Managed more future Hall of Fame players—Christy Mathewson, Rogers Hornsby, and Mel Ott among them—than any other skipper in baseball history
- As a player, ranks third all-time in on-base percentage with a .466 mark, behind only Ted Williams (.482) and Babe Ruth (.474)

sign him. That was Lou Gehrig, who had been a huge Giants fan growing up. Although he was hardly alone in this, McGraw didn't do a great job making the transition from the dead ball era to the roaring twenties. And the other thing that hurts McGraw is that he had his success such a long time ago—it was more than a hundred years ago when he won his first World Series, and you wonder how he'd relate to today's millionaire ballplayers sitting by their lockers with laptops. Barry Bonds and John McGraw, there'd be some fireworks there.

If you're going to pick a guy to represent those rough and tumble early days of baseball, McGraw has to be your guy. Tremendous success, tremendous legacy, tremendous impact on the game. Even when he was still alive, McGraw's greatness was recognized. When they needed a guy to manage the National League in the very first All-Star Game, the choice was easy. They chose John McGraw.

8. Great Scotty

All Scotty Bowman did was win . . . and win . . . and win.

If there was a category for the most underrated coach, Scotty Bowman would be right at the top of the list. Let's start out with the obvious stuff. He coached nine Stanley Cup winners. Nine. With three different franchises. He coached a bunch of Hall of Famers, from Guy Lafleur and Larry Robinson and Ken Dryden with the Canadiens, to Mario Lemieux and Jaromir Jagr with the Penguins, to Steve Yzerman with the Red Wings.

SCOTTY BOWMAN

- Coached 30 seasons in the NHL and holds all-time NHL coaching records for regular season victories (1,244) as well as playoff wins (223)
- His .654 winning percentage is the highest all-time.
- Coached a record nine Stanley Cup winning teams, including four straight cups in Montreal and back-to-back crowns with the Detroit Red Wings in 1997–98
- Only NHL coach to lead three different teams to a Stanley Cup championship

---

But try this on for size. In 30 seasons as a head coach, he never had a losing record in any full season in which he was behind the bench. Not one. Now, Casey Stengel had losing seasons. Red Auerbach had a losing season. Not Scotty Bowman. That is unbelievable. And his best teams weren't just decent, they were great. That Canadien team in '76–'77 was probably the best team in NHL history. They won 60 games. When he was with Detroit in 1995–96, the Red Wings broke that record and won 62 games, although they did lose in the playoffs.

And Bowman won in all sorts of ways. He had a nice run with St. Louis, getting the expansion Blues to the Stanley Cup Finals twice in a row. In Montreal, he took over the greatest franchise in the sport and he didn't just uphold the tradition, he made that team the best in hockey history. He won five cups, including four in a row. That in itself might be enough to make this list. But Scotty Bowman was just getting started.

He went to Pittsburgh and stepped in under incredibly difficult circumstances. Bob Johnson won the Cup and then he got sick with cancer and ultimately died. That's a hard, hard situation for a coach. It takes tact and character. But Bowman pulled it off and the Penguins won the Cup, and if Lemieux hadn't gotten Hodgkin's disease himself, they could have easily won a couple more.

Scotty Bowman is the kind of guy you'd like to play for. Here's one of my favorite stories. He's on the road and he wanted to check the team's midnight curfew. So he goes to the bellman at the hotel, gives him a goalie stick, and tells him, "Listen I'll give you a hundred bucks for every one of my players that you get to sign this stick after midnight." He goes up to bed to get some shuteye. Next morning, he goes downstairs to collect the stick. Sure enough, every guy on the team signed it. That's Scotty Bowman for you.

Then he heads to Detroit, one of the original six NHL franchises, a great storied team in a great hockey town that had fallen on hard times. They hadn't won for more than 40 years. He comes in and doesn't win one championship, he wins three.

DOGBITE: BOWMAN'S EARLY RETIREMENT

If it wasn't for the stick of Jean-Guy Talbot, Scotty Bowman might never have become the winningest coach in NHL history. In a junior playoff game at the Montreal Forum on March 7, 1952, a 17-year-old Bowman was skating down the ice on a breakaway when Talbot cracked him in the head with a stick. Bowman suffered a five-inch gash that took 14 stitches to close and was never the same player afterward. Talbot was suspended for a year. Were there hard feelings? Hardly. When Bowman got the head job in St. Louis, he signed Talbot, and he played three years for Scotty. "There was no history to it," Bowman said. "He wasn't that kind of a player. Jean just lost control. He wrote me a long letter explaining it, pouring his heart out. I figure he just started me on my career fifteen years earlier than planned."

And how does he go out? On top. He won the Cup with the Red Wings in 2002 at home in Detroit. Steve Yzerman brings the Stanley Cup over to Bowman. He hoists the Cup high, skates a lap around the ice, then heads over to the owner Mike Ilitch and whispers in his ear, "I gotta go, Mike." A storybook ending.

And that's a surprisingly rare thing in the world of coaching. A lot of great coaches go out on kind of a sour note. But Bowman did it the right way. He went out on top.

7. Let Brown Do It

Paul Brown turned football from a game into a science.

Don Shula. Chuck Noll. Bill Walsh. Mike Holmgren. George Seifert. Mike Shanahan. Those are all coaches who have won the Super Bowl. And every one of them can trace their coaching roots back to Paul Brown. Those first three guys are all-time legendary coaches; if you expanded this list to 20, they'd be real contenders. Honoring Brown is my way of honoring them.

Brown has a lot of things going for him. Along with Jimmy Johnson, he's the only coach to win a collegiate national championship and a pro football title. And although it was a long time ago, don't forget that Brown won a very significant game in modern football history. He coached in the old AAFC with the Browns, and then he played the Eagles who were the defending NFL champs in the first game of the season and destroyed them 35-10 and went on to win the championship. It wasn't quite Joe Namath beating the Colts, but it was still a very significant game, because the Eagles didn't respect the new Browns from some shaky league.

Brown is a bit of an unusual character. Most of the guys on this list had really strong personalities. Some coaches were like father figures, some scared the heck out of you, and some even made you laugh. Brown wasn't really any of those things. Not a charismatic leader like Lombardi, he was kind of a middle-of-the-road guy, personalitywise. As a player, you respected him, but you didn't love him, and you didn't fear him. What he had was intellect. Brown was a tremendous innovator, really the first modern coach. So many things that we now take for granted, Brown invented. He was the first coach to use game films. He called plays from the sidelines by shuttling offensive guards in and out of the game. He was the first to draw up pass patterns. He held team meetings, handed out playbooks, marked up Xs and Os on the chalkboard. He sequestered his team in a hotel the night before a home game. Those are all earmarks of modern football, the idea that you could approach sports as a science, that you could outthink the other team, and it all began with Paul Brown. He brought the classroom approach to coaching, and that really brought coaching into the twentieth century, getting all the players on the same page. He made football a game about the mind as much as about the body.

He was also about outworking the other guy. Eagles coach Buck Shaw would just hop on the train at the end of the season and say, "See ya." You wouldn't see him again until training camp. Not Paul Brown. He'd be working all summer. He was the first coach to make this a 12-month a year job.

One thing you don't like very much is the fact that Brown had Jim Brown, the greatest running back of all time, at a time when the NFL was much more of a rushing league, and he wasn't able to win a championship with him. Coach Brown had a falling out with Art Modell and Modell fired him and brought in Blanton Collier, who won the title with Brown. The bottom line with Paul Brown is that he didn't have as much success as you'd like to see. He won three championships, but Bill Belichick already has that many.

PAUL BROWN

- Compiled a 167-53-8 record with only one losing season
- Coached the Cleveland Browns to four AAFC crowns, six NFL championship games, and three NFL titles
- Coached the Ohio State Buckeyes to their first national championship in 1942
- Among his innovations were the playbook, game study, advance scouting, the face mask, use of intelligence tests, sending plays in from the bench, and the draw play. Brown helped break the NFL color barrier by signing two black players—Bill Willis and Marion Motley.

But the guys that Brown taught have won more than their share, and that's why he's worthy of a spot in the Mad Dog Hall of Fame.

CLOSE, BUT . . .

There are a bunch of NFL coaches who could certainly make your list:

• **Chuck Noll:** Coached the greatest team of all time in Pittsburgh. But aside from that six-year period, he was a very good coach, not a great coach.

• **Don Shula:** Won a billion regular season games, but when it came to championships, too many bad losses and close calls. Remember that he lost the '64 title game as a big favorite to Collier's Browns and, of course, he lost to the Jets in Super Bowl III.

• **Bill Walsh:** Great innovator, and in the middle of a great legacy, inheriting from Paul Brown and passing it along to Mike Shanahan, Mike Holmgren, and George Seifert. If he had won a fourth title, you'd have to give him some consideration for this list.

• **Tom Landry:** Similar to Shula. He was 2-5 in championship games. If he had another title or two, if Dallas could have knocked off the Steelers in the Super Bowl, he'd be a contender.

• **Joe Gibbs:** It's not like he had Joe Montana to work with. He won championships with Doug Williams and Mark Rypien in Washington, and you've got to like that.

• **Bill Belichick:** You'll know better about him in five years. He started a dynasty at a time, with the salary cap and free agency, when we all thought that dynasties were a thing of the past. If he can keep the Patriots in contention and win another title or two, he could crack this list.

• **Bill Parcells:** Great motivator, did a lot with a little, but bottom line, he's got only two rings.

6. Bear Necessities

With one part charm and two parts fear,
Bryant molded players into champions.

Talk about a great nickname. Bear. The only thing better than Paul Bryant's nickname is the way he got it. He wrestled a bear when he was a teenager. Talk about toughness. There's a lot that you like about Bryant. The first is that he was successful in a couple of other situations. His teams at Kentucky were very good, and if it wasn't for Adolph Rupp, he might have stayed there forever. But at Kentucky, Rupp was number one, and the football coach, no matter who he was, was number two. And Bear Bryant didn't play second fiddle to anyone, so that just wasn't going to work out. Bryant missed out on a couple of big jobs, and he ended up at Texas A&M and had three winning seasons and won a Southwest Conference title. Remember the Junction Boys? He took his team to Junction City, Texas, roasted these guys in the hot sun, out in the cactus fields, worked them so hard that he practically killed them. Now, I don't think it was about instilling toughness in these kids. I think it was simply about the fact that Bryant was ticked off that he was stuck at Texas A&M, and he took it out on the kids. And yet the guys on that team, like Gene Stallings, they love Bear Bryant. They had special rings made up to commemorate that boot camp.

And that's the mystique of Bear Bryant. He was a tough, no-nonsense guy. My way or the highway. And there are a lot of football coaches who are like that. But those guys are feared more than they're revered. Not Bryant. Joe Namath, he's the toast of Broadway, winning the Super Bowl, and all he talks about is the greatness of Bear Bryant. Ken Stabler, too, wins the Super Bowl and he's talking about Bear Bryant.

Bryant was the iron fist in the velvet glove. All of his players love him. His Southern charm has something to do with it, but I think it may have something to do with absence making the heart grow fonder. You're scared to death when you're 18, but by the time you're 28 you sort of look back on it and laugh. Bear mellowed a little bit as he got older and pretty soon it was a mutual admiration society.

And part of Bryant's edge was that charm. He would head into a recruit's house and pretty soon he's recruiting the parents as much as the kid. He's a big, strong, good-looking guy, gives dad a firm handshake, tells mom that this is absolutely the best lemon pie he ever had, and asks for the recipe for his wife. This high school kid sees Bear Bryant in his kitchen flattering his parents. What is this kid going to do, play at Auburn? No chance.

Sure, Bryant was charming, but he also had tremendous success. Bear won at least a share of six national titles and 14 SEC championships. He was the leader in all-time wins when he retired. Tremendous winning percentage. And remember, this is in Alabama. There's no professional football there. There isn't a major league franchise in any sport. The only real competition was Auburn, and they were pretty much a foil for the Crimson Tide when it came to football. Alabama football is like a religion there. They could play a Super Bowl at Legion Field and if Alabama had a spring scrimmage 50 miles away in Tuscaloosa at the same time, more people would care about the Alabama game.

It kind of ended in dramatic fashion for Bryant. He coaches his last team in 1982, and he dies a month later. It wasn't like he went to work in the booth for ABC. He couldn't live without Alabama football.

Why isn't he higher? Because he's not the number-one guy in his sport—Rockne is—and all the guys ahead of him are number one in their particular sports. And while Bryant was absolutely worshipped in Alabama, I think his impact outside that region isn't quite as huge as some of the other guys. But when it came to modern college football and the one guy who made himself a legend, Bear Bryant was the guy.

DOGBITE: BITTEN BY A BEAR

That story about Bryant wrestling a bear? All true. When he was 14, a carnival came to his Arkansas town and Paul Bryant—who stood 6'1", 180 pounds—was dared to wrestle a bear for one dollar. He took the dare. "I got the bear pinned, holding on real tight," he recalled. The trainer, hoping for a more balanced fight, whispered to Bryant, "Let him up. Let him up!" "The bear finally shook loose, and the next thing I knew, his muzzle had come off," recalled Bryant. "I felt a burning sensation behind my ear, and when I touched it, I got a handful of blood. The damned thing bit me. I jumped from the stage, ran up the aisle and out of the theater. I never did get my money."

CLOSE, BUT . . .

If you're naming great college football programs, you have to include Miami. That's been the dominant program of the last twenty years. But there've been four different coaches—Schnellenberger, Jimmy Johnson, Erickson, and Coker—and none of them individually have the résumé to crack this list.

• **Joe Paterno:** A great coach, a top program for a long period of time. Close to Bryant recordwise, but he doesn't have the same aura about him that Bear does.

• **Bobby Bowden:** Nice homespun guy, but he lost too many big games that he should have won, had too many times where he was the second best, or even the third best, team in the state of Florida.

• **Woody Hayes:** Great rivalry with Bo Schembechler, but he just didn't have the same level of success that Bryant did.

5. Casey on the Bench

Stengel acted like a checkers player,
but he usually ended the season with a checkmate.

When you think of a great baseball manager, you think of a guy who's sort of a chess player in the dugout. A guy like Gene Mauch or Tony La Russa, who knows what every hitter is likely to do in every situation. He's thinking two moves ahead of the other manager. Trying to squeeze out an advantage on every pitching change, every pinch hitter, even stealing signs. In short, a guy who's not only smart, but just a little bit smarter. Sometimes even, as was the case with Mauch, a little too smart for his own good.

And yet the guy that I'm going to pick seems like the very opposite of that. Casey Stengel. I know you're going to say, "C'mon Chris, Casey

Stengel? Are you nuts? You've got this Hall of Fame filled with guys like Vince Lombardi and Knute Rockne and Red Auerbach, and you're gonna put Casey Stengel in? The man sits there babbling. He couldn't put together an English sentence if his life depended on it. Get real."

I think Stengel gets a bad rap. People remember Stengel fondly—even guys who hated the Yankees can't really work up too much animosity towards him, maybe because he put some time in with the Dodgers as a player and later with the Mets, where he managed good but boy did they play bad. He was this colorful old guy, your friend's nutty grandfather, a real screwball. But when it came to baseball, there's this sense that he was a figurehead, that this Yankee juggernaut was rolling along on auto pilot and Stengel was just along for the ride. I don't buy that for a moment. For one, just look at the talent that he had to work with. Sure, he had Mickey Mantle, Whitey Ford, and Yogi Berra. But just look across town. The Dodgers had Duke Snider and Roy Campanella and Pee Wee Reese and Jackie Robinson. And guys like Gil Hodges, who just miss making the cut for the Hall of Fame. The Giants had Willie Mays. The Indians were loaded with pitching, with Feller and Lemon. It's not like Casey was the only guy with players.

Stengel got a lot of mileage out of guys like Moose Skowron and Billy Martin. There were a lot of pitchers, guys like Don Larsen, who had great moments for the Yankees, but they never did anything before or since. While most people think

CASEY STENGEL

- As skipper of the Yankees, Stengel coached seven world championship teams (1949–53, 1956, and 1958), including a record five straight.
- Only manager to win 10 pennants in 12 years
- Holds record for most World Series games managed (63) and the most World Series wins (37)
- Stengel is the only person to have worn the uniform (as player or manager) of all four Major League Baseball teams that played in New York City in the twentieth century (while each team was in New York City): the New York Giants (as a player), the Brooklyn Dodgers (as both a player and a manager), the New York Yankees (as a manager), and the New York Mets (also as a manager).

of Stengel as the guy who started the platoon system, he actually learned that under John McGraw, who really took him under his wing, but Stengel took it to a new level. As Jerry Coleman told me, Casey was a genius at using his whole 25-man roster. He got contributions from everybody.

Stengel was way smarter than he looked. A lot of that babbling idiot stuff was just an act. Remember that even then New York was the media capital, and there was a whole pack of newspaper beat reporters following the team. So when he didn't want to answer a question, he wouldn't stonewall the reporters, he'd just start some stream of consciousness ramble, and everyone would laugh, and forget what the question was. He'd make you laugh. He charmed the pants of those gruff old baseball writers. In a lot of ways, he was really the face of that team. What does anyone remember about Miller Huggins or Joe McCarthy? Nothing. But Stengel was more than just the guy filling out the lineup card. He was a personality. He'd walk out on the field with an umbrella asking the umpire to call a rain delay. He was really one of the first media-savvy managers, and you've got to give him credit for that, too.

Whitey Herzog always said that the toughest job in professional sports is to manage a Hall of Famer on the way out. And that's what Stengel had to do. He had to step right in there and manage Joe DiMaggio. And if DiMaggio wasn't exactly on the way out, he certainly wasn't the player he'd been in 1941. With the heel problems that Joe had, Stengel had to put him at first base. Joe didn't like that, but a manager's not running a popularity contest. Stengel and DiMaggio, they co-existed, and sometimes that's the best you can do. Same thing with Phil Rizzuto to a lesser degree.

On the other hand, Stengel groomed Mantle and Whitey from the time they were rookies, and he deserves some credit for that. He managed the transition from the DiMaggio era to the Mantle era without so much as a speedbump, and that's got to mean something. Which is not to say that Casey didn't make mistakes. He screwed up the 1960 World Series; we all know he did. There's no way they should have lost to the Pirates. They outscored them by a billion runs, but they lost all the close games. Stengel should have pitched Whitey Ford three times—he won the pennant comfortably and there weren't any earlier rounds to the playoffs, so he could have set up the rotation any way he wanted to. That was one of the biggest upsets in the history of baseball, and Stengel found himself on the short end of it, and he got fired because of it. Since he went out on that sour note—and Ralph Houk stepped right in and won the World Series in

1961—that's kind of been Casey's legacy. That bad loss and those awful Mets teams are what people remember.

If you really want to find out what kind of manager Casey Stengel was, you've got to get out the record book and do the math. Between 1949 and 1960, in 12 seasons, Stengel won ten pennants and seven World Series. And one of the pennants he lost, the Yankees won 103 games but the Indians won 111. That's as good as it gets. Baseball is not a sport of dynasties, like basketball and hockey, and there's really no one in baseball history who's ever had that kind of success. As Casey might have said, you can look it up.

4. Red Alert

Auerbach was the architect of basketball's greatest dynasty.

The only real question is where Red Auerbach belongs, categorywise. Do you categorize him as a coach, or is he a general manager? As a coach, he's got amazing credentials. He won nine championships in ten years, and the only year that they didn't win between 1956–57 and 1965–66, Bill Russell had a bum ankle. The Celtics did it year in and year out, through the drudgery of a long season, in a league where you can play five games in five nights, and in a town that didn't love the NBA the way they loved baseball and hockey. Red was a master at starting out the season well. Put the pedal to the metal early, get a big lead, and then regroup for the playoffs. But when they won four titles in row, Auerbach found a way to get them motivated to win five in a row.

And it wasn't like the Celtics were beating the Utah Jazz and the Indiana Pacers to win their titles either. Auerbach's Celtics beat the Philadelphia Warriors with Wilt Chamberlain and the Lakers with Jerry West and Elgin Baylor. Auerbach's teams had an uncanny knack for winning decisive games, working their way out of tough spots. They won Game 7 against St. Louis in 1957, double overtime, one of the greatest games in history. In '62, they beat the Lakers in overtime of Game 7 in the Finals. And again, in 1965, when Johnny Havlicek stole the ball in the closing seconds of Game 7 against the Sixers. Somehow or another Red always got the chance to light that victory cigar and stink up the joint. And then you talk about the players—Russell and Bob Cousy, two of the Top Ten players of all time. John Havlicek, Sam Jones, Tom Heinsohn, Bill Sharman. And when one of those guys retired, did they stop winning? No they did not. And while he's not Branch Rickey in this regard, Auerbach was the first to draft an African-American player, and the first NBA coach to start five black players at the same time.

If you've got to put a little bit of a knock on Auerbach, it's this: He may have been a better executive than he was a coach. After all, when Red retired, Bill Russell took the same team and won two championships. In that regard, he's more of an icon than he is an innovator. He only employed seven set plays. What made the Celtics winners is the players he got to execute those plays. Auerbach's detractors would make the argument that the talent was so good that anyone could win with this team. The response to that is simple. A) They might win, but not nine titles in ten years, and B) Auerbach has to get the credit for putting that great team together. The other thing that's funny is that Auerbach understood his limitations. We think of old Red as having been around forever—Isaac Asimov, the late science fiction writer, was his classmate, and he coached Bowie Kuhn in high school—but he was only 48 years old when he stepped down as coach and concentrated on being a GM. But by then he knew that his legacy was secure.

CLOSE, BUT . . .

The most controversial omission on this list of coaches is probably Phil Jackson. The man has nine titles after all, and it's hard to discount that. My counter argument is this: He won those titles with two of the greatest players in the history of the league in Michael Jordan and Shaquille O'Neal, and two perfect complementary players in Scottie Pippen and Kobe Bryant. These teams were pretty much set when he got there. He didn't build them. Jackson did a good job of establishing a relationship with his stars, but I don't think that he did anything that another coach couldn't have done with the same players. He wasn't an impact coach in my view, a guy who could make a good team great. How well did his Triangle offense work that season when Jordan wasn't around?

3. Made of Wooden

John Wooden was the master teacher behind UCLA's hoops dynasty.

To show you how tough a list this is, John Wooden has as many championship rings as he has fingers—including both thumbs—but he's still no higher than number three on this list.

Now, I know that a lot of people would disagree with this choice. You could make a very reasonable argument for putting Wooden at the top of the list. After all, he won seven championships in a row. Four undefeated seasons. That amazing 88-game winning streak. His overall record was 620-147. And along the way he coached all kinds of great players—Lew Alcindor, Bill Walton, Gail Goodrich, Walt Hazzard, Marques Johnson, the list goes on and on. And he really built the UCLA program from the bottom up. The first year they were barely .500 and they had to share the gym with the volleyball team. Nowadays if a coach makes the Final Four once, he's all over *Sports Illustrated* and the school is ready to rename the gym after him. Wooden made nine Final Fours in a row. Nine.

But that's exactly the point. Wooden couldn't have done that today. College basketball was a different sport back then. When Wooden had this amazing success in the 1960s and the early seventies, UCLA was in a lousy conference, and they got the automatic bid every

---

JOHN WOODEN

- Coached the Bruins to a record ten national championships (runner-up Adolph Rupp has four) and coached the Bruins to seven straight titles from 1966–73
- Led Bruins to four perfect seasons (1963–64, 1966–67, 1971–72, 1972–73) and a record 88 consecutive victories
- Under Wooden, UCLA won 38 straight NCAA tournament games and 19 PAC 10 championships.
- As a player, Wooden once sunk 138 straight free throws.

year. John Wooden did not coach in the ACC, where you had to beat North Carolina, Duke, and NC State. Name me another great program in the PAC-8 in his career. Name me one. What, USC one year? Come on— let's not get carried away.

And when the tournament rolled around, UCLA always ended up in the West region. They never got shipped out. They usually ended up playing 10 minutes from home against the Montanas of the world. And they only had to win two games to get to the Final Four. John Wooden had cakewalks into the Final Four. Nowadays, the NCAA tournament is so much tougher. You end up playing a tough game against a number six seed, and somewhere along the line you're going to get picked off. It happened to Dean Smith. It happens to Coach K. It would have happened to Wooden, too.

My knock on Wooden is his team only had to win a couple of tough games a year. That's it. To win those championships, Red Auerbach had to beat the Lakers and the Sixers. Lombardi had to beat the Colts and the Cowboys. Wooden was beating up on Oregon State.

The other thing, of course, is that when Wooden was coaching, college basketball was structured in a way that favored dynasties. Players had to stay in school four years. Had to. If you wanted to leave school, you didn't go to work for the Lakers, you went to work pumping gas. No, they couldn't play as a freshman, but then they stayed until they graduated. Do you think that Bill Walton and Lew Alcindor would have played as seniors if they were playing today? No way.

Still, you've got to give Wooden credit for recruiting these players and finding a way to get them to work within a team concept. He was a great teacher and he emphasized the fundamentals like crazy. He was also a great motivator in his quiet kind of a way. One time someone said to him, "You've got two sets of rules." And he replied "No, I don't. I've got twelve sets of rules. Each player is an individual and needs to be treated that way." His stars—and I'm talking about Alcindor and Walton—weren't your garden variety jocks. Both were very cerebral, so it took tact and intellect to be able to get them on your side, and to his credit, Wooden had that.

So I don't want this to come off as a criticism of Wooden. He's clearly the greatest college basketball coach of all time. No doubt. But I think that if Vince Lombardi came back and could coach in 2005, he'd be just about as successful as he was then. But in today's game, with the way that the NCAA tournament is set up, John Wooden would have a hard time being much more successful than Mike Krzyzewski.

DOGBITE: THE RUBBER MAN

Most people don't know this, but John Wooden was one of the nation's first great college basketball players. He was a three-time All-American, averaged 12.8 points per game, and led the Purdue Boilermakers to two Big Ten titles and helped them claim the national title in 1932. Dubbed the Indiana Rubber Man for the way he would dive on the court, he was named College Player of the Year his championship season. But rather than play professional ball, he spurned an offer from the Boston Celtics. Wooden decided to teach and coach . . . at a high school. Wooden's only one of two people to have been inducted to the Basketball Hall of Fame as a player and a coach. The other? Lenny Wilkens.

---

2. Solid as a Rockne

Knute lived a short life . . . and left an indelible legacy.

"Win one for the Gipper." Is there anyone in America who doesn't know that phrase? They might not know a third down from goose down, but they know that line. And they know Knute Rockne. That's why Rockne is number two on the list.

But who was Knute Rockne? First off, Rockne was a pioneer, a trendsetter. At the time that he was coaching, college football was probably the biggest team sport in the country, even bigger than major league baseball. And Rockne was a big part of that. Notre Dame was one of the first teams to play a national schedule, and he was instrumental in playing up rivalries with teams like USC. He was also one of the first to understand the role of the media in sports. Do you remember Harry Stuhldreher, Don

KNUTE ROCKNE

- Led his team to six national championships, including five undefeated seasons (1919, 1920, 1924, 1929, and 1930) and his .881 winning percentage is the highest in college football
- Rockne produced 20 first-team All-Americans, including George "Gipper" Gipp and members of the legendary Four Horsemen.
- At the time of Rockne's untimely death, he had an active 19-game winning streak and had just completed his second straight championship season.
- Eighty-nine of his former players went on to become coaches.

Miller, Jim Crowley, and Elmer Layden? Maybe not, but you remember the name that Grantland Rice gave them: The Four Horsemen of Notre Dame.

And Knute Rockne was Notre Dame football. Just like Yankee Stadium was the House That Ruth Built, Notre Dame Stadium was the House That Knute Built. The Golden Dome. The Subway Alumni. Touchdown Jesus. That all started with Rockne, and 80 years later it's still going strong. USC and Oklahoma don't have their own network television packages. Notre Dame does.

And Rockne deserves credit for building something that endured. The Packers fell apart when Lombardi left. UCLA wasn't successful in the post-Wooden era. But Rockne put Notre Dame on the map, sportswise, and they've stayed there for the better part of a century.

And while Rockne was so much bigger than his record, his record was still tremendous. In 13 years, he won three consensus national titles, had five undefeated seasons, and produced 20 first-team All-Americans. He lost 12 games in 13 years. Think about that. His .881 winning percentage is still the best in the history of college football.

How big a star was Knute Rockne? The Studebaker car company actually hired him to be their public spokesman and sales consultant in 1928, paying him a salary of $10,000, and in the winter of 1931, they announced the creation of a new firm to be called the Rockne Motor Corporation.

The other thing that people forget about Rockne is that he died in a plane crash in a place called Bazaar, Kansas, in 1931 while flying from

Kansas City to Los Angeles. He was only 43 years old. He won the last 19 games he coached, so who knows what he might have done over the next 20, 30 years? He could have easily finished with 10 or 15 championships.

DOGBITE: WIN WHAT FOR WHOM?

How do you separate fact from legend? When you're talking about Rockne and the Gipper speech, it's hard. Here's how the legend goes. George Gipp was Rockne's first All-American and an amazing player—a great runner, passer, punter, and defender, and his school record of 2,341 total rushing yards lasted until 1978. After beating Northwestern in 1920, Gipp came down with strep throat, which, in the days before penicillin, led to a fatal case of pneumonia.

In 1928 Rockne is said to have given this speech to his team at halftime of a scoreless tie against a powerful Army team: "Well, boys . . . I haven't a thing to say. Played a great game . . . all of you. Great game.

"I guess we just can't expect to win 'em all. I'm going to tell you something I've kept to myself for years. None of you ever knew George Gipp. It was long before your time. But you know what a tradition he is at Notre Dame. And the last thing he said to me—'Rock,' he said, 'sometime, when the team is up against it, and the breaks are beating the boys, tell them to go out there with all they got and win just one for the Gipper. I don't know where I'll be then, Rock,' he said, 'but I'll know about it—and I'll be happy.' "

Notre Dame went on to beat Army 12-6 that day, that much is clear. The legend of the Gipper was immortalized in the 1940 film *Knute Rockne All American* with Ronald Reagan playing Gipp. Less well known is the fact that Gipp was a notorious gambler (this was a common practice in collegiate sports at the time) and was expelled for cutting classes in 1920. And nobody ever called him the Gipper. As for Rockne, it's doubtful that he was at Gipp's deathbed, and the coach was famous for using half-truths to motivate his players, invoking everything from his not-so-sick son to a long-shot possibility of a Rose Bowl bid to get them to play harder. And the Irish didn't exactly blow out Army in the second half. The Cadets scored first, and Army was on the Notre Dame one-foot line and poised to score when the whistle blew—some believe prematurely. Does it matter? As Carleton Young said in *The Man Who Shot Liberty Valance*, "When the legend becomes fact, print the legend."

And Rockne's death was a huge deal at the time, a stop-the-presses news story, almost like when a president gets shot or something. Here's what Will Rogers said: "It takes a big calamity to shock a country all at once, but Knute, you did it. You died one of our national heroes. Notre Dame was your address, but every gridiron in America was your home."

1. In-Vince-Able

Lombardi was the very model of a modern football coach.

What do you need to know about Vince Lombardi? He lost only one playoff game in his life. One. When it comes right down to it, championships are how you measure a coach, and that is a tremendous record. Lombardi won five championships. Three in a row. The one playoff game that Lombardi lost? It was the very first one. It ended 17-13, when Jim Taylor was tackled by Chuck Bednarik on the 7-yard line on the last play of the game. But this wasn't some kind of moral victory for Lombardi. It was a lesson. Early in the game he had a chance at a field goal and decided to go for it on fourth down. At dinner that night in a Philadelphia restaurant, he told broadcaster Ray Scott, "I will never make that mistake again. Next time, I'll take the points."

The next year, he made sure the field goal wasn't going to matter. The Packers beat the Giants 37-0 for the title and held New York to about 40 yards of offense. Shut them down completely.

Lombardi showed you how important a coach was in the NFL. The year before he got to Green Bay, the team was terrible. Awful. Scooter McLean was the coach, and these guys just couldn't get out of their own way. But it wasn't that they didn't have any players. Bart Starr was there. Paul Hornung was there. But they didn't start winning until Vince Lombardi got there.

Lombardi is more than a great coach though. He was a tremendously important figure in American sports, in American culture. Even today, he epitomizes the classic image of a football coach, standing on the sidelines with his wool coat and his fedora. And even though the coaches today wear windbreakers, they still channel Lombardi's attitude. Rugged, unforgiving, tough on his players, never took a short cut. That's Lombardi. An NFL football coach has an aura around him that doesn't surround coaches in the other sports. A football coach is in control more than the other coaches are. No guaranteed contract, you can cut almost anybody any time you want, the idea that the players are interchangeable pieces. A football coach is like a great army general, a leader of men. That's what Lombardi was. Henry Jordan, his great defensive end, pretty much summed it up. "He treats us all the same. Like dogs." But it worked. Jordan also said, "I play for the love of the game. The love of the money. And the fear of Lombardi." That, in a nutshell, is Lombardi's motivational technique.

And when you're talking about the change-the-game factor, Lombardi is at the very top in that category, too. Did John Wooden reinvent college basket-

> ## VINCE LOMBARDI
>
> - Lombardi coached the Packers to six division titles, five NFL championships, two Super Bowls (I and II), and compiled a 105-35-6 record.
> - The Packers had a 1-10-1 record the year before Lombardi arrived; it took him only three seasons to lead the Packers to the NFL title.
> - Lombardi never had a losing season, and in 1969, two years after he retired from the Packers, he led the Redskins to their first winning record in 14 years.
> - Richard Nixon considered Lombardi as a running mate, but reconsidered after learning Lombardi was a Kennedy Democrat.

ball? No. Did Casey Stengel make baseball hugely popular? No. But Lombardi helped make the NFL what it is today, the biggest and best league in America. That trend began with the 1958 championship game between the Giants and the Colts. But Steve Sabol of NFL Films maintains that it was Lombardi who really represented Pete Rozelle's league during its growth period. He was a big-city guy, a New York guy, in a small town in the Midwest, creating an epic franchise, and that's an unbelievable combination. Titletown, USA. It was a story that had something for everybody. The Packers were the most important team in football—and who was the face of that team? It wasn't Bart Starr. It wasn't Paul Hornung. It wasn't Willie Davis. It was Vince Lombardi.

All of that mythmaking is fine. But the other part of Lombardi's legacy is that his teams always came up big in the big spot. He was under tremendous pressure to win those first two Super Bowls against the Chiefs and Raiders, and the Packers didn't just win, they dominated. Blew them out. In fact, that domination set up Joe Namath's big win in Super Bowl III, which was the last piece in the puzzle that set up football as the biggest game in America.

Even more than 30 years after his death, you still feel Vince Lombardi's impact on the league. What does Paul Tagliabue hand to the winner of the Super Bowl? The Vince Lombardi trophy. Named after the greatest coach of all time.

DOGBITE: THE GIFT OF LOMBARDI

Frank Gifford was the number-one pick for the Giants in 1952, and he had a rough rookie season. The team's awful, 3-9, and he's getting beaten up, playing both ways. Gifford told us that he talked to owner Wellington Mara at the end of the year and said, "I'm done. I'm going back to California to make movies." And Wellington said "I promise I'll make it better." Mr. Mara begged him to come back, and Gifford thinks about it the whole off-season and finally returns in July. Who is the first person that Gifford sees the first day of training camp? Vince Lombardi, his new offensive coordinator on the other side of the field, and a new defensive coordinator, Tom Landry. That was the way Mr. Mara did things.

Chapter 5

The Top-Ten NFL Players of All Time

LT or Butkus? Who's the game's most bone-crunching defender?
Which QB was the game's greatest winner?

More than any other sports league, the NFL has changed over the years. Go back 50, 60 years and you'll find guys playing in leather helmets with hardly any pads. They were playing two ways, offense and defense. On those old scratchy newsreels, the game practically looks like rugby. In baseball, the game has changed, but it's still fundamentally the same: throw the ball and try and hit it. You know that if you had a time machine, Christy Mathewson and Babe Ruth would be great players today.

But you can't have that confidence with pro football. Is Sid Luckman as good as Dan Marino? Is Sammy Baugh up there with Joe Montana? When he wasn't taking snaps, Baugh was punting and playing defensive back, for gosh sakes. Are you going to give guys extra credit on this list for playing both ways? It's not like Babe Ruth being a pitcher. *Everybody* played both ways in those days, so if you're going to place a huge emphasis on that, you're going to have a list completely filled with guys who played before the 1960s, and that's not going to give you a proper list.

The other thing you have to remember is that the NFL wasn't a big-time league for a long time. Before the 1950s, college football was the big game. So the pro football section of the Hall of Fame is going to have much more of an emphasis on modern players. Most of these guys, I saw them play for at least some of their careers, and the ones that I didn't see in their prime, I've heard all about them from people who did.

10. The Rule of Baugh

Slingin' Sammy defined the game's most important position.

Quarterback is by far the most important position in professional football. You just can't win consistently in the modern NFL without a great quarterback. But it wasn't always like that. In the game's infancy it was run, run, run, and a forward pass was a last resort, a desperation play, like a Hail Mary is today.

SAMMY BAUGH

- Won a record-setting six NFL passing titles, throwing for 21,886 yards and 187 touchdowns
- Led the league in punting average four times, including a then-career record of 45.1 yards per punt and the best single-season mark of 51.4 yards per punt (1940)
- In 1943 he led the league in interceptions, the same year he led the league in passing and punting.
- Baugh led the Redskins to five NFL Eastern division titles and two NFL championships in 1937 and 1942, the first one in his rookie season.

And Sammy Baugh of the Redskins was the first great quarterback in the history of the NFL, the guy who really defined the position, made it the center of attention. Baugh proved to people that you could throw a football with accuracy. He'd run, he'd throw deep, he made things happen. He was a swashbuckler, a guy who wasn't afraid to take chances. To give you a modern analogy, imagine Michael Vick, except that Baugh was a much, much better passer.

On this list, Baugh represents a nod to the early days of the NFL, the pioneers of the game. Why did I settle on Baugh? He had tremendous historical importance. And I get the sense that, more than most of the old timers, he could have held his own in the modern game. Sid Luckman was great, and so was Bronko Nagurski, but I wonder how they would have fared in another era. But I really don't have any of those doubts about Sammy Baugh. He was tremendously athletic—

the Cardinals signed him to play major league baseball. He had a tremendous arm, strong and accurate. Look at his stat line for 1947. In 12 games, he completed 210 passes for 2,938 yards, over eight yards a throw, completed 59.3 percent of his passes, threw for 25 TDs and was intercepted 15 times, and ran for two more touchdowns. You don't have to make any excuses for those numbers. Those numbers would look pretty good in the NFL in 2006. When he retired, Baugh owned every important pro passing record.

In 1943 Sammy Baugh led the league in passing, interceptions, and punting. Think about that. Never happened before, and it'll never happen again. Did you know that Sammy Baugh's punting record for career average was broken just a couple of years ago? This is a guy that averaged over 51 yards a punt one year. Baugh fits the definition of an impact player. He came into the league in 1937 and won the championship his first year, beating the mighty Bears 28-21. In 1942, he beat a Bears team that was 13-0.

Baugh had a flair that would have made him a huge star today. He was a star in movie serials, playing a gunslinging cowboy. And he had a quick wit. Remember the championship game December 8, 1940? The Bears blew out the Redskins in the most lopsided game in history. Early in that game, Baugh threw a touchdown pass that was dropped by one of his receivers. It would have tied the game 7-7. After the game, someone asked Baugh, "What if that guy didn't drop that pass? Would it have been a different game?" And he said, "Yeah. We would have lost 73-7 instead of 73-0." Terrible defeat. Great line. There's a lot to like about Sammy Baugh.

9. Pictures of Lilly

Bob Lilly anchored Dallas's famed Doomsday Defense.

The Doomsday Defense. You've got to love that nickname, especially the way John Facenda said it on those great NFL film specials. It was like the coming of the apocalypse. And the foundation of that great Dallas Cowboy Doomsday Defense was Bob Lilly. Actually, he was the foundation of one of the great franchises in the NFL—he was the first player ever drafted by the Dallas Cowboys. And before he was through, he had earned the distinction of being the greatest defensive tackle in the history of the NFL. For his day, Lilly was huge: 6'5" and 260, and still he was tremendously strong and agile, the kind of guy who could react when Gale Sayers tried to get past him with a shake-and-bake move.

Another factor that's much more important in football than in other sports is durability. We all know about those guys who would be All-Pros if they could ever stay healthy enough to play four games in a row. Bob Lilly never, never got hurt. He played in 196 consecutive regular season games. Think about that. Fourteen years in a row, folks. In the trenches, right in the middle of that pile of big bodies. How many guys can play 14 years in the NFL, period, much less suit up for every game? That's toughness.

But the real measure of a defensive player is how the opposing team reacts to him. Remember that classic Ice Bowl game? The Packers went for it on fourth and one against the Cowboys. Did they try to run over Bob Lilly? No, they ran over Jethro Pugh. In the 1971 Super Bowl, against the Colts, an offensive lineman who shall remain nameless went up to offensive line coach George Young, who would later become GM of the Giants, and said, "George, I simply can't block the guy. I can't do it." That's quite an admission for an NFL player in a Super Bowl. And when the Cowboys ambushed the Dolphins in the 1972 Super Bowl, who was the guy who made the big defensive play, sacking Bob Griese for a 29-yard loss? That would be Bob Lilly.

Try and block Lilly and you were in for a long afternoon. You couldn't double team him. Teams put three guys on him all day and he still found a way to make plays. That Cowboy defense was really underrated. They lost that Super Bowl to the Colts 16-13 because Craig Morton was awful, but the defense played well enough to win. For a long period of time, pretty much the whole length of Lilly's career, Dallas had probably the second or third best defense in the NFL. At the beginning Green Bay was at the top of the heap, and toward the end it was Miami and Pittsburgh, but Dallas was just a half step behind. And the biggest constant was Mr. Cowboy.

The 1960s were really the Golden Era of the defensive lineman. There were a lot of really good ones. Deacon Jones. Willie Davis. Henry Jordan.

BOB LILLY

- Played in five NFL/NFC title games and two Super Bowls, winning the championship in Super Bowl VI
- Named to the Pro Bowl 11 times, including 10 in a row
- Over his 14-year career, he played in 196 consecutive regular-season games. The 1973 championship game against Minnesota, which the Cowboys lost, was the only game he ever missed.
- In 1961 the Cowboys made Lilly their first-ever draft choice. He was also the first player to enter the Hall of Fame as a member of the Cowboys, and was given the nickname "Mr. Cowboy" by Roger Staubach.

Merlin Olsen. Lilly, I think, was the best of a great bunch. He had more of a physical presence than these other guys. He could play the pass and stuff the run. Tremendously rugged, and he made big plays on great teams. What more can you want than Bob Lilly?

DOGBITE: ONCE A COWBOY . . .

The thing that you like about Bob Lilly is that he had a sense for the big stage. The best moment of his career came in the Super Bowl, and so did the worst. The best would have been that sack of Bob Griese in Super Bowl VI. Griese scrambled right but Lilly was right with him. He kept retreating and retreating, but Lilly kept pursuing. By the time Griese finally realized he was done and took the sack, he was 29 yards from the line of scrimmage. That wasn't just a Super Bowl record—it was an NFL record. Lilly later said that chasing down Griese was like corralling a horse on his ranch.

A year earlier, the Cowboys were defeated in Super Bowl V by the underdog Colts on a game-winning field goal by Jim O'Brien. Lilly heaved his helmet downfield over 40 yards. "I have two Super Bowl records—the sack of Griese and the helmet toss," Lilly will tell you. "Unfortunately, the one people remember is me throwing my helmet."

---

8. A Bear Minimum

As the prototypical linebacker, Dick Butkus had everything . . . except a ring.

Football is a little tough from a championship point of view. In baseball, you really can't take away too many points from a player because he didn't win a lot of championships, or even any at all. Look at Ty Cobb. Look at Ted Williams. There's only so much impact that one player can have. On the other hand, in basketball having a ring is a must. In many ways it's a one-on-one game, and to be considered an all-time great, you have to have some titles under your belt. Karl Malone? I don't consider him an all-time great. Charles Barkley? Closer, but he still comes up a little short.

Professional football is right in the middle on this. The players at the very top of this list all have at least one championship, and a lot of them have more than one. Which brings us to Dick Butkus. No doubt that he was an all-time great, one of the most dominating players ever, one of the most intimidating figures in the history of the sport. He was the kind of defender who would literally strike fear in the heart of the opposition.

But he'd be higher on this list if he had won a championship along the way. In fact, during most of his time in Chicago, the Bears were lousy. Think about this. In 1969 the Bears had Dick Butkus, one of the greatest defensive players of all time. They had Gale Sayers, who was one of the greatest running backs ever, a guy you'd have to consider if you were doing an all-time Top 25. And they went 1-13. One and thirteen! One and thirteen! You can win one game almost by accident. Sure, they had no quarterback. But you'd think that a team with those two players would win four or five games just by showing up. And that season hurts Butkus on a list like this.

And it's doubly surprising given the way Butkus played. He was an animal. No one in the history of football played the game with the same level of intensity. Butkus was big and strong, but he wasn't that much bigger or stronger than anyone else in the league. He didn't have that unbelievable combination of speed and power and athleticism that you had in a guy like Lawrence Taylor. No. What made Dick Butkus an all-time great, a Hall of Famer, was raw effort. He had such a motor on him. All forward motion. He just stood there up the middle, frothing at the mouth, and if you were a running back or a quarterback, you knew that you were go-

DICK BUTKUS

- Played in eight straight Pro Bowls, selected to seven all-NFL teams
- Over nine seasons, recorded 1,020 tackles and 489 assists; third all-time with 25 fumble recoveries
- The year before Butkus arrived, the Bears defense surrendered 379 yards per game. With Butkus on the field in 1965, they gave up almost one-third fewer yards (275).
- As an actor Butkus appeared on *Wonder Woman*, *Simon & Simon*, *Magnum PI*, and *My Two Dads*.

DOGBITE: DOWNHILL FROM THERE

Funny thing about Dick Butkus's career. He started out at the very top. In his first game he had 11 solo tackles. In 1965 he led the team in tackles and interceptions. His six fumble recoveries were a team record, which set him on his way to a then-NFL record of 25 for his career. And the Bears went from 5-9 to 9-5. But Butkus didn't win the Rookie of the Year award—that went to his teammate Gale Sayers. And the Bears would never match that record of the first year, and would have only one more winning season while Butkus was playing.

ing to get hit and you were going to get hit hard. He was going to run you over. He was going to separate you from the football. He was going to try to separate you from your head. Butkus knew that he was going to pick up his share of bumps and bruises along the way, but he was happy to take the punishment as long as he could dish out even more. Remember Deacon Jones's little poem? "Roses are red/violets are blue/If you have any sense/You'll keep Butkus away from you."

You'd think that this would have rubbed off on his teammates. But it didn't. You either had that passion or you didn't. I think that's one of the reasons why today's NFL teams make mistakes when they're drafting players. They get too hung up on how fast a guy can run the 40, or how many times he can bench press a 225-pound barbell. At the combines, it's all about strength and speed and physicality. They figure that you can teach a guy to try, to keep going, play after play, to hit just as hard in the fourth quarter as in the first. But you can't. You can't teach a guy to be Dick Butkus.

And that's why Dick Butkus didn't really revolutionize his position, so much as he perfected it. He didn't play linebacker any differently than it had been played for 45 years. He just played it harder . . . and better.

CLOSE, BUT . . .

What's the greatest football team of all time? Probably the 1975 Pittsburgh Steelers. And guess what? Not one player from that team makes my Hall of Fame. Maybe you could put Mean Joe Greene toward the bottom of this list, but he's hardly a no brainer. Terry Bradshaw? That would be a stretch. If you don't like the Steelers, how about the Green Bay Packers? Great, legendary team. Again, not one player on this list. Who's it going to be? Bart Starr? Paul Hornung? Willie Davis? Henry Jordan?

And you look at the best team of the first decade of the twenty-first century, the New England Patriots, and again, they don't have that one guy who you could see cracking this list. The only individual who you might see being honored in a future edition of this book is their coach, Bill Belichick. It's a very interesting question. Even in the days before the salary cap, it seemed that the formula for a dynasty is finding six or seven Hall of Famers, even if you don't have that one shining superstar.

7. Sweetness and Light

Walter Payton was the ultimate running back.

Walter Payton is the greatest running back I've ever seen. Now, I didn't see Jim Brown, but I saw a lot of great ones—and Sweetness was the greatest. There's a little bit of similarity with his fellow Bear Dick Butkus. While Payton finally did win a Super Bowl, by the time he won it, he wasn't the best player on the team anymore. That Buddy Ryan defense was the focal point of the team, not Payton.

Let's play a little game. I'm going to name a bunch of guys who would rank right behind Payton among the great backs of the Super Bowl era. Barry Sanders. O.J. Simpson. Eric Dickerson. Earl Campbell. What do they have in common? Not one Super Bowl ring among them. Not even one Super Bowl *appearance* among them. That's not completely a coincidence. I think the problem is that many great backs need a lot of carries, 25 or 30 carries a game, and when you get too dependent on one option like that, a good defense will find a way to stop him.

The more successful backs from the point of view of winning championships—guys like Franco Harris, Emmitt Smith, John Riggins, even Roger Craig—have found a way to blend in with the offense, co-existing with the quarterback and the receivers rather than always being the first option.

And while his teams didn't have the same amount of success as these other guys, you still like Payton in that regard. He wasn't one of these prima donna backs. If you wanted him to carry 30 times, he'd take the ball. If you wanted him to block, he'd block. He never complained, he never fumbled. He could run for 275 yards, but you got the impression he'd be just as happy to run for 85 as long as the team won.

During the prime of his career, Payton was the guy who gave the Bears a level of respectability. He played on that cold, hard Astroturf on those frigid Chicago afternoons, wearing just short sleeves. He had that engine in him, too. That high-stepping, perpetual-motion gait, always moving forward as the defenders bounced off him. He was almost an offensive version of Dick Butkus. Chicago is a rugged, tough city, the city with broad shoulders. You get that cold wind off the lake in the winter time at Soldier Field, and it's rough. It's not like the summer breezes at Wrigley Field. Chicago is a place

DOGBITE: AIR PAYTON

Walter Payton's accomplishments running the pigskin are so legendary, it's easy to forget he wasn't too shabby catching and throwing it too. As a matter of fact, in 1984 Payton broke the Bears record for career receptions. Payton has 176 more receptions as a Bear than Hall of Fame tight end (and his former coach) Mike Ditka. Payton also threw eight TD passes with the Bears, including one to TE Pat Dunsmore in a postseason win against the Redskins. In 1984 Matt Suhey caught two TD passes from Payton. When asked if he was ever sorry he wasn't a quarterback in college, he responded, "Not at all. They don't take [African-American] quarterbacks that much."

with a great football tradition, going back to George Halas and Sid Luckman. And tough loyal fans. Da Bears. Payton fit right in with that—they
loved him there in that great city, and you've got to give him a lot of credit
for that.

6. Unblockable

Gino Marchetti was the NFL's original unstoppable force.

I know. You might be scratching your head right now. You're probably
saying, "Chris, how do you put Gino Marchetti in the middle of a list of
the greatest professional football players of all time?" That is, of course, if
you know who Gino Marchetti is. (He played for the Colts from the mid-
1950s to the mid-1960s.) Here's a great quote from Gil Brandt, the man
who helped build the Dallas Cowboys: "He's the only lineman in history
that Jim Parker could not block." Parker played against him every single
day in practice. Couldn't block him. Could not.

So before I talk about Marchetti, let me give you Parker's qualifications:
Pro Football Hall of Fame. One of the first full-time offensive linemen. All-
NFL eight consecutive years. He was the Immovable Object. The only guy
he couldn't block? Gino Marchetti. The Unstoppable Force.

When you're talking about Parker, you're talking about probably the
greatest offensive lineman in the history of the NFL. And you could argue
that Marchetti helped to make him great. After battling Gino all week in
practice, the game on Sunday almost seemed like a vacation.

When you're talking about defensive players in football, you can't rely
on statistics. You can't just count tackles or sacks the way you can count
home runs or touchdown passes. It's about the respect that you get from
your opponents. Teams—and teammates—respected Gino Marchetti immensely.

Now, I know that Marchetti's a little bit of a forgotten man. He went to
the University of San Francisco, and he played ten years with the Colts,
ten Pro Bowls, All-Pro seven consecutive years. You could say that Mar-

chetti was the first great modern defensive lineman. He was really the prototype of the contemporary pass rushing defensive end, just at the time when players began to have defined roles. Before Marchetti, defense in the NFL was all about stopping the run. Marchetti broke in at a time when the pendulum was starting to swing back the other way, and he was one of the first guys who made a living out of harassing the quarterback. Marchetti was a tremendous pass rusher, but he was also great against the run, and that's why he gets a very slight edge over Deacon Jones. He was named the top defensive end of the NFL's first 50 years. Deacon Jones could have been on that list. But Marchetti was better.

And he played in big games. In the 1958 championship game, he broke his ankle on that classic play where Frank Gifford claims he got a bad spot on third and short late in regulation. The Giants had to punt, the Colts went down the field, and in a lot of ways the NFL was born as a big-time sport right there. And the Colts don't win that game that day without Gino Marchetti.

The other thing you like about Marchetti is his toughness. When you talk about a player being a throwback, Gino Marchetti is the guy you're comparing him to. Marchetti epitomized that smash-mouth football that they played just as the league was getting popular. It was war in the trenches, and Marchetti was a warrior. How tough was he? One time he played half a game with a separated shoulder, and another time he played only two weeks after undergoing an appendectomy. After all, he fought in the battle of the Bulge in World War II when he was only 18. After that, even the toughest day in the NFL doesn't seem so bad.

GINO MARCHETTI

- Selected to 11 straight Pro Bowls (missing only one of them due to injury) and nine All-NFL teams. Chosen for the NFL's 50- and 75-year anniversary All-Star teams
- In 1958 Marchetti was named player of the year as a member of the Colts' championship team.
- In 1952 the New York Yankees football team made him their number-two draft pick.

DOGBITE: TAKE THAT, SMART GUY

Most NFL quarterbacks knew enough not to anger Gino Marchetti. Yet, ironically, it was Frank Ryan, a guy with a Ph.D., who wrote a thesis called "Characterization of the Set of Asymptotic Values of a Function Holomorphic in the Unit Disc," who learned this lesson the hard way. The trouble began during the fourth quarter of the 1964 title game. The Cleveland Browns were shellacking the Colts 27-0 with time about to run out. "We were feeling our oats," Ryan recalled. "We were about on their 15-yard line. The fans had started piling onto the field. There were about 20 seconds left, and the officials asked me if I wanted to end the game. I said I wanted one more play, and I threw a pass into the end zone to our tight end, John Brewer, who hadn't caught any passes. I thought throwing him a pass would make him feel more a part of the team. The pass was incomplete, but Gino Marchetti had overheard me talking to the officials." So a couple weeks later, before the Pro Bowl game at the Coliseum, Marchetti ran into Ryan at the Stardust Lounge and challenged him to a fight. The two players were restrained before any blows could be exchanged. In the game itself, which was the last game of Marchetti's career, he made good on his threat. He hit Ryan so hard in that exhibition game that— shades of Pete Rose and Ray Fosse in the 1970 baseball All-Star Game—the QB dislocated his shoulder, an injury from which he never fully recovered. Marchetti denied any intent to injure, but he did say with a wink, "Yes, sir, I was in on the tackle. I'd say it was a pretty good tackle."

5. Rice on the Side

When pigskins fly, you can bet that Jerry Rice will catch them.

When God thought about what a perfect wide receiver is supposed to be, the ultimate catcher of the pigskin, he created Jerry Rice. He doesn't have one weakness in his game, not one gap in his résumé. Rice could do it all. He had speed, he had leaping ability, he had great hands. He ran picture perfect patterns and he would block, too. Now, there were guys who may have done one thing or another better than Rice. Cris

Carter might have had better hands. Randy Moss is faster. Irving Fryar was a better blocker. But Rice did everything. Everything.

Throughout his career he was double-teamed just about every play of every game. All he did was catch more balls, gain more yards, and score more touchdowns than any wide receiver in history. It didn't matter who was throwing to him. He caught balls from Joe Montana. He caught balls from Steve Young. He caught balls from Elvis Grbac and Jeff Garcia. And he managed to be an effective player well into his forties. That's unheard of in football, but he did it.

On an individual level, he was like Jim Brown, a guy who rewrote the record book. But Rice also had tremendous team success. He was really the face of that great 49er dynasty, the constant that linked Montana and Young, Walsh and Seifert. He made the wide receiver on the other side better—players like John Taylor, J.J. Stokes, and Terrell Owens—because of the way he attracted attention.

Funny but one moment I'll always remember about Rice is that fumble streaking into the end zone against the Giants in that 49-3 loss. Maybe it's different if the Niners take a 7-0 lead.

If you want the consummate Jerry Rice moment, how about the 1995 Super Bowl against San Diego? Rice goes deep over the middle, splits the defense, 44 yards. Third play of the game. The Chargers are shell-shocked and that Super Bowl was pretty much over before it began. That's the kind of impact that Jerry Rice can have.

Why isn't Jerry Rice number one? It's simple. Wide receiver is not the most important position on the field. It just isn't. No matter how good a wide receiver is, he's still the end of the chain. The line has to block, the quarterback's got to get him the ball. Then and only then can the receiver catch it. But that said, there's never been anyone in history better at that than Jerry Rice.

CLOSE, BUT . . .

The first great wide receiver in NFL history was Don Hutson, the incredible receiver for the Packers between 1935 and 1945. He was really the guy who invented the position. He caught 500 balls for 8,000 yards, led the league in receiving eight consecutive years. He was the MVP in back-to-back years. If you were doing a list like this 12, 15 years ago, before Rice had really solidified his credentials, Hutson has to be on it. He was Jerry Rice before Jerry Rice. It's tough to leave him off.

DOGBITE: CAUGHT IN THE DRAFT

It's a Saturday night in 1984, and Bill Walsh is sitting in front of the TV with a margarita doing what Bill Walsh does. Watching a football game. He happened to catch the highlights of a Mississippi Valley State game in which a wide receiver scored four long touchdowns. That receiver was Jerry Rice. On draft day, Walsh traded multiple picks to the Patriots but couldn't get any higher than 16th. "I thought, 'Oh boy, one day we'll be playing against this guy and that's going to be tough.' " But because of concerns about his speed—he ran a 4.6 40 while other top receivers were timed at 4.3—and MVS's schedule, Rice was still on the board while the Bengals picked Eddie Brown and the Jets tabbed Al Toon. Even in his rookie year, Rice wasn't an overnight sensation. After one early game, a local newspaper ran the headline SNAP, CRACKLE, DROP.

---

4. Taylor Made

In my humble opinion, Lawrence Taylor is the greatest defensive player in the history of the National Football League. Now, there are plenty of guys, including guys on this list like Lilly and Butkus, who were tremendous, tremendous forces. But they didn't revolutionize the game, turn it upside down the way Taylor did. Before LT, linebacker was kind of a containment position. Stuff the run. But Taylor changed all that. He was all about attacking. He could get in there, blow right by the offensive tackle, and chase the quarterback down for a 25-yard loss. He could cover wide receivers coming over the middle. And he could stuff the run—flattening even the biggest fullback with his combination of speed and power. Offensive coordinators stayed up the night before the game trying to figure out a way to stop LT.

Normally it was the defensive coordinators who went to sleep thinking about how to stop one guy. LT put the shoe on the other foot. Remember the time on Thanksgiving Day when LT was standing in his own end zone, picked off a pass one handed, and ran the interception back 97 yards for a touchdown? Butkus couldn't have done that. And I don't think that the 1969 Bears would have gone 1-13 if Lawrence Taylor was on that team. He would have single-handedly

LAWRENCE TAYLOR

- Three-time Defensive Player of the Year (1981, 1982, 1986) and 10-time Pro Bowler; played on two Super Bowl championship teams, 1986 and 1990
- Retired with the second most sacks in history with 132.5, even though the league didn't start compling sack stats until after his rookie year
- Recorded 1,088 tackles, 33 forced fumbles, 10 fumble recoveries, and nine interceptions during his career. In 1986, led the league with 20.5 sacks
- LT did not play organized football until the 11th grade.

won four or five games for them. And LT is a big reason why Bill Parcells has two Super Bowl rings. He was the difference-maker on a team that won two titles, especially the first one.

LT was an interesting guy. Now, after his career is over, we're hearing about all the bad things he did, hanging out at crack houses, using someone else's urine to try to fake a drug test. Losing his temper with other drivers on the street. This is not a guy you'd hand your keys to and say, "Here I'm going away—can you take care of the house while I'm gone?" No. No. No. But as much of a mess as he was everywhere else in his life, when you put Lawrence Taylor on the football field—whether it was in a game or a practice—he was completely dedicated, 100 percent. Dr. Jekyll and Mr. Hyde in reverse, almost. He was kind of like a lot of great musicians in that way—no matter how much he messed up off the field, football was this sacred part of his life, his art, and on Sunday he always gave it his best, no matter what happened during the week. He had a real tough-guy mentality, going out there in that famous game against New Orleans with his chest muscles all ripped up.

When I think of Lawrence Taylor, here's what I think of—that old NFL Films clip where he's running around telling the guys in the huddle,

---

DOGBITE: HEY, WHERE'S MY HELMET?

How tough was Lawrence Taylor? His own team tried to keep him out of the game. Lawrence Taylor was famous for playing through injuries—a broken foot, torn chest muscle, fractured ankle. The problem was that doctors and trainers didn't want LT to risk further damage. Do you want to be the trainer who has to tell LT he can't play? In a 1983 game against the Eagles, the trainers came up with a solution to keep Taylor on the sidelines: hide his helmet. Giants trainer Ronnie Barnes recalls, "He'd say, 'Give me my helmet, I'm going into that damn game.' But we wouldn't let him find it."

"He doesn't heal like normal people do," said Dr. Allan Levy, an associate team physician back when Taylor played. "One time, when he played with an injury he shouldn't have played with, I said to him that you're either one of the bravest players I've seen or one of the stupidest." But to LT it was simple: "You get only 20 chances a year to play, so you can't miss one."

"We're gonna go out there and play like a bunch of crazed dogs." That's what LT brought to the game. Incredible ability and focus and intensity and, yes, just a little bit of craziness. Add that to a guy who was simply one of the most amazing athletic specimens of all time and it's an unbeatable combination.

Every year at the NFL draft they talk about how this guy or that guy may be "the next LT." Well it's 18 years later, and they're still looking. That's why Lawrence Taylor is among the top-five football players of all time.

3. The U Turn

Johnny Unitas would just throw, throw, throw the ball, deftly down the field.

There's a lesson in the story of Johnny Unitas. He was a ninth-round draft choice. He was cut by the Pittsburgh Steelers in 1955 after the coach said he wasn't intelligent enough. Think about that. One of the greatest quarterbacks in the history of the game, and his coach calls him into the office and, in effect, tells him he should be pumping gas. Unitas goes out and plays semi-pro ball for six bucks a game. Weeb Ewbank finds out about him and signs him as a backup. His first NFL pass went for a touchdown. For the *other* team, after it was intercepted. But by 1957, he's playing in the Pro Bowl.

Unitas was the quarterback's quarterback, the classic image of a great passer. Number 19 sitting back in the pocket, cool as a cucumber, with his arm cocked, ready to throw the bomb. Think about it. Johnny Unitas threw a touchdown in 47 consecutive games. Every Sunday for almost four years, Johnny Unitas completed one in the end zone. In a league where just playing quarterback for 47 consecutive games is an accomplishment, that's a mind-boggling record.

Here's Johnny Unitas in a nutshell. It's the last drive of the game in that classic contest against the Giants. The Colts were on the nine-yard line, already in field-goal position, and he throws a seven-yard down-and-out to the two-yard line. Here's a guy that's already in field-goal position to win the NFL championship. Unitas is calling his own plays, goes to the line of scrimmage, and has so much confidence in his ability that he calls a pass play. No need to! Take the knee and kick the field goal. I asked him about it once. "Why would you do that?" He says, "Well, if he wasn't open I was going to throw the ball into the stands." That's how great he was and how much confidence he had in his ability. And despite what that first coach said, Unitas was plenty heady. In the fourth quarter of the 1958 title game, Unitas and Raymond Berry noticed that one of the Giants' linebackers lined up in a certain formation. That was a cue for Berry to run a certain route. No verbal communication. Just eye contact and boom. A big play. The punch line? The last time the linebacker lined up in that position was in preseason, and Unitas picked it right up.

> **JOHNNY UNITAS**
>
> - Three-time NFL Player of the Year and was selected to ten Pro Bowls; led Colts to back-to-back NFL titles in 1958–59
> - Completed 2,830 passes for 40,239 yards and 290 TDs
> - Threw a touchdown pass in 47 straight games. The next closest is Dan Marino with 30.
> - Over the Baltimore Colts' 31 years, they had a winning percentage of .664 with Unitas (156-79), contrasted with a .378 winning percentage in years without him (74-122).

And that combination of flair and efficiency really helped him become one of football's first television stars, kind of the Mickey Mantle of professional football. He was much more accessible than Jim Brown, and more telegenic than Bart Starr. And he was the star of what was the league's coming out party, that great 1958 Championship game. The NFL owes a lot to Johnny Unitas.

You could certainly argue that Unitas was the best quarterback of all time. He threw a better ball than Joe Montana. But here's why I can't put him higher than third overall on the list. He only won the two championships. The Colts won the title back-to-back in 1958 and 1959, and then he never won another championship. And after that run of success there was a long down period. Over four seasons between 1960 and 1963, the

Colts were 29-25. They still had Raymond Berry and Lenny Moore. A team with the greatest quarterback in history shouldn't go 6-6 the way Baltimore did in 1962.

And then in 1964 he had a very bad championship game against the Browns. The Colts were 12-2 that year, and they were shut out in a game where they were heavily favored, and Unitas did not play well at all. He threw a couple of interceptions. Only 95 yards passing. And that's the knock on Unitas, if you want to call it that. For all his greatness, he needed another title or two to take the top spot in the Mad Dog Hall of Fame.

DOGBITE: MUST BE THE SHOES

When you think of the legendary Johnny Unitas, you think of the flat top haircut and his trademark black, high-top sneakers. But the truth is that Unitas started Super Bowl V in a pair of low-cut Adidas shoes. When asked by a reporter why he wore the high tops, he gave a typically Unitas answer: "Because they were comfortable." The Pro Football Hall of Fame wanted to put a pair of his trademark sneakers in the museum. Unitas responded that he couldn't provide them because "I've got just one pair, and I use 'em to work in the yard." In 2002 the NFL prohibited Peyton Manning of the Colts from wearing black high-tops in memory of Unitas, threatening to fine him $25,000. Manning, who wore black, high-top shoes at the University of Tennessee, had received permission from the Unitas family, but the NFL still wouldn't allow it.

---

2. The Perfect Runner

Jim Brown carried the football with power and grace . . . and unequaled effectiveness.

Jim Brown was the greatest physical presence in the history of the NFL. And the NFL is a physical league, so on that basis a lot of people would argue that Brown should be number one. Just look at his numbers. He averaged 5.2 yards per carry. Think about that. Hand the ball to Jim Brown—the safest play in the book, because he never fumbled—and when the dust settled, you'd be more than halfway to a first down. And that was over his whole career. In 1963 he averaged 6.4 yards per carry. Give the ball to Brown and you were two thirds of the way to a first down. Amazing. And no other back even comes close to that level of production.

Brown played nine years and led the league in rushing every year but one. Look at his numbers and remember that the NFL season wasn't 16 games back then. Remind yourself that the season was 12 games long when Brown broke in, and then look at his numbers again. He had such an incredible combination of speed and strength. He wasn't elusive like O.J. Simpson, or Barry Sanders, or Walter Payton. He didn't dance around tacklers. He didn't have to. He just bowled them over. Pure power. You couldn't tackle the guy.

JIM BROWN

- Selected to nine Pro Bowls, eight All-NFL teams, and named Most Valuable Player in 1958 and 1965. In his nine seasons with the Cleveland Browns, he led the league in rushing a record eight times, including a record five straight years, and held seasonal and single game yardage records.
- In those 118 games, he ran for at least 100 yards in 58 of them for a record 5.2 yards per carry.
- Over nine years, Brown never missed a regular season game, playing 118 straight.

Brown was also all-world in two sports. He played lacrosse at Syracuse, and people who know that game still talk about him in hushed tones. He was the greatest lacrosse player in the history of the game. So there's a little bit of Jim Thorpe in Jim Brown. So why isn't Jim Brown number one? In a way, Brown is the Wilt Chamberlain of football. He dominated a game physically, and it showed up in those amazing stat lines. He did things that no one ever did before or has ever done since.

But somehow that great dominance didn't translate into championships. Brown won only one title. Brown was all about the tangible parts of the game. You handed him the ball and he'd get you some yardage. He didn't relish blocking. He wasn't a great inspirational teammate. He also had a chip on his shoulder. And he ended his career in a bad, strange way. In the summer of 1966, he was off filming *The Dirty Dozen*, and there were some delays on the set, and Brown was going to be late for training camp. The Browns owner Art Modell got ticked off and started fining Brown. Brown got ticked right back, and he said "I quit."

Just like that, at the height of his powers. The Browns had won the championship in 1964, beating the Colts 27-0 as a heavy underdog. In

1965 he wins the MVP and the Browns lose the championship game to the Packers. And Jim Brown walks away from football because he's having a spitting match with the owner over a couple of bucks. Now, it was a bad move by Modell—you don't treat your star that way—but it didn't hurt Modell's legacy. It did hurt Brown's. I guess it was a matter of principle, but it's not exactly Muhammed Ali giving up his title because he opposes the Vietnam War. And the chance to be an action hero in the movies would have still been there in a couple of years. But despite all that, Jim Brown is one of the singular figures in the history of the NFL, and in the history of sports really. When they do the *all rights reserved* disclaimer on an NFL broadcast, they show a few guys who represent the history of the league. Lombardi, as the great coach, Namath for his great charisma and that great upset, and then Jim Brown for his incredible greatness on the field.

1. The State of Montana

Joe Montana wasn't flashy. All he did was win.

Call it the triumph of intangibles. Joe Montana isn't a guy who blows you away. He didn't drop back and throw the ball 60 yards in the air. His arm was so ordinary, he slipped all the way to the third round in the NFL draft. Dan Marino could throw the ball a country mile. Joe Montana couldn't.

And in an age where a lot of quarterbacks were throwing for three, four hundred yards a game, Montana wouldn't have put up gaudy stats at the end of the game. He'd be 19 of 25 for 195 yards. But he would have dominated the game. In that way, he's kind of football's answer to Magic Johnson—a guy who can dominate a game without putting up amazing individual numbers. Team sports are all about making your teammates better, making the big play, and that's what Joe Montana did.

The other guys at the top of this list don't really have that quality. Jim Brown is all about numbers. Unitas threw touchdown passes like crazy, but his claim to fame was more in his stats. Montana, on the other hand, was like an orchestra conductor. Quick step, quick throw to Jerry Rice or Roger Craig. He'd hit him in stride for a nice run after the catch, keep the defense off balance, avoid the big mistake.

Montana has credentials of a different sort. He won four Super Bowls. The first was in 1981 and the last was in 1990, so that's a good long spread. And even in the years the 49ers didn't win it all, they were still right in the thick of it. Joe Montana's teams didn't go 5-11. When they lost in the playoffs it was to the Giants—a dominant defensive team—or to the Redskins—and the team they lost to would go on to win the Super Bowl. And in the biggest game of all, Montana was the MVP three times. And that fourth time, in that great comeback against Cincinnati, the reason why he didn't win may be that a lot of the voters cast their ballot before the final drive.

Think about this. Montana doesn't really have a tremendous supporting cast full of Hall of Famers. Jerry Rice is the greatest receiver of all time, but don't forget that Rice wasn't there the first two times they won a championship. There are no great Hall of Fame offensive linemen. Dwight Clark is not a Hall of Fame wide receiver. Freddie Solomon? No. Roger Craig, Wendell Tyler, they're not Hall of Fame running backs. Russ Francis played at the end of his career with him and played well, but he's not a Hall of Famer. Montana didn't have an unbelievable supporting cast, a team that was just stacked with Hall of Famers like the Steelers or the Packers.

Montana had plenty of great moments. The Catch, with Dwight Clark kissing the sky to beat the Cowboys. John Taylor's Super Bowl catch. That huge 55-10 defeat of Denver. Montana was just unbelievable in that game.

JOE MONTANA

- An eight-time Pro Bowl selection, Montana threw 40,551 yards and made 3,409 completions. His career passer rating of 92.3 is third all-time.
- His Super Bowl QB rating is a gaudy 127.8, an all-time record. He also holds records for consecutive pass completions (13), career touchdown passes (10), passes completed (83), and yards gained (1,142).
- The comeback king led 31 fourth-quarter rallies in the NFL.

One of the things you like about Montana is the Regular Guy factor. He wasn't this larger than life character. As you're watching a game, you can't really imagine being Michael Vick, but you can almost see yourself being Joe Montana.

With Montana it was all about his demeanor. No matter how big the spot, he was as cool as a cucumber. Remember the story about that great drive at the end of the 1989 Super Bowl against the Bengals. A hundred million people are watching, and the 49ers are in the ultimate do-or-die situation—pinned back at their own eight-yard line, down by three points with 3:10 left in the game. What's his reaction? He's in the huddle and he points over to the sidelines. Is he pointing to Bill Walsh? No. He says, "Hey, isn't that John Candy?" That said a lot more to his teammates than any inspirational speech could have. The message was: A) Hey, it's only a game, and B) Don't worry, I've got a plan. And of course they executed that two-minute drill flawlessly and won the Super Bowl. That, in a nutshell, is why Joe Montana is the greatest professional football player of all time, and the first inductee into the NFL wing of the Mad Dog Hall of Fame.

DOGBITE: JOE, NOT SO COOL

Even Joe Montana had his moments when he lost his cool. On one play during that last drive of the 1989 Super Bowl, Montana got to the line of scrimmage and believe it or not he started hyperventilating. "It's a blur. I hyperventilated to the point of almost blacking out," recalled Montana. "You know how a TV screen gets fuzzy. Well, that's what my vision was like. I was yelling so loudly in the huddle that I couldn't breathe. Things got blurrier and blurrier."

He managed to take the snap and heave the ball out of bounds. To the millions of viewers, it looked like just another play by the coolest quarterback ever.

CLOSE, BUT . . .

Dan Marino is probably the best pure passer in the history of the game. But you can't rank him ahead of Montana. Here's why. If you replaced Montana with Marino, he certainly would have won a Super Bowl. He could have easily won that 55-10 game and maybe made it 72-10. But would Marino have performed in the clutch the way Montana did? Would he have blended himself into the game the way Montana did? Probably not. That's why he doesn't make this list. Maybe one day Tom Brady does.

Chapter 6

The Top-Ten Sports Venues of All Time

Picture yourself as a sports fan, a fan who loves all the sports, not just a guy who's a huge football fan but doesn't really care about baseball, golf, or tennis. You rub an old Coke bottle you find in grandpa's attic, and a genie pops out and gives you one wish: the ultimate sports trip. You've got carte blanche to go anywhere you want in the world of sports. Ten venues, cost is no object. You've got tickets, hotel rooms, airfare, whatever you need. Where are you going to go? That's the question we answer in this section. And remember, we're talking venues here, not events. The Super Bowl is a huge event, but believe me, if you've been to Jacksonville once, that's plenty. So we're looking for that ancient, historical, been-there-forever venue. These places are cathedrals of sport, hallowed ground if you're a big sports fan. Places that are worth visiting even when there isn't a game going on. A place where the greats have displayed their talents. When you walk into the venue, you need to feel the ghosts.

Let's look at it another way. Call it the Grandpa Factor. Is this a place that would mean something to your grandpa? Is it a place he would know about, a place he could tell you stories about, or at least the kind of place that he could appreciate? Is this the kind of place you feel you need to take your own son or daughter? Is it one of those places you've just got to see before you die? If it is, then it's got a chance at cracking this list.

And I'm trying to be a little bit objective here. I'm a huge baseball guy, and I could be perfectly happy hopping from ballpark to ballpark. I'd like to go to Roland Garros to see the French Open on the red clay, but not too many of you are going to want to come with me. These are places that I can sell to anyone on their merits. Got your bags packed? Let's go.

10. Tobacco Road Trip

Want to shake the midwinter blues?
How about Duke-UNC at Cameron Indoor?

I can hear it now. "Cameron Indoor? Hey, Chris, after what you just said, why would you even put this on the list? They haven't had any Final Fours there, and it's not like Duke was a huge program back in the nineteen-thirties and forties."

That's all true. Legitimate gripes. My response is simply that there aren't a lot of current college basketball venues that fulfill the criteria I laid out. The closest is probably the Palestra in Philadelphia, but you're not going to get a really great game there, maybe St. Joe's playing Temple. It doesn't have a real home team, and I'm sorry, Penn fans, Ivy League basketball doesn't cut it. The other one might be Allen Fieldhouse in Lawrence, Kansas, but Kansas–Oklahoma State doesn't have a huge amount of juice for me, either. It's a regional game with no national appeal. That's just about it. Pauley Pavilion is a new facility. North Carolina plays in the Dean Dome, not at Carmichael anymore. Rupp Arena? It's not cozy enough—23,000 seats will do that. Those older buildings, if they were still around, could have worked their way up the list. But they're not, which is why our college basketball experience can't rank any higher than tenth.

When you're talking about a classic arena with some character and some history, what's left is Cameron Indoor. Everybody who's been there calls it a dump, but it's a a great old building that was designed by the same guy who designed the Palestra. And the Duke Blue Devils have been the preeminent college basketball program of the last 20 years. No contest. Some people love the Blue Devils. Some people love to hate 'em. But you've got to give Coach K a lot of credit for building a no-excuses basketball power at a school where the players actually go to class and there's a real emphasis on academics. You may not like the school's preppy image, but it's not a place where you've got recruiting violations, players getting arrested all the time, or the coach throwing a folding chair onto the court. I won't kid you. This pick depends on Coach K being there. Who knows if Duke is going to be a big-time program when he leaves? But for now, if you go to Cameron Indoor, you know it's going to be a game with something on the line.

The game I want to go to is this one: Duke-UNC. Let me see those two go at it in that eight-thousand-seat arena on a Wednesday night at nine o'clock in the first week of February. Ask any big-time college hoops fan and he'll agree with me on this. It's a classic matchup and as close to a classic venue as you're going to get nowadays. It's a cozy building and there's a lot of juice in there. The Cameron Crazies make sure of that—when you get a lot of brains, mixed up with a little too much testosterone, that's what you get.

The two schools meet twice a year, and I want to go to the first meeting in a year when it's at Cameron Indoor. In my mind, that's the day that college basketball officially begins, the day those two schools play for the first time. In that second matchup, it's too late in the year. You're looking ahead, thinking too much about the ACC tournament and even March Madness. This first time, right in the middle of winter, has a special feel to it. These two schools are going to be right at the top of the rankings, and

> ## CAMERON INDOOR STADIUM
>
> - The first game was played on Jan. 6, 1940, when Duke beat Princeton 36-27.
> - In 1972 Duke University Gymnasium was renamed for athletics director Eddie Cameron.
> - Cameron Indoor has been home to three national championship Duke teams (1991, 1992, 2001). Entering the 2005–06 season, Duke has posted a 672-141 record at home, including a 37-30 mark against arch rival North Carolina.
> - The stadium was designed by Julian Abele—one of the first significant African-American architects in America.

at the end of the night at Cameron Indoor you're going to know some important things about two huge teams and a bunch of really good players. That's why it's worthy of a spot in my Hall of Fame.

9. Retro Chic

By turning back the clock,
Camden Yards set the standard for a new generation of ballparks.

Unlike most of the other places on our list, Camden Yards doesn't have a lot of history. It's only been around a little more than ten years. They've never played a single World Series game there, and in terms of all-time greats who played there you can only go back as far as Eddie Murray and Cal Ripken Jr. There was one big moment there, and that was Ripken breaking Gehrig's record.

But I think in 20 or 50 years, when historians—and fans—look back on the history of baseball around the turn of the millennium, Camden Yards is going to be one of those places that everybody points to. That's because of the way it changed the baseball landscape. It's been tremendously influential. Think about it. For almost 50 years, until Camden Yards came around, every time a baseball team opened a new stadium, it was worse than the place it replaced. Sure, Three Rivers Stadium in Pittsburgh had more bathrooms than Forbes Field. But it was too big, too sterile. It didn't have that charm that you want to see in a baseball stadium. It was too modern. You were too far away from the action. And most of these stadiums were plopped down in the middle of a bunch of parking lots instead of in the heart of a city.

But Camden Yards changed all that. It's got all the modern amenities, the luxury boxes, the cupholders on the seats, men's rooms that are big enough that you don't miss half an inning waiting in line. But it also has the feel of a great old park. It's located right on the waterfront, so it feels like it's part of downtown Baltimore. It's a cozy little stadium, so the sightlines are great. And you've got all those little nooks and crannies on the field. The awning over the stands. The bleachers in right field in front of that big old warehouse connected by that alleyway. The funky scoreboard with the big Baltimore Sun sign over it. The double-decker bullpens. And if you want real history, center field is located on the site where Babe Ruth's father once had a tavern. Camden Yards has got a little bit of a Wrigley Field feel to it.

Camden Yards took that classic ballpark idea and added something else to the mix. If you don't want a hot dog, you can go eat at Boog Powell's Barbecue on Eutaw Street. There are nice shops, activities for the kids. It's the kind of place where you'd go to see the park if you were in town, even

---

CAMDEN YARDS

- Camden Yards debuted on April 6, 1992. The Orioles defeated the Indians, 2-0, in front of a crowd of 44,568. Building the ballpark cost approximately $110 million and took about 33 months.
- On September 6, 1995, at Camden Yards, Cal Ripken broke Lou Gehrig's 2,130 consecutive game streak.
- The Camden Yards complex includes the Baltimore & Ohio Warehouse, the longest building on the East Coast (1,016 feet long).

if you really didn't give a hoot about the baseball game. Going to an Orioles game became a happening, an event, and it didn't matter who they were playing. Now, as a baseball purist I think this goes a little too far—the kids get so wrapped up in playing video games, and the casual fans are so busy looking at the menus, they forget there's a baseball game.

Still, this new ballpark really helped to revitalize a decrepit downtown. Camden Yards was simply the best of the old and the best of the new, and that's why they sold out just about every game there for five years.

That got just about every other team in baseball thinking, Hmmm, the Orioles have this great little park that everyone wants to come to, and they're making money like crazy. Why can't we have one, too? Before too long just about every owner started lobbying the mayor and the council and the legislature, threatening to move the team if they didn't get their own Camden Yards. And that ploy worked to a tee. The result was that between 1992 and 2003 there were 14 new stadiums opened, almost all of them incorporating some of the retro style of Camden Yards. It helped baseball from an economic point of view, and it also changed the way the game was played, because most of these new stadiums were hitter's parks, with the balls flying over the fences, which the casual fan likes. But I've still got to say that of all those new parks—Cleveland, Houston, Pittsburgh, San Francisco, Detroit—Camden Yards is not only the first, it's still the best. So, if it's a hot summer night, a perfect baseball evening, and I can pick any stadium that was built in the last 40 years, I'm going to Camden Yards.

DOGBITE: DIGGING UP HISTORY

In the early 1900s, on the corner of Conway Street and Little Pica, stood a bar called Ruth's Café, and on the second floor of that building was the birthplace of the greatest baseball player of all time. The site of that tavern is now in the middle of center field at Camden Yards, but there was an intermediate incarnation for the place: a warehouse. Ruth's sister, Mary "Mamie" Ruth Moberley, with the assistance of an archeological firm, unearthed the remains of the house under the asphalt of an old warehouse. Artifacts from the saloon on Conway Street, like drinking glasses and bottles, now reside at the Babe's museum nearby.

Here are two places that just won't make my list. I know that horse racing fans are going to get all over me on this one, but I just can't get excited about Churchill Downs. To me it's another racetrack. Saratoga has some charm to it. Not Churchill Downs. There's no romance to the stupid building. And 51 weeks out of the year, it's pretty much another racetrack. And the week leading up to the Kentucky Derby, it's the site of a huge social event. My sister-in-law goes to Churchill Downs with her husband so she can wear the latest hat design. Give me a freaking break. She could care less about the race. She doesn't know one horse from another. She's just there to see and be seen. Most of the fans there are more interested in the mint juleps than the history of the place. Me, if I've got to watch a horse race, I'd rather watch the Belmont Stakes when there's a Triple Crown on the line, and you've got people jazzed up, rooting for a horse like Smarty Jones.

Daytona? It's a dive. I've been to Daytona a million times. And I can tell you, it's a dive. The Daytona 500 does nothing for me—it's one of the weirdest events in sports because it's the most important race of the NASCAR season, and yet it's the first event of the year. It's like playing the Super Bowl the first week of the season. My biggest thrill at Daytona? Seeing Air Force One land when Ronald Reagan came to see Richard Petty's milestone race at the Firecracker 400 in 1984. Daytona? No thank you.

8. Bowled Over

The Orange Bowl may not be a garden spot,
but it's hosted huge football games.

Want to know why the Orange Bowl makes this list? The best college football game I ever saw was played there—Nebraska-Miami in 1984. And the best NFL game I ever saw, the Chargers-Dolphins, a 41-38 thriller, with Kellen Winslow being carried off the field with heat cramps, that was played there, too.

You can call the place a dump, and I'm not going to argue with you. But still, I like the view a lot, you can see the skyscrapers of downtown Miami in the background and the palm trees in the foreground. And when you're stuck in the middle of a New York winter, what more could you want to see than a little slice of the tropics? But the stadium itself is far from charming and that's why it's not higher on the list.

A great stadium needs history. Great games. Great teams. Great players. And that's what the Orange Bowl has. The only undefeated team in NFL history—the 1972 Dolphins—they played here. Dan Marino, the best pure passer in the history of football, he played here.

They also played the Super Bowl here. The NFL is unique in this way, but there have been a lot of great stadiums that housed great teams that never housed a Super Bowl. They never played a Super Bowl at Lambeau Field, RFK Stadium, or Soldier Field. But the Super Bowl was played at the Orange Bowl five times. Joe Namath won the most important game in the history of the NFL in the Orange Bowl. Super Bowl III was probably the most important game in the history of professional football. You could argue for the 1958 Championship game, but I'm going with Super Bowl III because of A) Namath's guarantee, B) the huge upset factor, and C) the huge impact it had in legitimizing the AFL-NFL merger. That adds to the mystique of the place.

And then there's the college football aspect. Over the last 20 years you can make the argument that year in and year out, Miami has been the best team in college football. They've gone through a bunch of coaches, from Howard Schnellenberger to Jimmy Johnson to Larry Coker. But they've won a bunch of national championships—five of them—and even in the years they don't win, they always seem to be in the hunt. And the Miami Hurricanes played in the Orange Bowl.

It's too bad that the Orange Bowl game isn't played in the Orange Bowl stadium anymore. It's played at the Dolphins' Stadium in Dade County, which is kind of a shame, because in the old days there was nothing better than tuning in the Orange Bowl on New Year's night with Don Criqui and Bob Trumpy in the booth with that smiling orange emblem at the 50-yard line.

DOGBITE: BROADWAY JOE'S SOUTHERN SWING

The guy who had the most big games at the Orange Bowl was Joe Namath. With John F. Kennedy looking on in the stands, Namath led Alabama to a 17-0 victory over Oklahoma in the 1963 classic, giving Bear Bryant his first Orange Bowl victory. Two years later, Namath lost a heartbreaker to Texas in the first prime-time Orange Bowl. Namath, who had injured his knee practicing for the game, came off the bench to mount a big fourth quarter rally, but he was stuffed on the Texas one-yard line on fourth down by Tommy Nobis after two straight failed QB sneaks. Although Alabama lost 21-17, Namath was named MVP. And four years later, on the same field, he would lead the Jets to one of the greatest upsets in the history of sports, beating the Colts in Super Bowl III, walking off the field in the end zone with his index finger held high.

CLOSE, BUT . . . THE LA COLISEUM

A lot of people will wonder where the LA Coliseum stacks up against the other great venues. It's a gargantuan building, and it has that Roman coliseum look to it at the far end of the end zone, and it hosted the 1932 and 1984 Olympics. All true. So why doesn't it make the list? Merlin Olsen said that although you can cram 90,000 people in there, he can never re-member the LA Coliseum providing a home-field advantage. The Rams were never a signature team, and while the Raiders won a title while playing there, you always kind of think of Oakland as their home town. And you never had that huge game there, that epic Nebraska-Miami kind of game, or even a really classic Super Bowl. So the reason why it didn't make the cut is simple: no great teams, no huge games.

7. Splendor on the Grass

Wimbledon sports a century's worth of tennis tradition.

They contested the first Wimbledon championships at the All England Lawn Tennis and Croquet Club back in 1877. Rutherford B. Hayes was the U.S. president and Queen Victoria was the monarch of England. That, my friends, is history. And at the All England Lawn Tennis Club they've done everything they can to keep the event the way it was then. The all-white dress code. The green lawns of center court. Center court itself is not used all year except for a ladies doubles match by four club members, just before the beginning of the fortnight. When you look up on the score-board it's always Mr. Federer or Miss Clijsters. You've got the strawberries and cream. That quote from Kipling about triumph and disaster, over the entry to Center Court. Play begins promptly at two P.M. Wimbledon is all about sporting tradition in the best sense of the word.

But make no mistake about it, this is not a museum. The fans are into it. British tennis fans are every bit as serious as Red Sox fans. They stand in line—overnight, practically—to get tickets, and when they get in, they know a great point when they see it. That's not the case at the U. S. Open, where a lot of the fans wouldn't recognize Andy Roddick if they saw him on the subway. Same with the French Open, where it's more about springtime in Paris than about tennis on the clay. Remember the Monday Final between Pat Rafter and Goran Ivanisevic? They let everyone in and these great grass-roots fans played a huge part in a dramatic match.

As far as I'm concerned, the best day of tennis of the whole year is the second Monday of the Wimbledon fortnight. If the weather is decent—and has been decent up to that point—you'll get eight men's matches in the round of 16, and eight women's matches. You're bound to get a couple of those classic Wimbledon nail-biters, where every set is headed for a tie breaker and you get the sense that the first guy to break serve is going to win the match. In a lot of ways, you might rather do this day than the men's final on that last Sunday, because you're bound to find a match you can get into, whereas the men's final can be Sampras or Federer blasting through in three quick sets. You like a little ebb and flow to a match, a break and a break back, and sometimes you don't get that with a great player in the finals, especially on the men's side, at Wimbledon.

The other thing is that Wimbledon is played on grass. While the Australian and the U.S. Open have switched around surfacewise, at Wimbledon they play on grass the same way they did 100 years ago. Now, grass court tennis, for the men, puts a little too much emphasis on the serve. You get a guy like Richard Krajicek or Goran Ivanisevic, they're not epic players, but they won the tournament because they got on a roll and nobody could touch their serve. Still, it's better than watching Gaston Gaudio hit a billion balls to win one point at the French. And the weather can be very irritating. It seems like it rains every second day in England at that time of year, and it can play havoc with the schedule. The roof that's planned for Centre Court and Court One in 2009 should help that problem.

And grass-court tennis is fun to watch. It's different. For example, it's much quieter. There's barely any sound when the ball bounces. And those low bounces are amazing. It has a really different feel from the game you can see down at the public courts, or even the local clay court club.

The other thing that's great about a grand slam tennis tournament, Wimbledon included, is that you get a chance to see both the men and the women playing on the same day. Women's tennis is a big-time sport, and you can even argue that on grass the women play more entertaining tennis than the men. So on a good day like that second Monday, you can get a little bit of both and watch Roger Federer and Serena Williams playing one right after the other.

If you're giving me my personal choice, Wimbledon would be right at the top of my personal list. I'm a big tennis guy, and I guess I'd get as much of a thrill going to the All England Club as any venue on this list. But tennis isn't a huge sport, so I can't justify putting it any higher than seventh.

DOGBITE: WIMBLEDON'S WAR SERVICE

When we talk about sports during wartime in the U.S., it's about an outfielder spending a couple of years in the army. In England, it was very different. During WWII, the tournament was suspended, and the All England Club was converted into a barnyard, with pigs, horses, donkeys, geese, hens, and rabbits calling the grounds home while the National Fire Service, the Red Cross, and Air Raid Prevention occupied the buildings. Center court itself was bombed near the royal box, and before the tournament could be resumed, holes in the roof had to be patched and the rubble cleared.

6. Monster Mash

Fenway Park is jam-packed with history. Lately, some of it has been good.

There are really only three old-time nostalgic baseball parks left today. Yankee Stadium, Wrigley Field, and Fenway Park. Now, you can say that Wrigley is a prettier place than Fenway, one of those Friendly Confines with the ivy covering the outfield walls. But the problem is that Wrigley Field, as long as it's been around, really has no history to it. There's more World Series history at Joe Robbie Stadium (or Dolphins Stadium as it's now called) than at Wrigley. And while it's hard to say bad things about Ernie Banks—let's play two!—let's face it, he's not anywhere near a top-ten player of all time, and he's the best player who ever called Wrigley Field home. None of this seems to bother Chicago fans very much. They're very loyal—perhaps too loyal. If they can sit outside in the sunshine, drink a couple of Old Styles, and watch Sammy Sosa, or nowadays, Derrek Lee, hit a couple onto Waveland Avenue, they're happy, even if the Cubbies lose 12-9.

Fenway Park still has plenty of that same kind of charm, a sense of intimacy that you really like. Little weird things like the manual scoreboard. The Pesky Pole. And the Green Monster. Sure there are some obstructed seats, and it's a pain in the neck getting around, but this little bandbox just reeks of baseball. Tris Speaker played here. Babe Ruth played

FENWAY PARK

- On April 20, 1912, Fenway opened its doors as 27,000 fans watched the Red Sox defeat the New York Highlanders 7-6 in the 11th inning.
- The current capacity of Fenway Park is 33,871, lowest in the major leagues.
- In 1934 the Green Monster made its debut. The left field wall is currently 37 feet high.
- Game 6 of the 1975 World Series, in which Carlton Fisk hit a 12th-inning home run, was the first World Series game played at night at Fenway.

here. Ted Williams, Lefty Grove, and Carl Yastrzemski played here. Roger Clemens and Pedro Martinez played here. Fenway has a huge sense of history.

Of course, for the Red Sox fan, a lot of the history at Fenway has been heartbreaking. Fenway Park has ghosts. Tell a Red Sox fan that the same weekend that Fenway Park opened up, the Titanic sank, and they won't be surprised. The Sox lost the 1975 World Series there, day after Carlton Fisk hit his classic "reaction shot." In 1978 you had Bucky Bleepin' Dent hit one over the Monster and into the screen. And just this decade alone, you've had some amazing games. Zimmer vs. Pedro and all that craziness. But 2004 exorcised a lot of those demons. Going down 3-0, and then beating the Yankees back to back, Game 4 and Game 5, with Mariano blowing saves on two consecutive nights, and David Ortiz getting the game-winning hits . . . that's sweet, sweet, sweet redemption.

I want to be here at this great classic old ballpark on a Yankees–Red Sox night in October. I think Boston is the best baseball town in America. The fans are hugely into it, and I want to be right there with them, booing the Yankees.

DOGBITE: MONSTROUSLY GOOD SEATS

It's amazing that somebody in Red Sox land did not figure this out earlier, but the best seat in baseball without a doubt is a Monster Seat at Fenway. What's so great about them? First off there's only 200 or 300 of them up there. You've got your own bathroom and your own concessions. So what's the big deal? Fenway Park is a 1912 ballpark and bathrooms are a disaster. Go to a regular concession stand in the bottom of the 5th, you'll get back in the top of the 7th. Not the case with those Monster Seats. But the best part is that you're so close to the field that you're on top of the players. There's not one spot on the field you can't see. And so many balls are hit in that direction—even from left-handed hitters—that you feel like the ball is coming towards you all the time. And they're not foul balls, they're balls in play. You feel like you're part of the action. And there's nothing better than seeing someone hit a home run that sails over your head and lands on the parking garages on Landsdowne Street. They're tremendous seats, the best seats in sports.

5. Masters of the Universe

Augusta National isn't populist, but it is a classic.

For a golfer, there are a handful of truly hallowed places. Pebble Beach, for sure. St. Andrews. Royal and Ancient. But the most hallowed has got to be Augusta. The reason why Augusta goes to the top of the list is that every year, when the azaleas bloom in the second weekend in April, there's the Masters, the most important tournament in golf. The U.S. Open comes back to Pebble Beach every now and then. The British Open rotates through its selection of courses every five or six years. But the Masters and Augusta are inseparable, year in and year out. A great tournament, the one everyone wants to win, and a great golf course.

And make no mistake, Augusta is a great golf course. Even after the Tiger-proofing of the late 1990s, it's still a fair test. You like the way it gives you the possibility to blow up—the way Norman did in 1996—or to be miraculous—the way Nicklaus did in 1986. You can reach the 3rd green in 2, get an eagle. You can reach 13 and 15 in 2, but then you can hit the ball in the water on 16 and be dead. You can hit the ball into the water of Ray's Creek on 12 and that's all she wrote. You can hit the ball in the water on 11 like Ray Floyd and it's bye-bye green jacket. And now that the club

AUGUSTA NATIONAL

- The yardage of the championship course is 7,270. There are 110 acres of fairway and 35 acres of rough.
- The fairways are composed of Bermuda grass overseeded with ryegrass. The greens are bentgrass.
- In 1997 Tiger Woods broke the 72-hole record at the Masters shooting 270.
- The name Amen Corner, for holes 11, 12, and 13, was coined in a 1958 *Sports Illustrated* article by Herbert Warren Wind, who borrowed the name from an old jazz recording, "Shouting at Amen Corner," by a band under the direction of Mezz Mezzrow, a Chicago clarinetist.

members have finally allowed us to see all 18 holes, you really get to know the course in the way that you don't know the sites of the other majors. You can almost play along with the players, figure out who's playing too conservatively and who's taking crazy chances.

All that said, there's an elitist aspect to Augusta. No women. Only a handful of African-American members. It's not democratic. The guys who run the club are a bunch of blowhards. Those old Southern gentlemen, some of them drive you crazy with their nineteenth-century attitudes— banishing Gary McCord from CBS. Very petty. But you've got to admit they're not phonies. You don't want to watch it? They don't care. Don't watch it. No women? They don't care. Go picket. They are not going to be intimidated by any interest group, by any politician, by any television executive, by any player. Part of you likes that. Part of you doesn't, but part of you does.

The other thing you've got to admit is that golf is not a mass-appeal sport. In 2004, when Phil Mickelson finally won, making that great comeback to catch Ernie Els for a dramatic storybook finish, it only got an 8 rating. The NCAA Finals gets a 15. The Super Bowl gets a 45. So golf, as a spectator sport, is definitely an acquired taste.

A ticket to the Masters is just about the toughest get on this list. It is by far the toughest ticket in sports. You want to go to a World Series or a Super Bowl, you might have to crack open your piggy bank, but somehow or another you can score a ticket. The Masters, you're going to have to pull in every favor you can think of and then some. But once you get inside there's a certain civility here. It's pretty easy to get around. The galleries are manageable. The lines aren't huge. Hamburgers are a dollar. A Coke's 50 cents. It's like you've turned back the clock to the 1950s. For better and for worse, you're one of the privileged few.

And with that lifetime exemption for former champions, you get to see some of the real legends of the sport up close and personal. I don't get too wrapped up in watching Arnold Palmer shoot an 85, but for some golf fans that's a dream come true. And it means something to the players, too. I remember Johnny Miller telling us very sincerely that his one great regret was not winning the Masters in 1975 when he had the chance, missing the putt on 18 that would have forced a playoff with Nicklaus. He said,

"I really wanted to win that one because I wanted to be able to go back there every year." I can see why.

DOGBITE: PLAYING FOR MONEY

Nowadays you can't buy the privilege of playing a round at Augusta. That wasn't the case when the club opened. In the mid-1930s, the initiation fee was $350 and the annual dues were $60. And despite the fact that Bobby Jones personally sent out letters to thousands of people asking them to join, the club struggled at first.

Augusta didn't even have enough money to pay the course designer, Alister MacKenzie, his $10,000 fee. MacKenzie reduced his fee by half in hopes of getting paid, but had no choice but to settle for two checks of a thousand apiece. And chairman Clifford Roberts suggested he not try to cash them in Augusta. Lenders actually foreclosed on the club in 1935, but the club's fortunes changed after the Augusta National Invitation Tournament—later renamed the Masters—began. In the mid-1930s.

---

4. Dome Field Advantage

South Bend has more than just Touchdown Jesus going for it.

In a lot of cities in America—Tuscaloosa, Alabama, Gainesville, Florida; Norman, Oklahoma—college football is king. The NFL isn't on the radar screen. And if you're from one of those places, or you went to a big football school, a trip to a big college football stadium is a must.

Which one? It's pretty much a no brainer to me. We're heading across the plains to South Bend, Indiana, to the Golden Dome, that great stadium that stands in the shadow of Touchdown Jesus. There's a tremendous sense of history here. "Outlined against a blue-gray October sky, the Four Horsemen rode again." Grantland Rice wrote those words back in 1924, probably the most famous line in sports journalism. And it wasn't about Florida State. You can start with the Four Horsemen and work your way up to Joe Montana and Rocket Ismail, connect Knute Rockne to Ara Parseghian to Lou Holtz. There's a sense of continuity here, of being part of something bigger than just this season, just this game, and you have to respect that. Even when Notre Dame is having a sub-par year, there always seems to be at least one game where you feel the ghosts. Autumn leaves. Green pants. NBC-TV. It's must-see TV.

But it's not like you're taking a trip to a museum. Even though they've fallen on hard times a little in recent seasons, Notre Dame has the biggest national fan base of any program. No question about it. There's a reason they have their own TV network. There are Notre Dame fans in Albuquerque. No Michigan fans, but plenty of Notre Dame fans. And for every Notre Dame fan in New York or Miami, there's someone else who just can't stand them.

So if you're a Notre Dame fan, a trip to South Bend is practically a pilgrimage. But what if you're a Notre Dame hater? Ask any college coach, player, or big-time fan where they'd most like to have a big win on the road. If you eliminate the few classic rivalries—Texas and Texas A&M, Auburn and Alabama—just about every one is going to say, "I want to beat Notre Dame at South Bend."

You're not just beating this year's team, you're beating the ghosts. I hate Notre Dame. I'd want to go to South Bend just to watch them lose. And the answer to that question would have been the same 70 years ago, or 50 years ago, or 20 years ago. That's why South Bend is number four on our list.

DOGBITE: ROCK FOUNDATION

Believe it or not, Knute Rockne had a huge part in designing Notre Dame Stadium. In the late 1920s, Rockne wanted a bigger stadium—the earlier facility had a 30,000 capacity—to accommodate the alumni he envisioned coming from around the country to see the Fighting Irish play. Facing resistance from the school president, who wanted to build dorms and academic buildings, Rockne submitted his own plan. "When Rockne first proposed the stadium," said former president Reverend Matthew Walsh, "he was almost laughed at." Legend has it that Rockne traveled to Ann Arbor and came back with the blueprints for Michigan's stadium. "This is not fiction, this is fact," former Notre Dame coach Lou Holtz contends. "He built 60,000, just like Michigan." (Notre Dame Stadium had an official capacity of 59,075). In any case, Rockne won over his opposition and before long, the Osborn Engineering Company, which had designed Comiskey Park, Yankee Stadium, the Polo Grounds, and the University of Michigan, began building the $750,000 stadium in the summer of 1929. But there were plenty of Rockne's ideas in the building. The sidelines were kept small with just enough room for coaches and players, and he was the mastermind behind the parking arrangements and traffic system that are basically the ones used today. Rockne coached only one season in the new stadium—the 10-0 national champions of 1930—before his death in that March 1931 plane crash.

3. Garden Party

Major sporting events? MSG hosted them by the score.

The first question you have to ask yourself about Madison Square Garden is which building you're talking about. There's the old Garden, which was a few blocks uptown, and the new Garden over on Eighth Avenue. But for the purposes of this list, we're going to consider it one building. While the new Garden could pretty much stand on its own on this list, the reality is that most of the classic venues have been around for a lot longer than 40 years. So we'll look at the combined legacy here.

The thing that makes the Garden stand out from just about every indoor arena is this: There have been a million different kinds of events here. It's got one of the great fights of all time: Ali-Frazier I. Okay, maybe the Thrilla in Manila was better, but Ali-Frazier I was like the first act of a great play. Just an electric atmosphere. Burt Lancaster called the fight. *Burt Lancaster.*

There have been a lot of great tennis matches—Connors-Vilas, McEnroe-Ashe—in the Masters, and plenty of great women's matches when the Virgina Slims championships were played there. It's got the Melrose Games track meet. It's even got the Westminster Kennel Club dog show. And Nadia Comaneci scored her first perfect 10 here in gymnastics. There's been lots of college basketball. Remember when St. John's with Chris Mullin took on Georgetown with Patrick Ewing in that classic second game between the two schools back in 1985? That was at Madison Square Garden. And for a while the NIT was even more important than the NCAAs. The Rangers had a nice run in the early 1990s, broke a long, long drought, and got a couple of all-time greats, Wayne Gretzky and Mark Messier, onto the ice here.

And there's the music thing, from Sinatra to Springsteen and back again. The concert for Bangladesh was here. John Lennon made his last public performance here. Marilyn Monroe sang "Happy Birthday Mr. President" to JFK here.

But the Knicks are really MSG's signature team. In the early 1970s you had Clyde Frazier pulling up outside of Toots Shor's in his white Rolls Royce wearing a mink coat and a purple hat. And it was at Madison Square Garden that Willis Reed dragged himself out onto the court, in one of the classic mind-over-matter moments.

And even though the Knicks don't have the same number of championships as the Celtics or the Lakers or the Bulls, there's still a lot of juice around this team. Call it star power. There are the regulars—Spike Lee, Woody Allen, Alec Baldwin—and they're big fans and they're really into the game. Watching Spike Lee jaw with Reggie Miller, that's worth the price of admission alone. And take a peek in the front row and you'll find the hot celebrity couple. When the Knicks are going well, the paparazzi don't need to stalk the trendy clubs, they can just come to MSG. They might have their cell phones, driving you crazy, but they're there. I don't care about any of that, but you might. I know that the ticket prices are absurd. Anybody who would spend $1,500 for an NBA regular-season ticket to see the Clippers is nuts. But there's no secret when a free agent is being wooed by a New York sports team, you always see them at the Garden that night, courtside. That aspect of it gives the place a big-time feel. It gives you the idea that Madison Square Garden is a happening place.

And I think there's something else that happens here. In basketball, especially, Madison Square Garden is the toughest home court to protect. Opposing teams really try to put on their best games here. Whether it's the Spurs or the Clippers, they're not going to fold their tents if they get down by nine late in the third quarter the way they might if they were in Charlotte or something. Madison Square Garden, in a lot of ways, is about New York, and although that might annoy some people in Kansas City, to be great you have to play your A-game in New York.

What about Michael Jordan dropping 55 points on the Knicks in his comeback game? Now, Jordan won a championship at the United Center. But I would bet if you asked Jordan where he would rather play, MSG or the United Center, and he could be completely honest, he'd say Madison Square Garden. I think he'd pick the old Chicago Stadium over Madison Square Garden, but among the active arenas, he'd say MSG. In short,

Madison Square Garden bills itself as the world's most famous arena. For once you can believe the hype.

DOGBITE: RIDING AROUND THE SQUARE

Madison Square Garden hosted some of the greatest boxing matches and basketball games of the last century. But in 1879, William Henry Vanderbilt built the original Garden for, of all things, bicycle racing.

Bicycle races were huge at the turn of the century, with guys like Major Taylor being huge stars, so Vanderbilt converted the building—it was a site of P.T. Barnum's circus—into a velodrome. That old MSG was also the site of the first artificial ice rink in North America, and hosted boxing exhibitions with John L. Sullivan and an indoor pro football game. But although the bike races are a distant memory—and good riddance—in Europe, they still refer to an indoor bike race as a Madison.

CLOSE, BUT . . .

What about the Boston Garden? Fair point. But the Boston Garden is a defunct venue. I don't consider the Fleet Center the same building. Same city, same two teams play there, but it's not the same, I'm sorry. The same thing goes for Chicago with the old Chicago Stadium and the United Center. Or even the old Montreal Forum or Maple Leaf Gardens for hockey fans. If we were doing this ten years ago, you could make a case for those great old buildings. But now they've been torn down and there's nothing left but great memories and some parking lots.

2. Lambeau's Frozen Tundra

Green Bay's a little town, but its football stadium has a giant legacy.

You can tell a lot about a venue by your reaction the first time you see it. And I sure remember the first time I laid eyes on Lambeau Field. When you're flying into Green Bay, there's a flight path that takes you right over the stadium—and Green Bay's airport isn't exactly LaGuardia, so there aren't too many flight paths. You look out the window, and you see this tiny town in northern Wisconsin. And I mean that; it's not a city, it's a town. And then boom, you see it in the distance, this big bowl of a stadium. There are no buildings around it. I love that bird's eye view of Lambeau, right in the middle of nowhere. It looks kind of like a football version of the Field of Dreams.

On a good day, Green Bay is one of the few NFL cities that has the great feeling of a college game. The Packers are really the only game in town, so everything kind of stops for three hours on Sunday afternoon. There's this great juxtaposition between small town Green Bay and the big league NFL. When you visit the town, it's hard to fathom that this is the home of the legendary Green Bay Packers.

As you know, one of my yardsticks for a great venue is whether you can feel the ghosts. And the problem with the NFL is that too many of the stadiums are so new that you don't have that. I felt a little bit of that at RFK Stadium in Washington,

LAMBEAU FIELD

- On September 29, 1957, Green Bay defeated the Chicago Bears 21-17 in the first game ever played at the stadium.
- On September 11, 1965, a year after Curly Lambeau passed away, the stadium's name changed from City Stadium to Lambeau Field.
- Site of three NFL Championship games: 1961, 1965, and the 1967 Ice Bowl
- The Packers hold an impressive 12-2 postseason record in Lambeau.

but it's gone. A little bit at Soldier Field in Chicago. Gone too. I like Arrowhead in Kansas City, because the fans are really into the game, but it's not old enough and the ghost of Elvis Grbac doesn't give me goosebumps. Of the stadiums still in use in the NFL, Lambeau is the place.

Part of it is the really forbidding weather—the frozen tundra as John Facenda called it. Ten degrees and light snow. That, my friends, is NFL football weather, and that's what you get in December and January in Green Bay. And with a bunch of indoor stadiums and stadiums with retractable roofs and so many expansion teams in Sun Belt states, those classic cold, crisp conditions are becoming more and more of a rarity. Don't like the cold? Bundle up.

And there's the legacy of Vince Lombardi and those great Green Bay Packer teams. You had Curly Lambeau and Don Hutson back in the day. Now you've got Brett Favre, tough as nails, plays every game, won a title. But the golden age of Packer football, and in many ways the golden age of NFL football, happened during that period. When you're in Green Bay, you think of Lombardi and you think of those nine Hall of Famers and those five championships. Vince Lombardi in Title Town, USA, that's what put the NFL as we know it today on the map. The NFL became America's most popular sport when the Green Bay Packers were winning five titles in seven years: '61–'62 and '65–'67. Five in seven.

And arguably the most amazing game in the history of the NFL happened in Lambeau Field. The 1967 Ice Bowl. Now, you got the '58 championship game at Yankee Stadium, and Super Bowl III. No question about it, they're up there, too. But for my money, the most memorable game in the history of the NFL is the Ice Bowl in Green Bay against Dallas in 1967. Amazing conditions. Arctic. It's minus-13 degrees without the wind chill. Hot Coffee freezing on the ledges of the broadcast booths. Third and goal at the one, Lombardi eschewed the field goal and went for the quarterback sneak. The Packers win in Lombardi's last year—that to me is probably the most famous game in the history of the NFL. It's also the first important game that I remember vividly as a kid. I had just turned eight. I remember the '66 championship game at the Cotton Bowl a little bit, but the first game where I can specifically remember calls and plays—Chuck Marcein, sliding on the ice in that classic last drive—is the Ice Bowl in '67. At Lambeau. And it's funny, when I went to Green Bay in '94, who did I sit next to in the press box for the whole four hours? Ray Scott, the legendary Packers broadcaster. And Ray Scott and I talked NFL football, talked the Packers for the whole Jet-Packer's game that day. And you know what I couldn't believe about Ray Scott? He lived in Minneapolis. I couldn't get over that. Here's the Packer voice for all those years, and I thought boy, here's a guy who's the Voice of Green Bay, so he must have a nice house on the edge of town. Nope. He lived in Minneapolis and flew in every weekend.

I have a fantasy about when I retire one day. You know what I'm gonna do? When my kids are old enough to appreciate it, and they want to understand what Daddy's all about, and they want to go to an NFL football game, I am going to take them to a Packer game during the Christmas season. Mid-December, bundled up with the hats and gloves. Hot chocolate. Watching the gladiators march onto the frozen tundra of Lambeau Field. That is the NFL. Lambeau, December, ice, snow, cold, blustery winds. Lambeau is number two.

DOGBITE: THE THAWED TUNDRA

Almost 40 years ago, Vince Lombardi had 14 miles of electric heating cables installed beneath the field at Lambeau. That was the year of the Ice Bowl, but Lombardi's $80,000 system was no match for the 13-below temperatures. Nobody was more upset than the coach, as his son, Vince Jr., recalls. "I'd never seen him quite that way on game day. He worried that if the thing didn't work, he'd be accused of tampering with it to make the field worse for Dallas." In the 1997 NFC Championship game against the Carolina Panthers, Lombardi's heating system thawed the playing surface, but the sideline remained frozen. As a result, the slush drained back onto the heated field, making for dreadful, sloppy playing conditions. The game was coined the Mud Bowl. After that season, the Packers decided to rip up the cables and install a new heating system—this time powered by natural gas–fired hot water.

1. The House That . . .

Ruth built it, but that's just the beginning of the story for Yankee Stadium.

Number one. How could it not be? What we have here—we have America's most famous franchise, we have America's most historic sport, and we have America's most historic building, all rolled into one. Whenever I have friends come into town, even if the Yankees are away or it's winter, I make sure I drive them up the FDR Drive, to the Deegan, down to the GW, and down the West Side Highway to see Yankee Stadium. Yankee. Stadium. What needs to be said? The most famous player in the history of sports built the place. Babe Ruth. Remember that before this stadium was built, the Yankees were sharing a stadium at the Polo Grounds—kind of like the Jets do with the football Giants today. The Yankees needed a place of their own, and, oh, what a place they got.

Look down the right-field line. That short porch is where the Bambino deposited a million home runs. A little further along, there's the facade. That's where Mickey Mantle almost hit one out of the Stadium. Center field? That's where Joe DiMaggio patrolled. That black batter's eye? That's where Reggie Jackson's third homer in the 1977 World Series landed. There's monument park. Past the bullpen, in the upper deck in left, that's where Aaron Boone deposited a Tim Wakefield non-knuckler to beat

YANKEE STADIUM

- Opened on April 18, 1923. Babe Ruth hit a home run in the inaugural game as the Yankees beat the Red Sox 4-1.
- Yankee Stadium hosted the 1938 heavyweight title fight between Joe Louis and Germany's Max Schmeling, the famous "Win one for the Gipper" game between Notre Dame and Army in 1928, and the 1958 NFL championship game between the football Giants and Colts.
- After the renovated ballpark was opened in 1976, the Yankees appeared in the next three World Series.

the Red Sox. The infield? That's where Lou Gehrig gave his Luckiest Man on the Face of the Earth speech. And where Yogi Berra jumped into Don Larsen's arms after his World Series perfect game. I can see George Brett going nuts during the Pine Tar Game.

And the players: Ruth, Gehrig, DiMaggio, Mantle, Berra, Ford, Jackson, Winfield; and now Jeter, and A-Rod, and Mariano. There have been more World Series celebrations here than anyplace else. (I assume that George Steinbrenner will forgive me if I point out that the most recent one was by the Florida Marlins in 2003.)

Now, I know that it's not exactly the same Stadium that was built in the 1920s. It's been refurbished. And I know that it's a nightmare getting out of there on a game night. An urban planner wouldn't put a stadium there today. But that's one of the great things about Yankee Stadium. It's not in Manhattan, it's in the Bronx. Not a great neighborhood by any stretch, but it's the home of the Yankees.

And you can talk other sports if you wish. The football Giants played here. Chuck Bednarik's hit on Frank Gifford in 1960. That frigid '62 championship game between the Giants and the Packers. (Guys who played in the Ice Bowl in 1967 claim that New York that day was colder than Green Bay.) Fights? Ali fought here. Joe Louis too. A papal mass. But

---

DOGBITE: THE RIGHT STUFF

Yankee fans talk about how many homers Joe DiMaggio would have hit if not for that left-field Death Valley. But by the time Joe D arrived, the fences had already been brought in. When the Stadium opened, the deepest part of the park was 490 feet away in dead center (although the right-field corner where Ruth and Gehrig made their living was only 296 feet away). In 1937 the Yankees took in the Stadium's deepest fences—center field went from 490 feet to 461, left center went from 460 to 457, and right center from 429 feet to 407. The fences have been moved in twice since then. Last year when A-Rod broke DiMaggio's record for home runs by a Yankee righty, the original 460-foot power alley in left center had been reduced to 399 feet, and the wall in dead center, originally 490 feet away, had been moved in to only 408. Imagine Joe D's reaction. He would have just rolled his eyes.

Yankee Stadium is about baseball. It's about the team that you either love or hate, but no matter how you feel about them, you've got to tip your cap to them. If you want to understand America, you need to understand baseball. And if you want to understand baseball, your first stop has to be in the borough of the Bronx to catch a game in the House that Ruth Built.

Chapter 7

The Top-Ten College Basketball Players of All Time

Who deserves top billing? Walton or Russell?
And which all-timer never played a single tournament game?

Cutting down the nets after the final game of the NCAA Final Four. It's one of the great, classic moments in sports. But can you make the Mad Dog Hall of Fame as a basketball player if you never did that?

In my opinion, you can. The reality is that there are plenty of all-time great college basketball players who never won a championship. That's because the NCAA tournament is really a game of Russian Roulette. One bad game and you're out. Done. History. Bye-bye. And before they expanded the field in the late 1970s, and it was one berth to a conference, there were some very good teams that didn't make it. If you were in a great conference like the ACC and you were 25-0 and you lost in quadruple overtime in the ACC tournament final, you didn't make the NCAA tournament. Wait till next year. And while the school or the coach has plenty of chances, as a player you've only got three or four shots at most to win the big dance. A couple of bad bounces or injuries can leave even a great player on the outside looking in.

What ties these guys together? A certain presence. The ability to dominate a game. These were players who were so good they forced the game's powers-that-be to change the rules. These were guys who were capable of having a perfect night. These were impact players in the best sense of that word.

Here's one thing I'm not going to include: pro performance. Some of these players would go on to become very good pros, a few would be Hall of Famers. And a few would be real disappointments. One guy wouldn't play pro ball at all. If you're going to give some extra credit for pro performance, a guy like Patrick Ewing could sneak onto this list. So without further ado, let's head to campus for the induction ceremony for the inaugural class of the Mad Dog College Basketball Hall of Fame.

10. The Shotmaker

It was the biggest basket in college hoop history, and Christian Laettner made it.

East Regional finals, Duke down by one in overtime. Two seconds left on the clock. Grant Hill throws an 80-foot pass to Laettner, who catches it, dribbles once, fakes right, turns left, and drains a 17-foot jumper. This wasn't a desperation shot. He almost made it look easy. That fake is what gets you.

A lot of people are going to have trouble with putting Christian Laettner in any kind of Hall of Fame. First, there's the Duke factor. Duke is one of those teams that polarizes people—like the Yankees, Notre Dame football, or the Dallas Cowboys—and flat out, there are a lot of people who just hate Duke. And that enters into peoples' perceptions of Laettner. In the second half of that Kentucky game, Laettner didn't make any friends when he drew a technical by stepping on the chest of a Wildcat player who'd fallen to the floor.

And as a pro, he's been a complete disappointment. He was the number three pick in the NBA draft, and people expected him to be the second coming of Larry Bird. But he wasn't even close in that regard. He was an All-Star just once, and he bounced around from team to team, kind of an overpaid journeyman. (A question for you trivia buffs: Who was the first [and, at this writing, the only] Duke player to win an NBA championship? It was Laettner's "twin," Danny Ferry, who won one in 2003 as a bench player with the Spurs.)

But let's put that aside for a second. That Duke team from the early 1990s was the closest thing you'll find to a dynasty in modern college basketball, and Laettner was the best player on that team. You can make the argument for Bobby Hurley or Grant Hill, but Laettner really was the guy. He's probably the best player in Duke history, and Duke is one of the three or four greatest programs in the game.

In four years, Laettner played in four Final Fours. Think about that. His first two years, Duke lost, first to Seton Hall in the semis, and then they got buried by UNLV in the finals. But in his junior year they played UNLV in the semis and no one gave Duke a chance. UNLV had all the guys back from their championship team—Larry Johnson, Greg Anthony, Stacey Augmon—and everyone figured they'd blow them out the same way. Not this time. Duke pulled off one of the great upsets in college basketball history, and it was because of Christian Laettner. He scored 28 points.

A lot of people are going to have a problem putting him as number ten, and I understand that. He doesn't have the sparkling résumé of some guys on this list. He averaged 20 points a game only once. He was a First Team All-American only once, and was MVP of the tournament once, in his junior year.

CHRISTIAN LAETTNER

- Led Blue Devils to back-to-back championships in 1991 and 1992, winning tournament Most Outstanding Player in '91
- In his record 23 games, he scored the most points all-time in the NCAA tournament (407) and is second in rebounds (169). He also leads in free throws made (142).
- In the 1992 East Regional, against Kentucky, Laettner made all 20 of his shots (10 FG, 10 FT), including the buzzer-beater.
- Holds Duke records for most combined points-assist-rebounds (3,882), three-point percentage (48.5%), free throws made (713), wins (122), and personal fouls (425)
- Laettner is second in NCAA history in games played with 148.

But love him or hate him, Christian Laettner was a big-time player in college. And a clutch player. He made the game ending shot in a regional final to beat U-Conn. And while everyone remembers that game-winner against Kentucky, here's what people forget about that day: Christian Laettner went 10-for-10 from the field. And he went ten-for-ten from the line. He was perfect. Nobody ever had a better game in a bigger spot.

And Duke won the title that year. If they hadn't—if Laettner misses one shot that day—there's no Duke dynasty. Since when is two titles a dynasty? Since the NCAA tournament went to 64 teams and six rounds. Until Duke did it, nobody had won back-to-back championships since UCLA, and nobody's done it since. That's why Christian Laettner is in the Hall of Fame.

DOGBITE: MR. KRYPTONITE

Hard to believe it now, but Christian Laettner had Shaquille O'Neal's number when they were in college. In their first meeting, Laettner burned O'Neal for 24 points on 10-of-14 shooting and 11 rebounds while holding Shaq, who had been averaging 27.9 a game, to a season-low 15 points. The Blue Devils won by 18 points, and Dale Brown said afterward, "I was very happy that Shaquille was able to go against somebody that's better than him. Laettner's the only person who's been better than him all year."

Their other matchup took place in Baton Rouge. Laettner scored 22 points and grabbed 10 rebounds while Shaq had 25 points and 12 rebounds. But, late in the game, Laettner was great. He scored 10 points in the final six minutes, while Shaq missed five free throws in the last five minutes. As the teams left the floor, Laettner went over to Shaq and told him, "Good game. Keep improving."

CLOSE, BUT . . .

Christian Laettner is the most contemporary player on this list, and he played 15 years ago. There's a good reason for this. For the really good players, college basketball has become a means to an end, not an end in itself; just a pit stop between high school and the NBA. Since 1990, how many really great pro players can you name who stayed in school four years? Tim Duncan. Maybe Grant Hill. That's about it.

The very best players—LeBron James, Kevin Garnett, Kobe Bryant—don't even go to college anymore. That's turned around 180 degrees from where it used to be. If you go back 50 years, college was much more important than the NBA. It was a huge deal. Look at Bob Kurland. He didn't even play in the NBA. The reality is that the level of play in college basketball—at least at the very top of the game—just isn't as high as it once was. I think it's really going to be tough for a contemporary player to crack this list in the future.

9. The Biggest Wildcat

Kentucky's legendary center made one giant mistake.

It's time for an ethics question. If you're looking strictly at the qualifications, Alex Groza deserves to be on this list. The Beak, as they called him, was a two-time First Team All-American, and MVP of the NCAA tournament in 1948 and 1949. And his teams never lost a game in the NCAA tournament. He was really the lynchpin of Adolph Rupp's offense. He was 6'7", a hard-nosed, slashing kind of center. They didn't keep track of assists and rebounds back then, but by all accounts he was a great passer out of the post and a tough rebounder. When he left the team for a while to do a stint in the army between 1945 and 1947, Rupp told a reporter who didn't understand what all the fuss was about, "You don't replace Caruso with a barbershop singer." Kentucky is one of the all-time great programs, and just like with Laettner and Duke, Groza is the best player in Kentucky basketball history.

And after he left Kentucky, he was

ALEX GROZA

- As the foundation of the Fabulous Five, he led Kentucky to its first national championship in 1948. The following year he scored 25 points to help deliver a second title.
- Top scorer and tournament Most Outstanding Player in both 1948 and 1949
- Three-time All-American and All-SEC (1947–49)
- In the 1948 Championship game against Oklahoma A&M, Groza scored more points than all the other players on his team combined.

All-NBA in 1950–51, ahead of Dolph Schayes. How good was Groza's Kentucky team? The Fabulous Five went straight over to London for the 1948 Olympics and they won the gold medal. The score in the gold medal game against France? 65-21. Yes. They beat the second best team in the world by 44 points.

What's the negative? He took money for point shaving against Loyola. $2,000. Now, that may not seem like much now, but back then two grand would buy you a car, so it's hardly pocket change. And Kentucky was a 10-point favorite in the game and ended up losing by five. It ticked Adolph Rupp off to no end. He bragged that "the gamblers couldn't get to our guys with a ten-foot pole" and then this came to light. Rupp didn't talk to Groza for years. Groza paid the price for what he did. He got a suspended sentence in the criminal deal, but the NBA banned him for life, took away a piece of a franchise he owned, and to this day he's not in the National Basketball Hall of Fame. His brother Lou, who was a field goal kicker for the Browns, recalls how devastating the news was. "My father was a strict disciplinarian, and we never got into any trouble as kids. When I heard about Alex—I got a call in the middle of the night—I just lay on the floor and cried. I couldn't believe it."

As far as the actual evidence, Groza admitted that he took the money,

---

DOGBITE: ABSOLUTELY FABULOUS

Remember how Antoine Walker, Ron Mercer, and Walter McCarty won the 1996 NCAA tournament for Kentucky and then were reunited with former Wildcats coach Rick Pitino on the Boston Celtics? Well, there was plenty of precedent for that. In 1949 the entire starting lineup of the NBA's Indianapolis Olympians came from the University of Kentucky. It included four members of the Fabulous Five team that won the 1948 NCAA championship: Ralph Beard, Cliff Barker, Wah Wah Jones, and Alex Groza. The fifth player was former teammate Joe Holland. Not only did the five Wildcats join the team at the same time—they owned it. In their first year they won the division. Groza finished second in the league in scoring, behind George Mikan. He continued his outstanding play the next year, leading the league in field goal percentage.

but he denied actually throwing the games. For whatever it's worth, Loyola's center Jack Kerris outscored Groza 23-12 in that game.

Where do I draw the line? Joe Jackson is a Hall of Fame baseball player. He should be in Cooperstown. He's one of the greatest hitters of all time. How is he not in there? He took $500 in the 1919 World Series; and he proceeded to play well in that World Series, by the way. But he took $500 and he's not in the Hall of Fame. Does that mean that we expunge all of Joe Jackson's records and pretend he didn't exist? I don't think we can do that.

It's the same thing for Groza. Kentucky not only has the banners of those two NCAA championship teams hanging proudly in the gym, they retired Groza's number. You look in the NCAA record book and there's no asterisk beside those two Kentucky championships. If you want to eliminate Groza because of what he did, go right ahead. But I'm not going to.

8. High-Wire Actor

No player ever thrilled like NC State's David Thompson.

If you ever saw David Thompson play, you understand why I put him in the Hall of Fame. Does the phrase "44-inch vertical leap" mean anything to you? The story is that Thompson could pluck a quarter off the top of the backboard, and if you saw his hops, you'd believe it.

He was such a great theatrical player, a real high-wire act. If you're looking for a guy who could do things that could take your breath away, David Thompson was the one. You didn't have to be a basketball purist to appreciate the amazing, gravity-defying things he did.

He was also a tremendously influential player ahead of his time in the mid-1970s. He was Michael Jordan before there was a Michael Jordan. For that matter, do you know who a young Michael Jordan idolized when he was a young kid growing up in North Carolina? Right. David Thompson. Thompson wasn't just fun to watch, he was a scoring machine. In his last three years he scored 24.7, 26.0, and 30 points a game while pulling down eight rebounds and shooting 55 percent from the field. The ACC is considered the best basketball conference in the country, and Thompson is the best player in the history of the ACC. Remember NC State went 27-0 in 1973, but couldn't play in the tournament because of recruiting violations.

He cemented that reputation in just a couple of weeks in the spring of 1974. Remember that classic ACC tournament final against Maryland, 103-100 in overtime? Maybe the greatest college basketball game of all time. That game pitted probably the two best teams in college basketball—there were five All-Americans and 11 future NBA players on the court that day—and in the days before at-large bids they were playing for the right to play in the NCAA tournament. David Thompson scored 29 points and made room for Tom Burleson to score 38, and they came back from 12 down in the first half to win. They don't even make the tournament if not for Thompson's heroics.

In the East Regional final against Pittsburgh a couple of weeks later Thompson had this *Friday the 13th* kind of fall, the kind of scary thing that makes you cover your eyes when you see the replay. Up to that point it had been a very physical game, with Pitt really shoving NC State around. Thompson got mad after getting hacked, which was very uncharacteristic of him, and said, by hook or by crook, I'm going to block their next shot. He jumped so high he got tangled up with Phil Spence, one of his teammates. He fell backward, hit his head, and lay on the floor in a pool of blood, not moving for more than four minutes. The arena was dead silent. Rumor has it that they put in a call to CBS News alerting Walter Cronkite that he might have to do a special report announcing that Thompson was dead. He got 16 stitches and a concussion, but he actually came back to Reynolds Coliseum with his head wrapped up in these huge white bandages and got a huge ovation. Forget Willis Reed. Thompson wasn't just limping, he practically came back from the dead that afternoon.

In the semis of the Final Four he upped the ante, scoring 28 points and grabbing 10 rebounds in double overtime against UCLA. NC State came back from 7 points down in that final overtime, and Thompson iced the game with his free throws. Simply, he did the impossible—beat Bill Walton's all-time great UCLA team when it really mattered, and sealed the deal in the finals, scoring 21 points in the championship game.

"David Thompson was clearly the best player we ever played against in college," Walton said after the game. That's why he's worthy of a spot in the Mad Dog Hall of Fame.

DOGBITE: DAVID'S DUNK

Know how many dunks Thompson had in his college career? One.

The NCAA ban on dunking was still in effect, but in his final home game at Reynolds Coliseum, Thompson couldn't resist. "I decided to give the crowd a little bit of something they had been missing," he said. "We were way ahead and it was my last home game. They had just retired my jersey before the game, so I decided to go out with a bang. I dunked and got my only technical of my career. The coach took me out of the game and I got a standing ovation."

Thompson also invented the alley oop. In a scrimmage, point guard Monte Towe threw an errant pass that sailed up toward the basket and Thompson made it seem like part of a plan. Towe recalls, "He went up, caught it, and dropped it in, and Coach Norm Sloan said, 'I think that's something we can use.' "

7. The First Dunker

Bob Kurland was so big and so good, they had to change the rules.

One of the criteria for enshrinement in the Mad Dog Hall of Fame is that you changed the game in some way. Well, no one changed the game of college basketball more than Bob Kurland. Kurland was probably the first player to dunk. Nobody made a big thing about it at the time—it was called the "duffer shot"—and it was considered kind of bad form, so it wasn't a huge part of the game. But that's just one way that Bob "Foothills" Kurland, the great center at Oklahoma A&M, made an impact.

Bob Kurland played so long ago back in the mid-1940s, that it's hard to get a handle on him, but Kurland really ushered in a new era of college basketball. He was the first seven-footer in the history of the college game. He literally made them change the rules. In his sophomore year with Oklahoma A&M, he just sat back under the basket and swatted away the shots before they went in. The next year they changed the goaltending rule so that you could only block shots on the way up, not on the way down. And to top it off, they actually stationed an official on a platform above the basket to make sure that he complied with the rule. Talk about changing the game.

In one year, in a game against Baylor

BOB KURLAND

- Led Oklahoma A&M to consecutive NCAA championships from 1945–46
- Back-to-back NCAA tourney MVP (1945–1946), the first player to accomplish this feat and one of only five players in history to have done it
- Won the 1946 national player of the year award, leading the nation with 643 points, 40 more than the runner-up
- The three-time All-American was the first athlete to play for the U.S. basketball team in consecutive Olympics. Both times, in 1948 and 1952, his team took home the gold medal.

in the first round of the NCAA tournament, Kurland shot 7-for-13. What's the big deal? In Harvard's first round game that year against Ohio State they shot 10-for-72. The average shooting percentage of teams in the NCAA tournament in 1946 was 25 percent. But Kurland was shooting over 50 percent from the floor.

Kurland didn't just dominate both ends of the floor. He was a winner. He played for the legendary Henry Iba at Oklahoma A&M, and his senior year they were 28-2. They were the first team ever to win back-to-back NCAA championships. Now, the NCAA wasn't the undisputed biggest tournament back then; the NIT was at least as big. But a championship is a championship. In 1944 there was a winner-take-all benefit game at Madison Square Garden between Oklahoma A&M and DePaul, which won the NIT with the great George Mikan at center. It was a huge game, billed as the Clash of the Titans. What happened? Mikan fouled out in the first half after scoring only 9 points (he had scored 53 against Rhode Is-

---

DOGBITE: BOB'S BLOCK PARTY

The other guy who got goaltending banned? Bruce Drake, who was the coach of Oklahoma when Kurland was playing at A&M. On February 18, 1944, Drake invited James St. Clair, the chairman of the NCAA rules committee, to a game between the two schools. He saw Kurland stand under the basket and not only swat shots on the way down, but actually punch them out of the basket from below, which was perfectly legal then. He also saw the Sooners stall, and the game ended with A&M winning by a final score of 14-11.

Drake lost the game but he made his point, and when the next season rolled around, there was a brand new rule: No goaltending. Drake, who once tried to get under Kurland's skin by having a football player named Merle Dinkins parade around the floor on stilts during a warm-up, probably thought he had stuck it to Kurland, but Foothills was actually happy that goaltending was banned. "I didn't like it," he said. "It didn't seem right. I'm glad it happened before we won back-to-back championships." Some have even suggested that Iba also quietly lobbied the NCAA to adopt the goaltending rule. "The change helped me because it caused me to develop the ability to defend man-to-man," said Kurland, "which was Iba's forte."

land earlier in the year), while Kurland scored 14, a really good effort in those days, and A&M beat DePaul 52-44. Mikan was Kurland's great rival, the Magic to his Bird. Over three years, DePaul did beat A&M three out of five, but the games were so close that A&M actually outscored the Demons by seven.

I think we'd remember Bob Kurland better, the same way we remember Mikan, if not for one thing. While Mikan joined the NBA, Kurland turned down an $11,000 offer from the Knicks. Instead, he played AAU ball for the team sponsored by the Phillips 66 oil company, won a second gold medal in the '52 Olympics, and ultimately had a very successful career as a big executive for the company. He probably made more money than Mikan during those years but he isn't remembered in the same way. But he was a great, game-changing player, completely deserving of a spot in the Mad Dog Hall of Fame.

6. Pete Performance

Maravich was the greatest scorer in college history.

How can you put a player on this list who never played in the NCAA tournament? You can when he's Pistol Pete Maravich. Maravich played on bad teams in a brutally tough conference, the SEC in the early 1970s. And LSU didn't even win the NIT the one year they played. But hand him the basketball and Maravich, with that mop of brown hair, was the unstoppable force. He led the nation in scoring three consecutive years, but that's only the tip of the iceberg. His sophomore year he averaged 43.8 points per game. The next year it was 44.2. His senior year, when he won the Naismith Award as the best player in college basketball? He averaged 44.5 points per game, which is the all-time single-season scoring record. Think about that. Today, a player scores 44 points once and he's got his own talk show. Maravich averaged 44 points for his whole career. This is a guy who scored 50 points or more 28 times. He scored 69 points in a game against Alabama. And this was all without a three-point line. So why didn't they foul him? They did. He made 30 free throws—in 31 attempts—in a game against Oregon State. Here's the really mind-blowing number. He scored a total of 3,667 points, which is still an NCAA record. That means that he scored more in three seasons than any contemporary player has been able to score in four.

He also pulled down six-and-a-half rebounds, too, which is a little like saying that John Updike is a good typist. Statistically, Pete Maravich is the most dominant player in the history of college basketball. And as we'll see in a minute, he put up those numbers while being double- and triple-teamed, scoring when everyone in the gym knew he was going to shoot.

He was not only a great shooter, he was a great, great ball-handler as well, in a flashy Harlem Globetrotters kind of way. When he was a kid, he would dribble the ball everywhere. He'd walk to school dribbling a basketball. He'd take the aisle seat in the movies so he could dribble while he watched *Fantastic Voyage*.

And he could pass—usually behind his back—not that he did so very often. He not only holds all kinds of records for scoring, he also holds just about as many records for shot attempts. He averaged 38 shots a game for his career. When he met Lefty Driesell at a camp, the coach took one look at his game and told Pete that Oscar Robertson didn't need these flashy moves. Here's what Maravich said, "I want to be a millionaire, and they don't pay you a million dollars for two-hand chest passes."

Maravich was the great individualist in the classic team game. His father, Press

PETE MARAVICH

- Holds many NCAA scoring records, including most points in a season (1,381) and career (3,667)
- Had a 44.5 scoring average in 1970, the all-time highest in a single season in NCAA history. Owns the top three spots on the all-time list (1968 [43.8], 1969 [44.2], and 1970 [44.5])
- First-Team All-American for three straight years (1968–1970)
- On February 21, 1970, Maravich and Dan Issel of Kentucky combined for 115 points, the most in history for two opposing players in the same game. Maravich outscored Issel 64-51, but LSU lost 121-105 in the last game of Maravich's collegiate basketball career.

Maravich, was the LSU coach, and he let him shoot whenever he wanted. Not only did he let him shoot, he made him shoot. His father was one of those Great Santini guys who didn't know when enough was too much. One story goes that when Pete was a kid, Press had him dribble the ball outside of a moving car, saying, "Let's see if you can really control that thing."

Pete Maravich is the only real "what if?" guy on this list. You wonder what might have happened if a guy with this talent had ended up somewhere else, playing for a John Wooden or a Dean Smith. You can make the argument that LSU might have been a better team if he had only scored 35 points a game and got the other guys involved. It's hard to refute that. During his three years there, LSU was only 49-35. And for whatever it's worth, the same trend followed Maravich into the pros. He scored a million points—remember the time he dropped 68 on the Knicks?—he thrilled the crowds, but his teams were never very good, and he kept bouncing from city to city. Pat Riley called him "the most overrated superstar."

I said that basketball is an individualist's game, and it is. Pete Maravich is the example of what happens when you take that too far. He was just electrifying to watch, but he tried to do it all himself. And after a while, teams caught on. They were happy enough to let Maravich score 42

DOGBITE: PETE'S BROKEN HEART

One of the tragic aspects of Pete Maravich's life is the fact that he died at a very young age. At the age of 40, while playing a pick-up game at a Pasadena church, Maravich collapsed on the court. His final words: "I need to do this more often. I'm feeling really good." He was rushed to the hospital where 50 minutes later he was pronounced dead of a heart attack. When they did an autopsy it turned out that Maravich had a serious hereditary heart condition—he was missing his left coronary artery. When they discovered that, the question changed from how could a guy die at age 40 to why didn't he die when he was 20?

"For a guy to go ten years in the NBA and have a congenital anomaly like that is, to say the least, very unusual," Dr. Paul Thompson of Brown University told the Associated Press at the time of Maravich's death. "How could a guy like that run up and down the court for twenty years?"

points, as long as his teammates were standing around watching and LSU ended up on the short end of the score. Maravich was more interested in being an entertainer than he was in being a basketball player.

All that said, Pete Maravich was probably the greatest player in the history of the SEC. It was his tough luck that Kentucky was a great team when he played there. And he absolutely put LSU basketball on the map—without Pistol Pete, there's no Shaquille O'Neal. He's such a legend there that they named the new gym after him, and they still have his old locker preserved in the basement of the old gym. I think that when you walk into that place, you remember some breathtaking moves and mind-boggling numbers. But it's also a little bit about what might have been.

5. The Big O-My

The legend of Oscar Robertson began in college.

You all know what a great pro Oscar Robertson was—and if you don't, I'll just direct you to our chapter on the greatest NBA players.

Here's what you need to know about Oscar Robertson as a college player. He led the nation in scoring in his sophomore year, with 35.1 points per game, and two more times after that. He was college basketball's all-time leading scorer when he left Cincinnati, scoring almost three thousand points and averaging 33.8 points per game. He was voted the national player of the year by the Sporting News and UPI three years in a row. What's the big deal about that? Three other guys playing college basketball at that time: Elgin Baylor, Jerry West, and Wilt Chamberlain.

Then add in the rest. While he was at Cincinnati they went 79-9, they went to two Final Fours and he averaged 32.5 points and 13 rebounds in 10 games in the NCAA tournament. He scored 56 points in a consolation game.

The only problem with Oscar Robertson was just that. In the Final

OSCAR ROBERTSON

- Established 14 NCAA scoring records. His career scoring average of 33.8 is third all-time.
- Seventh all-time in scoring with 2,973 points, despite a career of only three years. (Pete Maravich is the only player to score more points in a three-year collegiate career.)
- Third all-time in combined points and rebounds with 2,973 points and 1,338 boards
- The first player to win National Player of the Year honors three straight years
- After graduating from Crispus Attucks, Robertson was recruited by at least 75 colleges.
- As a sophomore Robertson scored 56 points in Madison Square Garden against Seton Hall on January 9, 1958. The Bearcats won 118–54.

Four, the games that meant something, Oscar didn't play great. That's the chink in his armor. And you have to remember that the year after he graduated is when Cincinnati won the first of its back-to-back championships, which doesn't help his cause.

If he had won a championship in both of those years, you would have to think about making Oscar a contender for one of the top spots on this list, but even so he's still one of the college game's all-time greats.

4. Remembering Dr. Memory

Post play and rebounds galore made Jerry Lucas a college legend.

A lot of sports fans remember Jerry Lucas as the guy who memorized the New Testament and wrote books about ways to help improve your memory. I think, deep down, one of the reasons why Lucas got into that business is the fact that people don't really remember Lucas at his best, from his college days of the late 1950s and early 1960s.

I think a lot of people think of Lucas as a pro, a kind of borderline Hall of Famer, the second banana to guys like Oscar Robertson in Cincinnati and Willis Reed and Dave DeBusschere on that second Knicks championship team. That's true.

But oh what a college player Jerry Lucas was. He was probably the best high school player in Ohio history, leading his team to 76 straight wins, with 150 colleges knocking at his door. He was one of the greatest rebounders in the history of college basketball, leading the nation in rebounds three years in a row, averaging 17.2 per game for his career. He was almost to rebounding what Pete Maravich was to scoring. And he could score, too. He didn't look like much of a shooter, but that one-handed push shot of his from around 20 feet was so deadly they called it the Lucas layup. He never shot less than 60 percent from the field for a season. Think about that.

More to the point, Ohio State had incredible success while he was there. He went 78-6 during his three years there. One of his teammates was the great John Havlicek. Another was Bobby Knight, who would go on to coach at Indiana. They went to the NCAA title game all three years that Lucas played. In his junior year, he was the MVP of the Final Four. He came back the next year, and although Ohio State didn't win, he repeated as MVP. There are only four other guys to win the award back-to-back, and they're all on my list: Bob Kurland, Alex Groza, Lew Alcindor, and Bill Walton. Trivia buffs will want to know that after college, Lucas signed with the Cleveland Pipers of the short-lived American Basketball League, a team owned by none other than George Steinbrenner.

Lucas was a sophomore on the 1960 Olympic team, probably the best Olympic team ever, a Dream Team before there ever was such a thing, and Billy Packer says he was the best player on that squad—and his teammates included Oscar Robertson, Jerry West, and Walt Bellamy. Jerry Lucas is the ultimate example of a guy who got the most out of his abilities. He was a great center in college, but at 6'8" he was too small to play center in the pros and not quite agile enough to be an elite forward. But there's a lot to like about Lucas. He was probably the best player in Big Ten history. He was the first guy to win a championship at every level— high school, college, the Olympics, and the NBA. And that's reason enough to remember him.

DOGBITE: TOTAL RECALL

Probably Lucas's most memorable off-court moment came in 1972. He was on the *Tonight Show* and he blew Johnny Carson away by memorizing every name in the crowd. He would memorize the Manhattan phone book. Who needed 411 when you could just ask Jerry Lucas. More to the point, Lucas claims to have memorized every play by every team in the league and the strengths and weaknesses of every player he faced. But Lucas will be the first to tell you that you only retain those things that you commit to memory. "A lot of people will come up to me, tap me on the shoulder and say, Who am I? What I always say to them is, 'If you don't know who you are, how do you expect me to?' "

---

3. The Original Mr. Bill

Russell was the catalyst behind USF's historic streak.

Quiz time. Who held the record for the longest winning streak in college basketball before UCLA ran off 88 in a row? Give up? It was the University of San Francisco, with Bill Russell at center. They won 60 in a row. Before Bill Russell got there, USF was nowhere on the basketball map—they held their practices in a high school gym. But when Russell arrived things changed in a hurry. With Russell around, USF won two championships—his junior and senior years—and he was the MVP of the NCAA tournament.

There's a lot to like about Russell. He's one of only five players to average 20 points and 20 rebounds for his career. He averaged 23 points in nine tournament games and, most importantly, he won them all. And he was the greatest defensive player in the history of college basketball. Russell was a selfless player who made the guys around him better. This USF team just smothered you on defense. At a time when good teams would average 80 a game, the Dons would hold their opponents to just over 50 a game. In his junior year, in the '55 championship game, Russell had a huge game, 23 points, 25 rebounds, and stopped LaSalle's great Tom Gola. In his senior year they won every regular season game by double-digit margins except for two. The closest they came to losing his senior year was to Marquette, beating them by 7 on a neutral court. And his senior year they beat Iowa in the championship game even though his teammate K.C. Jones didn't play because he was declared ineligible. Russell, for his part, was just Russell; he had 26 points and 27 rebounds, a Final Four record that still stands almost 50 years later. Iowa center Bill Logan scored 36 in the semis. With Russell guarding him, he scored only a dozen.

Russell was also an amazing athlete. In 1956 he was ranked as the world's seventh best high jumper by *Track and Field News*, with a top jump of 6 feet 9¼ inches, the 11th best mark in the world that year.

Russell also fulfills the changed-the-game test. After his junior year, the NCAA doubled the size of the three-second lane from 6 feet to 12 to give teams a fighting chance against his defense. And on the offensive end, they outlawed offensive goaltending—it was called the Russell Rule—to keep him from getting putbacks.

Why isn't he higher on the list? Simple. This is rarified air, and in his sophomore year, Russell was improving, but he wasn't yet a force and the team wasn't that good. They went 14-7 and didn't make the NCAA tournament.

DOGBITE: RUSSELL'S ONE SCHOLARSHIP

This is one of those paragraphs you should show your kids. You know how many scholarship offers Bill Russell got? One. And the only reason he got that one is because he graduated midyear and other players weren't available.

Russell, who didn't start playing basketball until he was 15, was the furthest thing from a superstar in high school at McClymonds High. He was cut from the junior varsity basketball team, and baseball star Frank Robinson recalls that the best part of his game was being tall. "He couldn't even put the ball in the basket when he dunked," Robbie said. Russell worked day and night on his game at the Boys Club, but he was still a second stringer on the varsity. But a teacher pleaded with USF to give him a scholarship because he was a really good student, and the rest is history.

---

2. Big Red

UCLA's Bill Walton was one win away from the top spot on this list.

Bill Walton's UCLA team won the first 60 games he played in college. Going back to high school, he won 129 consecutive games. Think about that. One hundred twenty-nine and oh. Walton was the central figure in one of the most impressive streaks in sports history.

That UCLA team in Walton's sophomore year went 30-0. They beat Florida State 81-76 in the finals. What did he say? "I'm really embarrassed. I can't believe how bad I played. I'd have to say it was one of my worst games. We should have beat these guys with ease. I guess I should be happy that we won, but in all honesty I'm not."

The next year, he didn't mess around. Another 30-0 season and in the championship game against Memphis State he was just about perfect. He went 21-of-22 and scored 44 points. All of the other stuff kind of flows from those two perfect seasons. He was the national player of the year three times running.

For those of you who know Walton just from his basketball commentary, which is a little bit off the wall at times, you've got to realize what an amazing player he was. Sure, at seven feet he could shoot and rebound and defend. But he was also probably the best passing big man in the history of the game. He'd get the ball in the post and he'd find the open man like a great point guard. Imagine a really great passing center of today like Vlade Divac or Arvydas Sabonis and then square it. That's how good Bill Walton was in college.

Walton was one of those guys who could make everyone around him better, a guy who could dominate a game without scoring a ton of points. And when he did keep the ball, he had that nice little bank shot, a bit like Tim Duncan today.

Part of the reason why his greatness has been a little bit forgotten is all the injury problems he ran into when he was a pro. He was amazing for Dr. Jack Ramsay's Portland Trail Blazers during their championship run, but he broke his foot and that was really the end of him as a dominant player.

Now, Walton was also a true character, a real child of the 1960s. He says he went to something like 600 Grateful Dead shows. Once he got arrested for protesting the Vietnam War and John Wooden had to go and bail him out. I can't imagine that the Wizard of Westwood was all that happy about that. And then there's this story that's been repeated so much it's taken on a life of its own. Depending on which version you've heard, Walton shows up at practice with a beard and/or long hair, which was against

Wooden's team rules. He says to Wooden, "Coach, you can't make me shave/get a haircut." And Wooden says to him, "I admire people who have strong beliefs and stick by them, I really do. We're going to miss you." Bill Walton went to the barber that day.

Why isn't Walton number one on this list? One game. Actually a basket or two. If UCLA won the NCAA championship his senior year, I think you'd have to put Walton on top of this list. But they lost that brutal game to NC State in the 1974 semis in double overtime by a score of 80-77. They had beaten the Wolfpack by 18 earlier in the year, and they were up by 11 points in the second half and 7 in that second overtime, but they didn't slow down the tempo because Wooden hated that. Walton wasn't bad—he scored 29 and had 18 rebounds—but still it was a bad loss, and Walton knew it, too. "It was the most disappointing, embarrassing event of my life," he said. "I think about it almost daily. If I had one week to bring back and live over, that would be it."

But for a couple of years there, Bill Walton was as close as you could come to the perfect college basketball player: an unselfish center who didn't miss, on a team that never lost.

1. Sweet Lew

Success, dominance, and style: UCLA star Alcindor had it all.

There are two things that you need to know about Lew Alcindor, who would, of course, later be known as Kareem Abdul-Jabbar. The first thing was that they changed the rules of the game for him. Just the way that they changed the goaltending rule for Bob Kurland, and the offensive goaltending rule for Bill Russell, the reason why dunks were outlawed in college basketball was Lew Alcindor. His first year, the dunk was legal. After that it wasn't. And it showed up in his stat line. He scored 29 points and shot 66 percent his sophomore year, and the next year it was down to 26.2 and 61.3 percent. (For whatever it's worth, John Wooden insists that the rule change was about keeping players from hanging on the rim and breaking backboards.) Alcindor's reaction? He further developed his signature sky hook, probably the most unstoppable single shot in the history of basketball.

Ferdinand Lewis Alcindor Jr.—didn't know that, did you?—is essentially the perfect college basketball player. Bob Cousy said that Alcindor "pretty much combines what Bill Russell and Wilt Chamberlain have individually specialized in." Bill Walton called him the best player he ever played against and said,

KAREEM ABDUL-JABBAR

- Led UCLA to three consecutive national championships (1967–1969)
- The first three-time NCAA tournament Most Outstanding Player
- Scored 2,325 points from 1967–69, making him the leading scorer in UCLA history
- One of only eight players to have been named national college player of the year and to later win the NBA regular season MVP award (the others: Russell, Robertson, Walton, Bird, Jordan, Robinson, O'Neal)
- The last man to have over 200 career rebounds in the NCAA tournament, second to rival Elvin Hayes (222)

"His left leg belongs in the Smithsonian." One thing separates him from everyone else on this list. Lew Alcindor never lost a game in the NCAA tournament. Not one. Three years, three titles. Three times the tournament MVP. Perfect.

And not only did Alcindor win games, he took names. In January 1968, UCLA lost that game to Elvin Hayes and Houston. Elvin Hayes outplayed him, dropped 39 points and grabbed 15 rebounds while Lew only got 15 and 12. Huge game, nationally televised from the Astrodome, the biggest crowd ever to see a college basketball game. Huge upset. Ended UCLA's 47-game winning streak. Alcindor had suffered an eye injury a week earlier and he wasn't his usual self. And this was only the second game he'd ever lost. The only other one was when DeMatha beat his high school team, Power Memorial, in 1965. After the game, Wooden said that he wouldn't trade Alcindor for two of Elvin Hayes. In the rematch in the Final Four you could see why. UCLA just demolished Houston. Crushed them. They led by as much as 44 points before Wooden called off the hounds, and they finally won 101-69.

DOGBITE: VARSITY BLUES

How's this for a freshman debut? The UCLA varsity, the defending national champions who had lost two games over the past two seasons, played the freshmen in the first game at the Pauley Pavilion in front of 12,051 Bruins fans.

And they lose. Big. 75-60. In his very first game, freshman Lew Alcindor scores 31 points, grabs 21 rebounds, and blocks 7 shots. "I just felt kind of odd that we could beat a varsity Pac-8 team like that," Alcindor later recalled. "All I remember is they couldn't press us and we were faster than they were. That was an easy game for us."

The problem of course is that Alcindor and his freshmen teammates weren't eligible to compete in varsity games. So they had to settle for compiling a 21-0 record by destroying junior colleges and other freshmen teams by an average of almost 57 points. The intrasquad game in Pauley Pavilion had a slightly different result the next year. The varsity team, led by Alcindor, managed to beat the freshmen. The score was 127-56.

So Alcindor is the complete package. Tremendous personal success. Played for a legendary coach at the greatest basketball school of all. Had an amazing record in big games, a perfect three for three in championships, three for three in MVPs. And a huge, almost unprecedented, impact on the game.

Chapter 8

The Top-Ten Sports Moments of All Time

What's the most unforgettable football moment?
And which famous homer didn't make the cut?

Let's talk for a moment about what makes a great sports moment great. The first thing, I think, is that it has to be a positive moment. There are plenty of important sports moments that have a negative aspect to them. Buckner in the 1986 World Series. The final moments of that U.S.-Soviet basketball game. Even the Ali-Liston phantom punch. You remember them, of course, but not for the right reasons.

So when we're talking about great sports moments, we're going to put those aside. Quite frankly, there's enough ugliness and negativity in this world. You want a moment that's about winning, not about losing. Here's my bottom-line criterion: You want a moment where you walk away with goose bumps, not a moment that causes you to cringe. The other stipulation I'm going to make is that it's a moment. There are plenty of great games that have a great see-saw tension to them, but they don't have that one great pivotal moment, that one indelible play. They're not going to make this list. The other part of this is that it's got to be a moment that happens within the context of a game. It's a play, not a post-game celebration. That's why the Miracle on Ice isn't here. The defining moment of that game was Al Michaels's call after it was over, saying, "Do you believe in miracles?"

And finally, the moment should contribute to a championship, or at least some kind of larger victory. What good is winning Game 6 in a dramatic fashion if you lose Game 7? So with all that said, here are the ten greatest sports moments of all time.

10. Braves New World

'll say it flat out. In my 37, 38 years of watching baseball, this is the greatest ninth inning rally I've ever seen. Braves-Pirates, 1992, Game 7. It was a tremendous pressure situation, and a tremendous clutch performance by an unlikely hero.

Let's set it up a little bit. We all know about the Braves in the 1990s, but it's easy to forget what a good team Jim Leyland's Pirates were in the early 1990s. They made it to the NLCS three consecutive years, losing to the eventual champion Reds in 1990, losing to the Braves in Game 7 in Pittsburgh in 1991, and then this rematch against the Braves that went the full distance. They were down 3 games to 1 so they felt they were on the verge. Adding to the drama is the fact that the Pirates knew that the clock was ticking. Their two best players, Doug Drabek and Barry Bonds, were both free agents, and everyone knew that the club didn't have enough money to sign them. So this was a potentially great team's last chance, a kind of last hurrah.

And as far as the Braves were concerned, they seemed like they were pretty much just coming into their own. They had surprised the baseball world a year before, went from worst to first and then to the seventh game of the World Series, and they had a feeling that this was going to be their year. The series of postseason disappointments that had plagued them during the 1990s hadn't yet begun.

And that day Doug Drabek of the Pirates pitched a tremendous, tremendous game. He pitched with guts and determination. You couldn't ask for more, and he was never quite the same after that. He got his team into the ninth with a 2-0 lead.

But then the Pirates began to unravel. Terry Pendleton leads off the ninth with a double that's fair by two feet. Jose Lind, who was usually surehanded, misplayed a hard-hit but routine ground ball. Drabek's completely out of gas, not a drop left in the tank, and he walks Sid Bream on four pitches. Bases loaded, no out. The Pirates bullpen has been shaky all year, but Leyland has no choice but to bring in Stan Belinda. Ron Gant hits a bomb to left, Barry Bonds makes the catch, and Pendleton scores on the sac. It's 2-1. Belinda walks Damon Berryhill, and Brian Hunter pops out. It's two outs and the bases loaded. Bobby Cox sends Francisco Cabrera to the plate to pinch hit for Jeff Reardon. Who is Francisco Cabrera?

The last guy on the Braves bench. He spent most of the year in the minors. He was the last guy added to the postseason roster, he had batted ten times for the Braves that year. On the 2-0 count Bobby Cox gave Cabrera the hit sign, a gutsy move since Belinda, thanks in part to home-plate umpire Randy Marsh, couldn't get the ball over the plate. On a 2-1 count he lines a ball to left. David Justice scores the tying run from third. Barry Bonds, who's the best left fielder in baseball at this point, comes up throwing. The winning run is Sid Bream, who is the slowest runner in baseball, and he's chugging around third. The throw's a little up the line, Bream makes the best hook slide since Jackie Robinson, and the Braves win the pennant! The Braves win the pennant! This is, after all, the first time since Bobby Thomson that a team scored three in the ninth to win a playoff series.

There was a little side drama to this, too. On that hot night, umpire John Mc-Sherry had to take himself out of the game in the third inning because of dizzy spells. I bring that up because his re-

1992 NLCS GAME 7: BRAVES-PIRATES

- With their Game 7 win, the Braves became the first team since the 1977–78 Los Angeles Dodgers to repeat as N.L. pennant winners.

- For the Pirates, it was their third consecutive NLCS championship loss, one of only three teams to lose three straight league championships.

- Atlanta right-hander John Smoltz, who won Games 1 and 4 in the series and pitched six innings of Game 7, was named MVP.

- Doug Drabek was charged with the defeat in Game 7. The Pirate right-hander became the first pitcher in league championship series history to lose three games.

What a difference a foul ball can make. Listen to Barry Bonds's recollection of that amazing inning. "If you recall, Francisco Cabrera hit a bullet right off the wall, but foul. We were playing shallow at the time to take away (the winning run), but when he hit that bullet, we took four or five steps back to prevent the ball from going over our heads." Which might have been the difference between a close play and a punch out. As for Cabrera, he had a different thought. When Bobby Cox asked Cabrera to pinch-hit, he wondered who would play second base in the 10th inning. Cabrera knew that with second baseman Rafael Belliard out of the game, it would likely be him, although the catcher/first baseman had never played that position in the big leagues. "I appreciate Sid Bream for coming in from second," Cabrera said. "It usually took a triple to score him from second."

placement, Marsh, squeezed the heck out of the Pirates in that ninth inning. If McSherry is behind the plate, some of those balls might become strikes and the game could turn out differently.

Amazing moment for the Braves. A terrible franchise-altering defeat for the Pirates—you'll remember that Drabek allowed only one earned run. And yes, you can quibble with the fact that the Braves didn't go on to win the World Series. They got beat by a very good Toronto Blue Jays team, but the fact that they lost does tarnish this moment just a bit and that's why it's only ranked 10th. Still, this is a very underrated moment. And I'm not the only one who saw its significance. Jimmy Carter climbed out onto the field and into the middle of the celebration. He found Cabrera and said, "Hello, Francisco. Wanted to tell ya that's one helluva way to win the pennant for us, son. They'll probably be talking about you 'round here after they've forgotten me." Don't know about that, but it was a classic, classic baseball moment.

CLOSE, BUT . . .

Now, I know that a lot of people would put Carlton Fisk's home run in Game 6 of the 1975 World Series right at the very top of any list of great sports moments. I don't. Here's why. The Red Sox lost the series. They won Game 6. They lost Game 7. I'm not going to go into the question of whether Bernie Carbo's homer was more dramatic. Bottom line: Fisk's homer didn't change the outcome of that series at all, except that they had to play one more game. Now, I know that the Braves didn't go on to win the World Series in 1992. But they did win the series against the Pirates. And I know that the 1951 Giants ended up getting beat by the Yankees. Fair point. But at least they did win the pennant and move on. The Red Sox just postponed defeat by another day.

9. The Man of Steal

Havlicek's swipe—and Most's call—made this the
NBA's most memorable moment.

"Johnny Havlicek stole the ball!" Johnny Most's call is pretty much the basketball equivalent of "The Giants win the pennant," the most famous call in the history of the sport.

There are a couple of things that you really like about this moment, Game 7 of the 1965 Eastern Conference finals, Celtics vs. the 76ers. First, it involves the two greatest teams of the day, Philly and Boston. It's Wilt and Russell. And this is kind of the rekindling of that great rivalry, because Wilt's back in Philly after a few years on the West Coast with the Warriors. So you get the sense that if this game goes a different way, basketball history might have been a little bit different.

Here's the situation. Deciding game. Boston Garden. Five or six seconds left on the clock, and the Celtics had the ball up by a point and a chance to just run the clock out. But Russell threw the ball inbounds and it hit the guide wire that supported the basket, and the Celtics lost possession. A huge turnover. Time out. Down one. Hal Greer inbounds the ball. K.C. Jones is guarding the inbounds pass, jumping like a madman. Greer looks for Chet Walker, seemingly open at the top of the key. But Havlicek was a crafty defender and he played just a little off the passing lane to make Greer think that Walker was open. Great decoy. Then he just stepped in front of the pass and tipped it to Jones, who dribbled out those last couple of seconds, and the Celtics had survived. There was absolute pandemonium on the court, fans coming down from the stands. Someone ripped Havlicek's jersey right off his back. He'll tell you that years later a woman came up to him at a party and showed him this little brooch holding a little piece of white material. It was a piece of his jersey from that game.

The most important thing about this moment is the way it epitomizes this incredible Celtic dynasty. They had a bad fourth quarter. They frittered away a 7-point lead late in the game. Russell committed that bad turnover. This would have been a huge loss in Celtic lore. And just when it seemed that they might be mortal after all, they came up with this huge play, one of those right-place-at-the-right-time plays. If you had to sum up the Celtic dynasty in a 30-second clip, this would be the play you'd show. They always found a way to win.

And the other side of the equation is Wilt Chamberlain. Statistically, he's the greatest player in the history of the game, bar none. But he's got this huge Achilles heel with his free throw shooting, and Dolph Schayes, the Philadelphia coach, doesn't dare call a play for him. He knows that if Chamberlain gets the ball that Russell's going to play him as tight as he can, and the worst that will happen is that he sends a guy who misses half his free throws to the line.

And you've got to love Most's call. It's one of those times where the guy in the booth stops being a broadcaster and starts being a fan, and I love that. Most is the ultimate homer, and this is his greatest moment. He's yelling and screaming just as loud as a guy in the cheap seats. "Havlicek steals it! Over to Sam Jones. Havlicek stole the ball! It's all over! Johnny Havlicek . . . stole . . . the . . . ball!"

DOGBITE: HIGH-WIRE ACT

"Will somebody please take these goat horns off my head? They are growing longer by the minute." That's what Bill Russell said in the huddle before Havlicek's famous steal. You remember that one of his rare mistakes—throwing the inbounds pass off the guide wire—set this one up. The wires had been lowered prior to the game as additional support for the baskets and, ironically, in a pregame meeting, Philadelphia coach Dolph Schayes had suggested that any ball off the guide wire should *not* count as a turnover. Auerbach shot that idea down, but it didn't stop him from complaining later. Havlicek summed it up: "Thank God for Bill Russell. What was going to be the most disappointing moment—the low point of his career, really—is what made me famous."

CLOSE, BUT . . .

You would think that NBA basketball would be the perfect game for dramatic moments. Games are often very close and don't get decided until the very last second. But strangely enough there aren't too many of those moments that have enough drama and enough import to crack our list. I know that a lot of people really like Jordan's parting shot against the Jazz. People want to put that one in a picture frame because it's Jordan's last moment. I won't. First, it's a Game 6 not a Game 7. It was the winning shot, but it wasn't the last play. And no one really thought that the Bulls were in any danger of losing that series. They always beat Utah, beat them a million times. The Bulls weren't staving off elimination. Jordan was just sealing the deal.

The Magic baby hook against the Celtics in 1987? It came in Game 4 of the series, and the Lakers were up 2-1. Willis against the Lakers? Not really a game moment. It was Walt Frazier who was the star of the game for the Knicks. Frank Selvy's shot against the Celtics? That was a miss. Gar Heard's shot against the Celtics? The Suns lost that game. So it's harder to find these great NBA moments than you think.

8. The Kicker, Iced

Vinatieri's cold weather kick jump-started the Patriot dynasty.

There are few things that have as much built-in excitement as a last second field goal in the NFL. There's incredible anticipation. Make it, and you're a hero—like Jim O'Brien of the Colts. Miss it, and you're a goat. We're talking about you, Scott Norwood. And it makes it that much more dramatic that the field goal kicker spends most of the game just watching, waiting for his close-up.

And when it comes to clutch field goal kicking, Adam Vinatieri of the Patriots is right at the top of anyone's list. He made the field goal to beat the Rams in the Super Bowl, when the Patriots were huge underdogs. He made another one to beat the Panthers, two years later. Both of those kicks decided a Super Bowl . . . it's up, it's good, it's over.

But I'm not going to choose either of those kicks. The most important one, from my point of view, is the kick in that wacky winter storm in a divisional play-off game against the Raiders. Why do I like that one? Because without that play, there's probably no Patriot dynasty. With free agency today, three of four is a dynasty. That win put Bill Belichick on the road of great NFL coaches and started Tom Brady on the path to the Hall of Fame. If Vinatieri misses that kick, maybe the history of the NFL is different. Huge, huge play, and not just in that game.

And the other thing to remember is, this kick wasn't a game-winner. It was a field goal to stave off elimination. Adam

VINATIERI VS. OAKLAND

- Vinatieri kicked a total of three field goals that night, including a clutch 45-yard kick to tie the game with 27 seconds left and send it into overtime and a 23-yard boot to win the game.
- New England has never lost in four snow games at Foxboro Stadium, while Oakland has lost five straight road playoff games dating to 1981.

misses, New England's season is done. In those two Super Bowl field goals, the game was tied, so the game would have still gone on even if Vinatieri had missed.

The conditions in Foxboro that night were about as bad as they can be. Cold. Snowy. Blowing. An absolute blizzard. On a chewed up grass field. And it wasn't a chip shot field goal. It was a 45-yarder, not an easy field goal under the best of circumstances. This is the best pressure kick I've ever seen under the toughest possible conditions. Now, you have some other issues with the game. By all rights the Raiders should have won. On that drive, Tom Brady fumbled and it wasn't called. The referee invoked that silly "tuck rule," but the Raiders knew it was a fumble, Brady knew it was a fumble, and everyone in America watching the game knew it was a fumble. And if that's a turnover, Vinatieri doesn't get his chance to be a hero.

But a rule's a rule, the refs didn't give the ball to the Raiders, and the Patriots went on to win the game in overtime. They beat the Steelers in Pittsburgh the next weekend. And then they went into New Orleans, 14-point underdogs against the Rams. Remember that they didn't introduce anybody that day in warm-ups because they wanted to be that no-name team? And they came up huge. They had a lot of heart. And they went out there and beat the mighty Rams . . . on an Adam Vinatieri field goal.

The Patriots over the last three or four years have had God looking over them. Or karma. Or just good fortune. Call it what you want, but the ball has bounced right for the Patriots in every big game. They put themselves in the right positions, but the balls bounced right. The ball began to bounce right in that tough game against the Raiders. And 20 years from now, when you ask me about the Patriots, the first thing I'm going to think about is Adam Vinatieri's amazing do-or-die kick.

7. Horse Sensation

Alydar and Affirmed fought from wire to wire in all three legs of the Triple Crown.

Is there anything better in sports than a great rivalry? Two great competitors who are evenly matched and bring out the best in each other. The Lakers and the Celtics. Ali and Frazier. The Yankees and the Red Sox. But one of the all-time classic rivalries is between two horses, Alydar and Affirmed.

I wasn't a huge horse racing fan, but these races captured my imagination. In 1978 these horses ran one-two in each of the Triple Crown races. You wouldn't think that two animals could bring out the best in each other like this, but they could.

As two-year-olds they raced twice and split the two races. In the Kentucky Derby Alydar was a narrow favorite, and in the beginning of the race found himself 17 lengths off the pace. He mounted a furious charge that fell short by a little more than a length. In the Preakness it was the same scenario. Jorge Velasquez, Alydar's jockey, kept him closer to the pace, but Alydar gained on the backstretch and Affirmed held him off to win by a length.

And then away we go to the Belmont. After the way that Alydar came on so strong in the last couple of furlongs of the Preakness and the Derby, everyone figured that he'd have Affirmed's number at a mile and a half. In this race, it was a small field and these two horses facing off, *mano a mano,* so to speak. After just a half mile, Affirmed and Alydar were 1-2 and by the halfway mark they were running neck and neck, stride for stride. Alydar took a slight lead in the backstretch, and it seemed that what the handicappers predicted was coming true, that Alydar's late speed would be the difference in the race. But Affirmed was one of those horses who just didn't have any quit in him. He won six photo finishes in his career and five of them were against Alydar. Sensing where the line was, Affirmed dug deep, found something, and somehow won the Belmont, and the Triple Crown, by a neck. That's an amazing performance, and a classic sports moment.

In the years since, we've come to appreciate what a special thing this was. In the mid-1970s we had a few Triple Crown–winning horses clumped together—Secretariat in 1973, Seattle Slew in 1977, and Affirmed in 1978. But in the interim, we've come to realize how rare a feat a Triple Crown really is, and when it's as close as this one, it's something for the ages. You also had the jockeys. Jorge Velasquez is an all-timer. And Affirmed's rider, Steve Cauthen, was a young star, only 18, and he landed on the cover of *Time* magazine. Everyone figured he was going to be the next Bill Shoemaker, the next Eddie Arcaro, but as he got older he had trouble making weight and went to England where he had a great career. All of that added to the juice of these races.

ALYDAR-AFFIRMED

- In the 1978 Kentucky Derby, Alydar was the 6-5 favorite while Affirmed was the 9-5 second choice in the field of 11.
- Affirmed's margin of victory over Alydar narrowed during his chase for the Triple Crown: He would take the Kentucky Derby in 1½ lengths, the Preakness by a neck, and the Belmont by a head.
- Affirmed is the last horse to win the Triple Crown. It was the second year in a row that a horse had earned the Triple Crown, after Seattle Slew had won it in 1977.
- In Affirmed's first 18 races, Alydar was the only horse to beat him. Only once in their ten career meetings did either horse finish worse than second.

And Alydar was a great horse. In most other years he would have won a couple of legs of the Triple Crown, maybe even the whole thing. These horses were so evenly matched you would have thought that if they raced 51 times, it would have been 26-25. I rooted for Alydar to win that last one. It's funny though, Affirmed seemed to have something over Alydar. Even in their last race, at Saratoga, Affirmed again crossed the line first, although he was disqualified for blocking Alydar on the backstretch. It was while watching these races that I began to understand why people get into horse racing. It's pretty hard to find a better six minutes in sports than these three races, and you couldn't have scripted a better ending.

DOGBITE: SIRE GROUND

Affirmed might have won the duel on the race track, but there's no disputing that Alydar was the real stud off the track. Alydar sired two Derby winners—Alysheba and Strike the Gold. He also sired Easy Goer, Criminal Type, and Althea. Upon his mysterious death in 1990—he was put down after a leg injury that some claim was intentional—Alydar led the sires list, having produced 77 stakes winners out of 707 foals. He was bred to as many as 100 mares a year for fees that totaled $12 million annually.

Affirmed's best offspring was Flawlessly, who won 16 of 28 starts and was a two-time winner of the Eclipse award as best female turf runner. Flawlessly's maternal grandfather on her mother's side was Nijinsky II, England's last Triple Crown winner.

---

6. Iron Miked

Tyson's sudden fall epitomizes the kind of upset that makes sports riveting.

I'll be the first to admit that this is a moment that has lost a little bit of its luster over the years. Mike Tyson has done a lot of stupid, crazy things in and out of the ring, really wasting his talent. Over the course of his career, Mike Tyson has proved that he is not an all-time great boxer. He lost to Kevin McBride. He bit off a piece of Evander Holyfield's ear. He went to jail. But let's forget that for a moment and rewind to February 1990.

The fight took place in Tokyo, so very few writers traveled to cover it, and not very many people even saw it on HBO. I was at TJ Tuckers, East Side, 59th Street and First Avenue, with my pal Ernie Cashonis. I watched this fight start to finish. Watching Tyson get knocked on the ground and looking for his mouthpiece, trying to put it back in his mouth was one of the most amazing things I've ever seen in sports. I was just shocked. We talked about it for two weeks on the air.

Before that Douglas fight, Tyson looked like a modern day Sonny Liston. He was one scary hombre. Mike Tyson was a dominating presence in the sport from 1985 until 1990. He scared people so much that he often won fights before they even started. James "Bonecrusher" Smith danced away from him for 15 rounds. Michael Spinks wasn't that

> ### MIKE TYSON-BUSTER DOUGLAS
>
> - Tyson was a 42-1 favorite in the heavyweight title fight in Tokyo on February 11, 1990.
> - Coming into the fight, the undefeated Tyson had 33 KOs in his 37 consecutive wins.
> - Douglas went on to fight Evander Holyfield in October, only to get knocked out in the third round of what was the first pay-per-view telecast in boxing history.
> - Douglas's mother had died of cancer 46 days before the fight. After winning the title, he tearfully dedicated the victory to her.

lucky, and he got knocked out in 91 seconds. We used to make bets. Would you go in the ring for $100,000 for one round with Mike Tyson? Would you do that? We all said no way. Give me a million. After this fight, you would have done it for $100,000, maybe less. This fight wiped the aura of Mike Tyson away.

This was one of the great shocks of all time. Everyone figured that Buster Douglas was just a bum. He was the ultimate flash in the pan. It wasn't like Ali knocking out Liston, coming in as a huge underdog and then showing his greatness, letting us know it wasn't a fluke but a coming-out party. But Douglas never did anything at all after that. The next time you saw him in the ring he weighed 500 pounds.

With all of that, why did this moment make my list? I'll tell you why. Nights like that are the reason you watch sports. You figure that Tyson's going to murder him. But there's always that little nagging voice in the back of your head that says, "Maybe not." This was like *Rocky*, except that this time Rocky actually won.

In a way this moment was a turning point. In my eyes it was really the beginning of the end for boxing, especially in the heavyweight division. There's a sense of progression, passing that heavyweight belt from one

DOGBITE: DOWN FOR THE COUNT

Call it the Long Count, Part II. In the eighth round, Tyson landed a devastating right uppercut that sent Douglas to the canvas with six seconds left. Going by the time-keeper's count, which began as soon as Douglas's backside touched the surface of the ring, the eventual champ was down for 12 seconds after Tyson knocked him down. But a hesitant referee, Octavio Meyran, began his count two beats behind. Douglas rose as Meyran signaled nine.

Following the fight, promoter Don King, worried about how Tyson's loss would affect his plans for future fights, filed a protest. "The first knockout obliterates the second knockout," he argued. King even brought Meyran out to speak at a press conference after the fight. The referee said, "I don't know why I start my count and make my mistake. Yes, he was down longer than ten seconds." But look at the videotape, and you'll also see that in the 10th round, Tyson's count lasted for 14 seconds. The protest was disallowed.

great champion to the next, from John O'Sullivan and Gentleman Jim Corbett, to Jack Johnson, to Jack Dempsey, to Jess Willard, to Joe Louis, to Rocky Marciano, to Sonny Liston, to Muhammad Ali, to Joe Frazier, to George Foreman, to Larry Holmes, and then to Mike Tyson. You wondered for a moment if Buster Douglas might fit into that line somewhere, but when you saw him come into the ring in his next fight so big he needed his own area code, you knew that wasn't going to happen. Looking back on it now, it seems like Tyson might be the end of the line. That amazing night was the beginning of the end.

5. The Ice Bowl Cometh

The decisive play of the Packers-Cowboys playoff game cemented Vince Lombardi's legacy.

One of the things that people respond to when they're talking about great sports moments is the plays-of-the-week factor. Is this a moment that would make the highlights on ESPN if it happened in the middle of a game between two last-place teams? Is it the kind of thing that makes you say "Wow!" pick up the phone and call your buddy and say, "Did you see that?"

I will be the first to tell you that this play had none of that. If Bart Starr's quarterback sneak occurred in the third quarter, it wouldn't crack the list. But this was the do-or-die moment in the greatest game ever played, the 1967 Ice Bowl, the NFL championship game between the Cowboys and the Packers.

And one of the things that made this game one of the all-time greats is the awful, brutal weather in Green Bay. Those frozen conditions. Those temperatures. Thirteen below zero. Wind chill factor was what, 50 below? The NFL thought about canceling that game at noon, and the NFL never cancels anything.

Ray Scott, the voice of the Packers, told me that it was the greatest mind-over-matter drive in the history of football. This was an old team

- The victory gave the Packers a record third straight title and their fifth in seven years.
- Green Bay had jumped to a 14-0 lead before Dallas scored 17 unanswered points.
- Dallas had taken the lead when running back Dan Reeves connected with Lance Rentzel on a halfback option pass for a 50-yard TD on the first play of the fourth quarter.
- Dallas had sacked Starr eight times.

and they knew it was their last chance, their gunfight at the OK Corral.

That play was absolutely do or die. The Packers are down 17-14. If the Cowboys's great defense can stop the Packers on one play, they win the NFL title and probably the Super Bowl. It changes the way we think about the NFL during its formative years of the 1960s.

After the Cowboys scored to take the three point lead, the Packers got the ball and methodically drove down the field. On second down and short, Bart Starr handed the ball off to Donny Anderson. Stopped. On third down at the one-foot line, Green Bay called their last time out. Sixteen seconds left. Last play of the game.

This play could have ended Vince Lombardi's career as coach of the Packers. Think about that for a second. If the Cowboys stopped the Packers on that play, it would have tarnished Vince Lombardi's legacy. He only lost one playoff game in his life, and that was his first one. If he loses that game, that means his career is bookended by two losses, and he ends his run with the Packers with a bad loss. And the responsibility would have fallen squarely on Lombardi's shoulders. "Vince, why didn't you kick the field goal?" That's what every reporter would have asked him after the game. (And remember, the guy on the other sideline was Tom Landry, and there was never any love lost between them, back to when they were both assistants with the Giants.)

And with all that hanging on his decision, Lombardi made this tremendously gutsy call. He could have kicked the field goal and played for the tie and the chance at overtime. But he went all in, win or lose on one play. "We didn't want to tie," Lombardi said. "We had compassion for those spectators. We wanted to send them home right then."

The key to that play was one of the little things that make the difference in a classic game: Jerry Kramer's great block on Jethro Pugh. In these icy conditions Starr just didn't have the traction to push guys out of there—it was all he could do to stay on his feet. But Kramer opened a hole and Starr stumbled across the goal line, and the Packers were the NFL champions. (Remember, this was before the NFL-AFL merger.)

Even when he was still thawing out, when he was talking about the game with reporters in the locker room, Lombardi understood what this team had accomplished, the way this game had capped his legacy.

"This is what the Packers are all about," he said. "What we did in the last two minutes—they don't do it for individual glory, they do it because they respect each other and have a feeling for the other fellow. It was a question of the team knowing what they had to do with time running out," Lombardi said. "They arrived." Arrived right at the Mad Dog Hall of Fame.

DOGBITE: SNEAKY STARR

The final play of the game for the Packers was supposed to be "31 Wedge" in which running back Chuck Mercein gets the hand-off from Bart Starr. And that's what everyone ran . . . except Starr. Mercein explained that in the huddle, Starr called "31 Wedge," which Vince Lombardi had designed during the week "after guard Jerry Kramer had noticed a weakness in the Cowboys's short-yardage defense and suggested the play."

Mercein didn't know about the sneak until after the ball was snapped. "After a couple of steps I realized I wasn't going to get the ball. But I couldn't really pull up because it was so icy," Mercein said. After Starr ran it himself, lunging into the end zone behind the big blocks of Kramer and Kenny Bowman, Mercein raised his hands—but not to signal a touchdown, as most people have assumed. "What I'm actually doing is I'm showing the officials that I'm not assisting or aiding Bart into the end zone," Mercein said.

But it wasn't an audible. Starr says that Lombardi knew about it. "I told Coach Lombardi the backs can't get any footing, but I can shuffle my feet and lunge in. Typical of the kind of leader he was, he said, 'Let's run it and get the hell out of here.' I was running back to the huddle, chuckling." So why did Starr keep his teammates in the dark? "There was no need to tell anybody else," he said, "because nobody's blocking assignment changed."

4. The Put-Back

Lorenzo Charles's unlikely field goal put the madness in March Madness.

There are two things that make college basketball great when March Madness comes around. The chance of a game—and a team's season—hinging on one shot, one possession. It happens in the NBA some—in a Game 7, but even then it's not sudden death but lingering death. To get to the Game 7, one team had to be down 3-2 and facing elimination. In the tournament, it's four quarters, go on or go home. And sometimes that game hinges on one shot. It's fun if you're a sports fan. You get sweaty palms, sitting on the edge of your seat. They play for four months, and one game, one shot, and one way or another, one team's season is over.

The other thing that goes hand in hand with this is the possibility of a huge upset, a Cinderella team that comes out of nowhere and captures your imagination. Over the course of a seven-game NBA series, the better team is going to win 90 percent of the time. But in a college game, a team's shooters get hot at the right time, and all of a sudden, David is ahead of Goliath by 6 points with 4 minutes to go. Remember North Carolina beating Wilt Chamberlain in 1957? Harold Jensen shooting like he was unconscious and Villanova toppling Georgetown?

Well, there's one classic college hoops moment that has both of those aspects going for it. That's North Carolina State's huge upset of Houston in the 1983 finals. You remember how good Houston was? They had two future NBA Hall of Famers on that team—Hakeem Olajuwon and

LORENZO CHARLES'S PUTBACK

- NC State was the first team with ten losses ever to win the NCAA championship.
- The 54-52 game was the lowest-scoring final since 1949.
- A major reason Houston lost was their performance on the foul line—they hit only 10 of 19.
- In all but two of the Wolf Pack's last nine victories that season, they had trailed in the last minute.

Clyde Drexler. Phi Slamma Jamma. Talentwise, this was one of the all-time great teams. A prohibitive favorite.

NC State had just barely squeaked into the tournament by the skin of its teeth. They had to beat Virginia in the ACC tournament or they wouldn't have even gotten a bid. NC State, with Cozell McQueen and Dereck Whittenburg was not a great team. None of these guys had any kind of pro career. But they managed to survive the early rounds of the tournament and cemented their legacy in the Final Game.

Just as you would have expected, Houston jumped out to a lead. But instead of continuing to play, they got a little nervous. Tried to run out the clock, play the four corners offense, and that wasn't their style. Guy Lewis took the air out of the ball. And that played right into Jim Valvano's hands. He said to his guys, "Keep it close until the last four minutes and I'll think of something."

Here's what he thought of: Dereck Whittenburg taking a terrible shot. Just throwing up a Hail Mary from 40 feet. Not even close. Everybody could see that. But Lorenzo Charles was sitting underneath the basket.

DOGBITE: HAIL TO MCQUEEN

The Lorenzo Charles putback was probably the *second* most amazing finish of NC State's tournament run. During NC State's first-round double-overtime win over Pepperdine, the Wolfpack was down by 6 points with 24 seconds left. "We had them beat, hanging-on-the-rope dead," said Pepperdine coach Jim Harrick. They clawed back and Dereck Whittenburg was at the line with a chance to send it into overtime. They dodged a bullet earlier when Dane Suttle, an 89 percent free-throw shooter, missed a one-and-one opportunity that would have sealed the game. Jim Valvano looked at the way his players were lined up and insisted that Lorenzo Charles and Cozell McQueen switch places so that the left-handed McQueen would have a better angle on the ball in case of a miss. Whittenburg missed, the ball bounced right back to McQueen, who tipped it in to send the game to over-time. "The way it worked out, only a goofy six-eleven left-hander could have made that shot," Charles said. "People talk about the shot I made in the championship game? Well, if Cozell doesn't make that, we lose to Pepperdine. And we're not even talking about this. That was the difference-maker."

And with all those big bodies that Houston had, nobody boxed him out. Nobody. He catches the ball, and just lays it in. Game over.

Bottom line, this was one of the huge upsets in the history of college basketball. It happened on the biggest stage. And it happened in the most dramatic way possible. What NC State did in that March of '83 was so good for college basketball it is mind-boggling. It gave you hope that if you had a crazy little team, maybe your coach could be Jim Valvano and your team could win it all. This game is what the NCAA tournament is all about. Go to any small school in March after they win their small conference tournament to squeak into the NCAAs as a 16th seed. The coach is going to put together a little motivational film. Why not us? They're going to end it with this game, this basket. Everybody remembers this basket.

Almost as much as the shot itself, you remember Valvano running around the court looking for someone to hug. Valvano became a superstar with this win. Valvano had such charisma, his New York chutzpah made this moment all the more memorable. Then he got sick, and it adds to his legacy. You think Jimmy Valvano would have been the same kind of inspiration for people if he hadn't won a championship before he got cancer? I'm sorry, he wouldn't have. He would have been just another college coach who got sick. The fact that he overcame all odds and was the architect of this colossal upset—that gave him a platform to get across his message about battling and not quitting, a message that continues on with his Jimmy V. Fund.

I love this basket. It's an enduring moment. The NCAA tournament wants to promote the idea of wholesome nonprofessionalism as much as they possibly can. Well, this is their signature moment for that. This is their *Hoosiers*. A team out of nowhere rides an incredible wave of momentum, survives, and advances, plays the epic game in the championship match against Houston, trails, wins on a last second shot that looks to be way short, and suddenly this improbable team has won the national championship. This moment is the madness in March Madness.

3. The Catch

Dwight Clark's touchdown grab marked the birth of a dynasty . . . and a legend.

It's not very often you can trace the beginning of a dynasty to one moment. It's even rarer when you can pin the start of a Hall of Fame career to one play. But that's what you've got with The Catch.

In 1981 the San Francisco 49ers had been pretty bad for a pretty long time. They hadn't made the playoffs since 1972 and had had only one winning year since then. Two years before they were 2-14. Sure they went 13-3, but that happens in the NFL, where a team catches a couple of breaks in the schedule and goes from bad to good, and then they go right back to bad.

And Joe Montana wasn't a super quarterback prospect, a guy like Peyton Manning who had this pedigree a mile long. He was a third-round draft pick, a guy who was a little small, didn't have a cannon for an arm, won that Cotton Bowl for Notre Dame, but didn't have superstar written all over him by any means. To put a modern spin on it, it was a little like the 2004 San Diego Chargers and Drew Brees. A surprise team that put up a nice regular-season record, and a young quarterback who's starting to play pretty well.

And in the NFC championship game, Montana and the 49ers were playing the Dallas Cowboys. They were America's

---

THE CATCH

- A record crowd of 60,525 was on hand to witness the playoff game on January 10, 1982, at Candlestick Park.

- With 4:54 left in the game, down 27-21, Montana drove 89 yards for the winning touchdown.

- The 49ers went on to beat Cincinnati, 26-21, in Super Bowl XVI, the first of four Super Bowl wins for Montana.

- On the final drive, Montana missed an open Freddie Solomon in the end zone, causing the 49ers' normally reserved coach, Bill Walsh, to yell and leap high in the air. "He looked pretty disgusted," Montana recalled.

team, and with Tom Landry standing on the sidelines in that fedora, they had dominated football for 15 years, pretty much from 1966 on. They played in a million championship games, were in the playoffs every year.

Here's the situation: Candlestick Park, and the Cowboys lead the game 27-21 with four minutes to go. The Niners have their backs against the wall. But they start one of the great drives in the history of football from their own 11-yard line. How did they move the ball down the field? They ran it. That's one of the misnomers about the game. People think this drive was all Montana. It was actually running back Lenvil Elliot who kept moving the chains. The Niners move the ball until it's third and three on the Dallas six, 58 seconds to go. Bill Walsh sends in a play called Sprint Option Right that's designed for Freddie Solomon, but Clark is the second option.

Montana gets flushed out of the pocket by Larry Bethea, who runs him almost out of bounds on the right sideline. Montana throws the ball almost up for grabs right along the end line of the end zone. And Dwight Clark jumps out of nowhere to catch this ball, with the fingertips of both hands, and just barely gets both feet down, while Everson Walls, who was a great cover guy, can only watch. (Walls got his moment of redemption in playing for the Giants in Super Bowl XXV when he made a game-saving shoestring tackle on Buffalo's Thurman Thomas.) You can see from the photos just how high Clark, who was 6'4", had to jump. He just gets the very tips of his fingers on the ball. Another inch higher and it's incomplete.

And Clark will tell you that it was designed that way. San Francisco still had another play and some time on the clock, Joe Montana understood the percentages: throw the ball where it's either going to be caught or go out of bounds, with no chance of the interception. It's probably the most famous catch in NFL history. And it wasn't some All-Pro who made it. It was Dwight Clark. Clark came out of Clemson, and the 49ers went down to scout his teammate Perry Tuttle, and they got a look at Clark and decided to take a chance on him. And with that one moment, Clark assured himself a place in history. He's never going to have to buy a drink in San Francisco the rest of his life.

And just like this play was the beginning of things for the 49ers, it was also sort of the end for Landry's Cowboys. This was a turning point moment, a changing of the guard. The Cowboys were very close to going to the Super Bowl, a Super Bowl they probably would have won, and they'd never get that close again. The next year they would lose to the Redskins in the title game, and it was pretty much downhill from there. Which was sweet for old-time 49er fans who had watched John Brodie lose to the Cowboys three years in a row in the early 1970s. So this game got the monkey off their back in a big way.

Now, if you want, you can niggle a little about this one. You can point out that it wasn't fourth down. You can point out that it wasn't the last play of the game, that the Cowboys got the ball back and drove the ball to midfield, but Danny White fumbled. But this great play has taken on a life of its own. Go up to any sports fans and say The Catch, and they're going to know you're talking about Joe Montana to Dwight Clark.

DOGBITE: THE BALL FROM THE CATCH

Joe Montana wasn't the only Super Bowl quarterback in attendance at Candlestick Park on January 10, 1982. The other one? Tom Brady. He was only four-and-a-half years old—but clearly already taking notes on how to mount a winning drive at the end of a game. "When Joe threw that touchdown to Dwight Clark, everyone in front of me jumped up and I couldn't see anything," recalls Brady.

And where's the ball from the most famous catch in football? The ball sat, forgotten, in the garage of 49ers PR guy Jerry Walker, who, when the topic came up at the office, remembered it and gave it back to Clark. Clark displayed it for a while at his restaurant, but now that heirloom pigskin is sitting in a cardboard box in a closet in his home.

CLOSE, BUT . . .

• **Lynn Swann:** Incredibly spectacular play against Dallas near midfield with a huge wow factor. But it didn't decide the game, much less define the Steelers dynasty.

• **John Taylor:** Again, incredible moment, but it kind of came in the middle of the Niners run. Great play, important play, but it doesn't have the resonance of the Clark catch.

2. The Shot Heard Round the World

Call it The Miracle, call it The Shot,
but either way Thomson's home run was monumental.

"The Giants win the pennant! The Giants win the pennant!" There isn't a more memorable call in the history of sports broadcasting. Russ Hodges getting wrapped up in that moment as much as any Giants fan, letting his emotions, his shock and elation, at what transpired come through.

This is of course the culmination of the '51 pennant race. Giants vs. Dodgers. We can talk about this race absolutely forever. I'll give you the origins of it. The Dodgers have a 13½-game lead in early August. They'd just swept the Giants in a three-game series at Ebbets Field, and in the locker room after the game, the Dodgers were whooping it up. "They're dead. We'll never see them again. We just won the pennant." Leo Durocher heard it and said, "We'll see." From that moment on, the Giants went 37-8. At one point they won 16 in a row. They were relentless. The Dodgers were 26-23 down the stretch. Not bad. And don't forget, the Dodgers had to win their last game in Philly in 14 innings just to clinch a tie. The Giants had won earlier in the day, and Jackie Robinson saved the game for Brooklyn in the bottom of the ninth with an unbelievable play behind second, then won the game in extra innings with a home run.

And it's amazing how a season can turn on one small decision. This one sure did. Back in 1946 when the Dodgers played a playoff against St. Louis, Brooklyn won the coin flip and elected to play the first game in St. Louis and the next two at home. They lost the first game, and after the long train ride back, they were flat as a pancake and lost the second game, too. So Mr. Chuck Dressen vows he's not going to make the same mistake twice, and elects to take the first game at home but give up the chance to have the decisive Game 3 at home. This backfired five ways to Sunday. Bobby Thomson hit a home run in Game 1 that probably wouldn't have been out at the Polo Grounds, and the Shot Heard Round the World would have likely been just a long fly ball at Ebbets Field. As for the homer itself, there are so many things about this moment. Don Newcombe was the Dodger pitcher, and he had a 4-1 lead. Roy Campanella, the Dodger catcher, was hurt and didn't play that day, and Campanella always told Newcombe, "I would have been able to get you home in that ninth inning."

Dressen decided to make a pitching change. He wanted to bring in Clem Labine. And just as the phone rang in the bullpen, Labine threw a 59-foot curveball in the dirt, and they said, "You know what? It doesn't look like Labine has it today. Better bring Branca." Thomson, from middle of the season on, had absolutely destroyed Branca. He hit a billion home runs. And, as I said, he hit a homer off Branca in Game 1 of this playoff. Branca was worn out.

Thomson vs. Branca. Willie Mays on deck. On the second pitch, Branca threw an inside fastball, got too much of the plate. Going, going, gone. And this, my friends, is the Miracle of Coogan's Bluff. An epic baseball moment. You have the video of it, still. Durocher and Thomson hugging each other going down the third base line. You have Thomson jumping onto home plate. You've got Andy Pafko jumping at the fence as the ball sailed into the stands just out of reach. He was traded to the Dodgers by the Cubs in mid-season and he thinks he's going to the World Series. Think again. If that's Ebbets Field, Pafko makes the catch. And you don't think God plays in some of these games?

And even 50 years later people are reliving this moment. Were the Giants stealing the Dodgers's signs? Durocher evidently had this elaborate system worked out with a telescope and a buzzer system back to the

> **THE SHOT HEARD ROUND THE WORLD**
>
> - On October 3, 1951, the Giants defeated the Dodgers 5-4 to win the tiebreaker; official attendance: 34,320.
> - On August 11, the Dodgers were in first place by 12½ games but the Giants won 37 of the last 45 games, including the last seven in a row, to finish with the same record and force a best-of-three series.
> - In *The Godfather*, Sonny Corleone is driving his car, listening to a broadcast of the game just before he is gunned down, half an inning before Russ Hodges's call of Thomson's home run.

dugout. But it didn't taint this moment. Even the players who admitted the scheme noted that the Dodgers changed the signs with a runner on base, and with Rube Walker in there instead of Campanella, they were in the dark again in that ninth inning. Thomson, for his part, says that he never wanted the signs, that he thought they'd be distracting, and I believe him.

This is sort of the epitome of the Dodgers, a kind of close-but-no-cigar team. In this ten-year period, before you got to '55, they were a tough-luck team: '41 World Series, '42 they won 102 games, '46 they lost to the Cardinals in the playoffs, '47 they lost to the Yankees, '49 they lost to the Yankees, '50 they lost the last game to the Phillies in extra innings. This is a great team, with Hall of Famers, but they couldn't get over the hump and wouldn't until 1955.

And of course Branca and Thomson have gone on to become friends, signing autographs and retelling the story, and there's something nice about the way they've preserved the moment instead of tarnishing it with bitterness and regret.

You could argue very easily that this should be number one, but there's one reason I can't. The Giants lost the World Series. Got beaten for the World Championship. But still, this is The Shot Heard Round the World.

DOGBITE: GIANT CALL

Russ Hodges's great call was a highlight of that amazing game, but it was a fluke that it survived at all. WMCA didn't record the broadcasts themselves back then, but a guy in Brooklyn named Lawrence Goldberg knew he was going to miss the game to go to work. So he asked his mom to press a reel-to-reel tape recorder against the radio speaker and tape the end of the game for him. Good thing, too, because Hodges's call wasn't the one that most people heard live. The national broadcast on the Liberty Radio Network was by Gordon McLendon. The Old Scotchman's call wasn't quite as memorable as Hodges: "I don't know what to say. I just don't know what to say. This is the greatest victory in baseball history." Red Barber always hated Hodges's call. Thought it was way over the top. I think he resented the celebrity it gave Hodges. Red Barber was wrong.

1. The Miracle of Mazeroski

The upstart Pirates beat the mighty Yankees in baseball's ultimate walk-off.

There are 100 things to like about Bill Mazeroski's home run in the 1960 World Series. The first is that it decided the Series on one swing. That's happened surprisingly few times.

This is a far more significant moment than Joe Carter's home run in the 1993 World Series. It was fun, but the Blue Jays were up 3-2, and they were the defending champions. They weren't facing elimination. It's a little like Jordan's Parting Shot. It was an exciting end to the game, but you never got the feeling that the outcome of the series was in doubt.

The other thing is that it's such an unlikely moment in so many ways. The Pirates were supposed to get slaughtered by the Yankees. And in many ways, they did. New York beat them 16-3, 10-0, and 12-0. The Pirates won their games 6-4, 3-2, and 5-2. This was a World Series that bothered Mickey Mantle to his dying day. He knew the Yankees should have won this Series easily.

There are so many things that make this a great moment. You've got a Hall of Fame player at the center of it. Bill Mazeroski is in Cooperstown. There are three reasons for that: A) He's the greatest fielding second basemen of all time. B) He hit this home run. C) The old-timers on the Veteran's Committee liked him. The homer sails over the head of Yogi Berra and into the stands at Forbes Field. Yes, Yogi Berra. That's who was playing left field. And this was Casey Stengel's last game as manager of the Yankees. A really sour ending to a sweet run for the Old Professor. You want controversy? You can argue until you're blue in the face about how Casey handled his pitching staff. I think that he should have pitched Whitey Ford in games 1, 4, and 7, and then Mazeroski would have never gotten his chance.

Still, Mazeroski's homer was the culmination of a classic game. The Pirates were trailing 7-6 in the bottom of the eighth. Hal Smith hit a three-run homer and the Pirates took a 9-7 lead. They looked like they were on their way. The Yankees tied the game in the top of the ninth after Mantle made a great play on the bases. On a grounder hit to first, Mantle took off to second. But once he realized he was going to be thrown out he scurried back to first, eluding the tag and allowing the runner to come home from third safely to make it 9-9. Uh-oh. Usually when that happens, it's like a reality check. Order has been restored and the Yankees are on their way, like in the 2003 ALCS. But not this time.

Let's focus for a moment on Ralph Terry, who gave up the home run. As dramatic and unexpected as the Maz homer was, it wasn't the defining moment of his career. It's funny to compare Ralph Terry to Ralph Branca, who gave up Bobby Thomson's home run. Branca had been a very good pitcher, a guy who had won 20 games, but after that home run his baseball career was pretty much over. He won 12 more games and was out of baseball at age 30. Terry shook it off. The next year he went 16-3, and the year after that he went 23-12. Ralph Terry came back two years later in '62 with men on second and third and two outs in a Game 7, 1-0, against the Giants, and got Willie McCovey to line out. How about that for some stick-to-it-iveness? He's the goat of the all-time greatest World Series moment and comes back two years later in Game 7 and comes up huge, 1-0. Impressive.

And here's the other thing I can't emphasize enough. This was the ultimate situation. Game 7, tie game, do or die, sudden death. And the game ends with one swing of the bat. Walk-off homer. In more than a hundred years, it's never happened before or since. Every kid swinging a bat in his backyard dreams of this moment. That, my friends, is why it's the number one greatest sports moment of all time in the Mad Dog Hall of Fame.

DOGBITE: SECOND CHANCES

Maz hit the most amazing World Series home run of all time, but guess what: He didn't win the MVP award. The award went to the Yankees's Bobby Richardson, the first and only player in history to win the award as a member of the losing team. His 12 RBIs set an all-time record for the Fall Classic, and that's even more amazing when you consider that Richardson often batted eighth and had only 26 RBIs all season. That means a third of his RBIs that year came on the biggest stage. In Game 3 alone, Richardson drove in a World Series record six runs, including a grand slam that came after a failed bunt attempt. And in Game 7 it was Richardson's single in the ninth that helped the Yanks tie the game. And although he missed out on a ring in 1960, he did receive a shiny new Corvette for winning the MVP. "I couldn't get my family in it," he said. "So I traded it for a Jeep."

Chapter 9

The Top-Ten Other Sport Athletes of All Time

Does Muhammad Ali KO the competition? And which honoree isn't even human?

One thing I came up against in making these Hall of Fame lists is how to deal with those athletes outside of the big three sports. The Olympians. The golfers. The tennis players. The boxers. The hockey players. You can't just leave them out. But on the other hand, there's not much juice in debating the ninth and tenth best golfers of all time. The solution to this was simple: Toss these athletes together into one category and sort them out. And it's a really interesting mix. You have athletes from different sports, from different time periods, some guys who were amazing at their given game, others who excelled at practically everything. You even have one who wasn't a human being.

It was a really strong list of contenders, and to some degree you have to compare sports as much as compare athletes. There were some tough choices here, but it was a fun challenge. I think while you might make an argument for some of your own favorites, it's pretty tough to argue that everyone here is worthy of a spot in the Mad Dog Hall of Fame.

10. Rocket's Red Glare

Rod Laver's grand slams are tennis's greatest deeds.

We got all excited about the idea of the grand slam when Tiger Woods was threatening to complete one a couple of years ago. Well, Rod Laver did that in men's tennis not once but twice. And let's put that accomplishment in perspective. Among today's active players, Andre Agassi is the only one who could manage a career grand slam. Sampras couldn't do it. McEnroe couldn't do it. Borg? No. Connors? Nope. Federer? We'll see.

The tennis grand slam is really a tremendous accomplishment. And Laver won the grand slam in 1962 and 1968. The first one might have a little bit of a taint, because before 1968, tennis was split in half, pro and amateur, and the pros couldn't play in any of the grand slam tournaments. In that first one, Laver didn't have to face guys like Pancho Gonzalez. That's fair. But remember that plenty of other players had the same opportunity and none of *them* won the grand slam. And that second grand slam in 1969 was as pure as can be. It was the second year of open tennis and Laver beat all comers.

Laver won 11 major championships in his career, but there should be a big asterisk next to that number. If he had been able to play at Wimbledon and the French, Australian, and U.S. championships between 1962 and 1968, which was really the prime of his career, he would have won another eight or ten majors easily and ended up with 20 or more. And Pete Sampras, who ended up with 14, would be a distant second.

Laver was an amazing player. He hit the ball hard, with tremendous spin. Great speed, great net game. Reminds you a little bit of what Roger Federer does today. Laver didn't have the best serve in the world, that huge overpowering weapon, but once the point started, there wasn't a better player.

Some old timers talk about Lew Hoad's ball-striking ability, and on any given day he could be as good as Laver, but Laver was more consistent, a better competitor. It's a little like the way Ilie Nastase used to be able to give Jimmy Connors all he could handle, or Marat Safin can play with Roger Federer on a good day.

The other thing you like about Laver is his tremendous impact on tennis history. He was part of the amazing Australian tennis boom of the late 1950s and early 1960s. You had Harry Hopman, the coach, who was this Vince Lombardi figure, a guy who preached fitness and toughness. He'd have his Davis Cup teams practice for five hours in the baking hot sun, and then do squat thrusts and all kinds of calisthenics afterwards. Absolutely brutal. But it was also all about sportsmanship. No tantrums. Just try your best and behave the same way whether you're winning or losing. Laver was Hopman's prize pupil.

Laver's influence stretches on through today. McEnroe was coached by Hopman for a while when he was young, and he had more than a little Laver in his game. Sampras was a huge fan of the Australians, and he'll be the first to tell you that Laver is the greatest player of all time. And Federer emulated Sampras, who emulated Laver. In one of Sampras's first Wimbledons, Laver made a point to find Pete and take him out on those hallowed courts and hit for a while. Afterward Laver said that he belongs. It's almost like Laver indoctrinated him into that Wimbledon club.

And Laver was supercompetitive. Let's rewind a little for this great story that John Newcombe told me. He said that when he was 18 years old he beat Laver in a match in a mid-size tournament in White City, Australia. Then Laver turns pro, Newcombe stays an amateur, and they don't play again for five years. The next time Laver plays Newcombe, he cleans his clock. When they get up to the net, Laver shakes his hands and says,

"You know, Newk, I've been thinking about that last match for five years." He proceeded to beat Newcombe seven consecutive times. That's competitive spirit. And that's why Rod Laver's worthy of a spot in the Mad Dog Hall of Fame.

DOGBITE: ARM AND THE MAN

Arthur Ashe called it a two-by-four with freckles. A foot in circumference at its widest point, and seven inches at the wrist, it's the legendary left arm of Rod Laver. Cliff Drysdale, who played against Laver, recalls that his left arm was almost twice the circumference of his right. Laver said, "I was stunned when Dave Anderson of *The New York Times* tape-measured me one afternoon in 1968 and reported that my left forearm was 12 inches around—as big as Rocky Marciano's!"

While some suggested it was a result of kangaroo hunting, the real story is a little more pedestrian. Training with veteran coach Charlie Hollis, Laver would spend hours upon hours pumping pulley weights and squeezing tennis and squash balls. "After a session, the muscles in my arm would pulse," he recalled.

---

9. Tiger Burning Bright

Tiger Woods is the world's most popular athlete . . . and he's not done yet.

If we do this list again in 15 years, we might have Tiger Woods a lot higher. Right at this moment, Tiger Woods is probably the biggest, the most recognizable, athlete in the world. He's huge in America, but he's also huge in Europe and the Far East. He brings eyeballs to the television set. If he's in contention on a Sunday afternoon, that tournament gets a better rating. It's automatic. And that doesn't just go for the Deutsche Bank Championship. More people watch the Masters if he's in contention.

Tiger appeals to the sports fan—as opposed to the golf aficionado—because he grinds. He never takes anything for granted, always gives his best effort, always brings his A game (or almost always, as we'll see in a moment). No matter how far behind he is, Tiger goes out there on the last day trying to make the cut. I don't care if it's the Western Open or the Masters. He will give you everything he's got. So if you're at the Phoenix Open, and Tiger's had a lousy Thursday, and he's out there on Friday on the back nine and needs two or three birdies for the last five holes to make the cut, he'll bust his butt to make up those strokes. There's no quit in him. His run of consecutive cuts made was really remarkable. It's about consistency, but it's also about competitiveness. And Tiger's got plenty of both.

Tiger's had a tremendous impact on the game. Just look at Augusta National. It's the most famous course in golf, and they had to lengthen it and toughen it. Not to keep him from winning, but to keep him from turning it into a pitch-and-putt and going 20 under par. They called it "Tigerproofing." Now, they probably would have had to do it eventually anyway, with the longer balls and better clubs. But they didn't call it "Ernie Els-proofing." At the U.S. Open at Bethpage, they made the course incredibly long, where you had to whack the ball 375 yards, and that was because of Tiger, too.

Tiger took this country club sport and made it accessible. All of a sudden you had fans in the inner city getting excited about the Masters because Tiger was playing. A little like Venus and Serena Williams in tennis.

Tiger was really the first great athlete to play the game of golf at its highest level. He's not some fat golfer who's out there huffing and puffing, 25 pounds overweight. When you looked at Tom Watson did you think, "Hey that guy's a tremendous athlete"? Jack Nicklaus? If he wasn't playing golf, he'd probably be sitting behind a desk. But you could almost see Tiger Woods playing center field in the majors. And Tiger worked hard, lifting weights, working out in the gym. It raised the bar for everyone else, and now you see guys like Vijay Singh out on the driving range hitting balls until his hands bleed. I think you'll see that impact even more in a few years, as the kids who got turned on to golf by Tiger when they were 12 start turning 20 and 25.

Why is Tiger only number nine? Well, there are a couple of things you don't like about him. He's taken his cue from Michael Jordan. There's an aloofness there. He never bares his soul, never lets you get close to him. He thinks that's a weakness. It seems strange to say it, but he's boring. His game isn't boring, but the personality he shows is just dull.

In 2005, just a little short of his 30th birthday, we had the first knock on Tiger in his career on the golf course, in the PGA at Baltusrol in New Jersey. On Sunday, play is delayed several times by thunderstorms and is ultimately suspended. Tiger finishes his round and he's the leader in the clubhouse, but some of the guys who hadn't finished, like Phil Mickelson, were a couple shots ahead of him with three or four holes left. Well, Tiger decided he didn't have a chance and he hopped on his private plane and left for Florida. See ya. And remember this isn't the Buick Open, this is the PGA, a major championship. You've got to have problems with this. The first thing is the effect his mere presence on the driving range Monday morning can have on the other players. They think, "Tiger is lurking." But the bigger problem with him leaving is that he essentially has to root against himself. Because if the leaders falter—and that course was impossible—he could find himself in a playoff that afternoon, and he'd be disqualified because he's 1,000 miles away.

And Tiger didn't see anything wrong with this. The fact that he left the PGA is a disgrace, and the fact that he didn't acknowledge his mistake is even more of a disgrace.

TIGER WOODS

- His ten major championships as a pro place him third on the all-time list behind Jack Nicklaus (18) and Walter Hagen (11). His 46 PGA Tour wins, as of December 2005, ranks seventh all-time.

- Woods holds or shares the records for the lowest 72-hole scores in relation to par in every major championship.

- Made a record 142 consecutive cuts before missing one at the Byron Nelson Classic in 2005.

- In 2000, Woods became the first player to be under par in every event played on the PGA Tour for an entire year. His actual scoring average of 68.17 was the lowest in PGA Tour history, besting the 68.33 average by Byron Nelson in 1945.

But the real reason Tiger's not higher on the list is that he's still in the middle of his career. Anything can happen. Tiger could blow out a disc in his back on the driving range tomorrow and that could be it for him. If I were going to bet, I'd say, "Sure, he's going to beat Nicklaus's record." He's got ten, and he's only 30 years old. You've got to love his chances. But for the moment, he hasn't done it yet. Jack's got 18 majors. And that's a magic number for Tiger, too. When he was growing up in California, it's up there on his bedroom wall, the list of Jack's majors. If you want to be the greatest golfer of all time, Jack Nicklaus is the guy you have to beat, and Tiger Woods will be the first one to tell you that. But I think in 20 years you're not going to be able to say that anymore.

DOGBITE: SWEET SIXTEEN

Talk about a guy who was born to play. When he was less than two months past his sixteenth birthday, still a sophomore in high school, Tiger Woods got a sponsor's exemption into the Nissan Los Angeles Open. He used a three-wood on his first drive. "I was so tense I had a tough time holding the club," Tiger said later. "It was like rigor mortis had set in." Rigor mortis or not, on that first hole he shot a birdie. The rest of the afternoon wasn't quite so smooth. His dad recalled, "He was playing Army golf: left, right, left, right. But he was getting up and down like a thief. He recovered and made pars from positions that Riviera hasn't seen in a long time." He ended up shooting a 72 on his first day, and a 75 the next, and missed the cut by six strokes.

Nobody was all that blown away, though. Here's what *SI* had to say. "The touring pros, while conceding that Tiger may be the best junior golfer ever—he has won a record six junior world titles—steered away from hyperbole. They noted that Doug Clarke, who won the Trans-Mississippi Amateur at age 17, never made it on the Tour and now gives lessons at a driving range in Del Mar, California . . . Even [Scott] Hallberg, a four-time college All-America, was once billed as the next Nicklaus—but has fallen 18 majors short."

CLOSE, BUT . . .

• **Lance Armstrong:** I can't justify including a guy in a sport that nobody in America pays attention to. Bike racing is a niche sport. He's inspired cancer survivors, and he was hanging around with Sheryl Crow for a while. But riding your bike up a mountain isn't a sport to me, and the doping allegations don't help either.

• **Martina Navratilova:** I would love to have Martina Navratilova on our list, because in my opinion she's the greatest women's tennis player of all time, and she's in her late forties and still playing competitive doubles. Her love of the game is unsurpassed. And she really remade herself through training—look at her in 1976 and look at her in 1990 and it's like two different people. Martina's serve is the best weapon I've ever seen in women's tennis. If we had a couple more spots, she'd make it.

• **Jack Dempsey:** If I put another boxer in here, I think it'd be Jack Dempsey. The Manassa Mauler is one of the top three or four boxers of all time, and when he was fighting, he was right up there with Babe Ruth and Bobby Jones and Bill Tilden as the biggest athletes in the world. He was an American idol.

• **Richard Petty:** In some parts of our country people would say, "How can you not put Richard Petty in here?" My reply: You cannot be in the top ten in the history of American athletes if you are not big in the major media markets. New York, Boston, Chicago, LA, San Francisco, those kinds of cities. If you put a NASCAR race in New York City it wouldn't draw flies. I've been on talk radio for 17 or 18 years in New York City, and outside of Dale Earnhardt's tragedy I can't remember the last NASCAR call I took.

• **Arnold Palmer:** With Palmer it's a style-over-substance issue. He has a tremendous following. Hitch up the pants, grip it and rip it. Arnie's Army. And he was a tremendous marketer—IMG, the world's largest sports management company, got started because Mark McCormack started out handling Arnold Palmer's fan mail. But Palmer's only got seven majors. He's not as good as Hogan or Snead, much less Nicklaus or Tiger, so he's not going to make the cut.

8. Big Red

Secretariat is the horse every thoroughbred must be compared to.

One of the all-time memorable images in sports is the backstretch of the 1973 Belmont Stakes. Secretariat is galloping down the stretch and all the other horses are still rounding the turn. He crossed the line ahead by 31 lengths. Thirty-one lengths. Thirty-one. That's amazing. Incredible. And any other word you'd like to toss at it.

Now, I'm not a huge horse racing guy, but I know greatness when I see it, and Secretariat is the greatest horse of all time. No doubt about it. He won the Triple Crown in tremendous fashion. In the Derby, he was the first and only horse ever to officially crack two minutes, and each quarter-mile was faster than the one before, which is unheard of. In the Preakness, he probably set another record—that's what all the guys timing the race with a stopwatch said—but the official timer malfunctioned and his official time was short of the record. He more than made up for that in the Belmont.

He went off a 1-10 favorite in that race. His time of 2:24 for a mile and a half was a world record, and a lot of horse racing experts think it will never be broken. He broke Belmont's 16-year-old track record by more than two and a half seconds which is the equivalent of 13 lengths. I can still hear Chic Anderson's classic call of that final leg of the Triple Crown. "He is moving like a tremendous machine." He was so far in front that they had to go back to the

SECRETARIAT

- In 1973, became the first Triple Crown winner in a quarter century
- As a three-year-old, set a new track record at the Kentucky Derby and a world record at the Belmont Stakes, which he won by 31 lengths
- The only horse to make the covers of *Time*, *Newsweek*, and *Sports Illustrated* in the same month; this came before he had captured the Triple Crown at the Belmont Stakes

videotape and the photographs to figure out just how enormous the margin was. And he recorded that amazing time without the slightest bit of competition. His jockey, Ron Turcotte, said, "The horse did it by himself. I was just along for the ride."

The things he accomplished were mind-boggling. Looking back, you have to realize they've been running these Triple Crown races for more than a century, and the sport of horse racing has changed less than just about any other sport. And he was the only horse to set a record—that clock malfunction aside—in each of the three races. When you take a look at the record books, you see that no horse has come within two seconds of his Belmont time, and you wonder if his records aren't like Joe DiMaggio's hitting streak, something that's not going to be broken in your lifetime.

Secretariat just completely revived interest in the sport of horse racing. For a long time in the early part of the century, horse racing was the biggest sport there was. But it kind of waned in popularity, until Secretariat came along. There hadn't been a Triple Crown winner since 1948, so when he did it, it was front page news, a huge story not just on the sports pages. After his final race, almost 33,000 people came out to Belmont just to see this horse's final public appearance. He's been put on a postage stamp for crying out loud. That horse was a freak, and I mean that literally. When Secretariat died, they discovered that his heart weighed 22

DOGBITE: HORSE SENSATION

Summer 1969. Belmont Park. It was time for the annual coin flip between the Chenerys and the Phippses. Christopher Chenery's Meadow Stable had sent two broodmares—Somethingroyal and Hasty Matelda—to Phipps's Claiborne Farm to breed with their stallion Bold Ruler. As part of the long-standing agreement between the two families, a coin toss would decide who would get the first choice of foal. Owner Ogden Phipps won and took the Bold Ruler–Somethingroyal offspring. The name of that horse? The Bride. Penny Tweedy, Chenery's daughter, who had taken over Meadow Stable from her father, was "stuck" with The Bride's little brother. "I lost the toss, and got Secretariat," said Tweedy of the horse who would be named after Elizabeth Ham, her father's secretary.

pounds. The average thoroughbred's heart weighs less than nine pounds. That's amazing.

For as long as they keep running these races—and the Triple Crown races are true classics on the American sporting scene—every horse will be compared to Secretariat. It's been more than 30 years, and there hasn't been a horse that's close, and maybe there never will be.

7. King of the Courts

Billie Jean King was a true pioneer in women's sports.

Billie Jean King has three tremendous qualifications that earn her a place on this list. First off, she's an all-time great tennis player. She's right up there in the top five with Martina, Chris Evert, Margaret Court, Steffi Graf. She was a tremendous competitor, a great, flamboyant, attacking player. Amazing doubles player. She was never afraid to lose—she'd spill her guts on the court. And I think that a lot of the players she competed against had more going for them in the way of natural ability. Court was bigger and had more power. Evert was younger and steadier. Evonne Goolagong had beautiful strokes and tremendous touch. But Billie Jean wanted it more. There may have been a few players who were better than her, but I don't think there's ever been a better competitor than Billie Jean King, and as a sports fan, you admire that.

She also won the most important tennis match of all time. I mean the Battle of

> **BILLIE JEAN KING**
>
> • Between 1966 and 1975, King won six Wimbledon singles championships and four U.S. Open titles.
> • She was ranked No. 1 in the world five times, winning a total of 39 Grand Slam titles in singles and doubles.
> • In 1972, she became the first woman to ever be named *Sports Illustrated* "Sportsperson of the Year."

the Sexes match against Bobby Riggs. Nowadays you'd say to yourself, "How does a 55-year-old guy who's patting the ball back and forth, who won the 1939 Wimbledon and here it is 34 years later, how does this kind of guy even think about getting on the court with the best women's tennis player in the world?" Say what you will about Riggs, but he beat Margaret Court, psyched her out completely, and most people thought he was going to do the same against Billie Jean. And the Battle of the Sexes completely captivated people. There were 30,000 people in the Astrodome, and 90 million people watching at home. That's right up there with any Super Bowl, any World Series. Ask anyone who's old enough and they can remember watching that match, even if they never watched a tennis match before or since. It was an incredible spectacle, a huge prime-time event. And it would have been a horrible thing for Billie Jean if she lost

---

DOGBITE: FIT FOR A KING

Here's a story about Billie Jean King, and you could take this as a positive or a negative, it's up to you. Four years ago, I hosted this tennis event at Rockefeller Plaza. It was a bring-tennis-to-the-masses kind of thing. David Dinkins was there. Daisy Fuentes. James Blake. Andy Roddick. Patrick McEnroe was there as the Davis Cup captain. And so was Billie Jean King, who was then the Federation Cup captain. I met Billie Jean King before the event and she really wanted to make sure that she was introduced first and that she was introduced properly. Almost like Joe DiMaggio at Yankee Stadium. Pat McEnroe wasn't like this. Blake, Roddick, it didn't matter to them. But it mattered a lot to Billie Jean. And you saw that later in the year when she had it out with Jennifer Capriati at the Fed Cup. She was ticked off about Capriati bringing her own coach. She thought, "I'm the coach, and you shouldn't be off working with your coach or your hitting partner. This is a group effort." I thought she was right, but Pat McEnroe told me the other side of the story. To get Sampras or Agassi or Roddick to play in the Davis Cup, you had to accommodate them, let them bring their own coaches, give them whatever they want. But Billie Jean King said we're going to do it the way it was done in the 1970s. And that's what I saw at that event at Rockefeller Center. Billie Jean, both proud and prideful, wanted things done her way.

to this self-proclaimed male chauvinist pig. It would have set the sport of women's tennis back 20 years if she lost to Riggs. But Billie Jean was un-flappable. She took care of business and beat him in straight sets.

And probably most importantly, Billie Jean was a key figure in the for-mation of the WTA tour. Gladys Heldman was the organizer, but Billie Jean, more than the rest of the original nine, was the key, the top player, and the one with something to lose. They needed a great player to lend this tour legitimacy. Margaret Court and Virginia Wade didn't join right away. Billie Jean King did. She was the pioneer, and she is the reason why Maria Sharapova, Venus, and Serena are making all this money on and off the court today. All women's sports, really—WNBA, women's soccer, women's golf—are an outgrowth of what Billie Jean King did. Billie Jean King did what she believed was right, and because of it, any little girl who plays sports owes something to Billie Jean King.

6. The Bear Necessities

He was always great, but only near the end did Jack Nicklaus become loveable.

If we were doing this list in the mid-1960s, at the height of Jack Nick-laus's career, I don't think you would have put him in here. If you're looking for a golfer, you might have put Ben Hogan or even Arnold Palmer on the list. At that point in his career, Nicklaus was a great player, but he wasn't a commanding figure. He was a big, heavy guy from Ohio State, kind of boring. It was kind of hard to root for him, but it was pretty hard to hate him, too. It was a little like Roger Federer in tennis now. Nicklaus won so much you just kind of wanted someone else to win, so you rooted for the upset a little. You marveled at his perfection, but you kind of wanted a little competition, so you got behind someone else on Sunday afternoon in a major.

Tiger Woods is experiencing the same thing a little right now. He's good for the game because he establishes a benchmark, but you want someone else to win every now and then. And once Tiger becomes mortal for a while, loses a few majors, the pendulum starts to swing back the other way. You start to root for him again, because you realize that he's not going to be with you for that long. You want to hang on to his greatness. But if he starts winning too much, you start rooting against him again. It's the American way. Fans put their superstars on pedestals, and they can't wait to knock them off. And they can't wait to put them back up there again.

That's how it was for Jack Nicklaus in his prime, but that changed when Jack got older. He let his hair grow, lost a little weight. He became more likeable. And he also became more fallible. When he got older, and wasn't winning so much, we started rooting for him.

And his best moment by far came well after his prime. With that great charge on Sunday in the 1986 Masters, Nicklaus really defined himself. He was 46 years of age, and he was an old guy who hadn't won a big tournament in a long time. It became okay to root for him. And he played great that day, shooting a 30 on the back nine. He had to shoot a great score to catch Greg Norman and he did, making all those great putts. When did it become okay to root for Nicklaus? When Verne Lundquist said, "Yes, sir!" on seventeen. And because that moment came in golf, it wasn't just a swan song. In golf, once you're a legend, always a legend. You don't fade to black in golf. You get exemptions and you can still play at the Masters until you're 70 years old. So even though he was no longer what he once was, we could see the Golden Bear out there, at least until the last couple of years, and we could get all warm and fuzzy reminiscing about his career.

Think about it. Jack Nicklaus has been part of the American sports scene from 1960 until 2004. That's 44 years that Jack has been around. In 1960,

> **JACK NICKLAUS**
>
> • Won a record 18 major championships as a professional, earning victories in all of them at least three times each.
> • Second all-time with 73 tour victories, nine short of Sam Snead's 82
> • He won at least one PGA Tour event in 17 consecutive years (1962–78).
> • Nicklaus was the runner-up in a major 19 times.
> • Shot 19 aces; his last was in 2003 at the Senior British Open Pro-Am at Turnberry

at Cherry Hills, Jack was playing as an amateur and he had a great run against Palmer and Ben Hogan. Yes, Ben Hogan. And in 1997 he's in the field with Tiger Woods. I don't say that he was a threat to win the tournament, but he was certainly a threat to make the cut and play the weekend. What other athlete in what other sport has a longevity quotient of 40 years? What other sport allows you that panoramic of a career? No other.

And even now that he's not playing anymore, he'll still be around as a kind of eminence grise, not to mention the architect of a million golf courses.

But the bottom line of why Jack Nicklaus makes this list is simple. Once you get past the big four team sports, golf is the biggest and most important game that there is. And Jack is the greatest golfer of all time. Right now he's got more majors than anyone, and it isn't even close. And he could have had more. Lee Trevino told my partner Mike and me that if Jack didn't get married and have five kids he would have won five or six more majors. He never practiced in the sixties. He was busy being a father. He showed up at the Masters and just went out and played. He didn't lift weights or hit balls. He had five kids running around his house. Maybe that's why under different circumstances Nicklaus finished second a bunch of times and some of those could have become wins.

DOGBITE: HANG IT ON THE FRIDGE

Heading into the 1986 Masters, Jack Nicklaus looked like he was washed up. He hadn't finished better than 39th in a tournament all year, and was 160th on the money list. Tom McCollister of the *Atlanta Journal* wrote a column stating the obvious, that it might be time to retire.

A friend tacked the story up to Jack's refrigerator. "I kept thinking all week, 'Done. Through. Washed up, huh?' " Nicklaus said. After the first day he was six shots off the lead. On Sunday morning he was still four shots behind. His son Steve called and asked him what he thought he needed to shoot to win. Nicklaus said "Sixty-five." Steve said, "Go do it." And the rest is history.

Nicklaus spotted McCollister in the post-tournament interview room. "Thanks, Tom," he said, smiling at the reporter. "You just write that same article next year and put [age] forty-seven in it."

Now, there's a good chance that Tiger will catch him eventually. But it's going to take a while, and it's not a slam dunk. He's only a little more than halfway there and a lot can happen over the next 10 years. An injury, some 18-year-old coming out of the woodwork, who knows? So if and when Tiger wins his 19th major, we'll put him ahead of Jack Nicklaus. Until then, Jack Nicklaus is the greatest golfer of all time, and deserving of a spot in the Mad Dog Hall of Fame.

5. The Babe Factor

*Whatever she lacked in charisma,
Babe Didrikson made up for with sheer prowess.*

One of the most amazing records in sports belongs to Byron Nelson. In 1945 he went out and won 11 consecutive golf tournaments. Amazing feat. Well, imagine this. Imagine that someone had won not 11, but 17 tournaments in a row. And this competitor did this after being an All-American basketball player. And a double Olympic gold medalist in track and field.

That's what Babe Didrikson Zaharias did. She's the greatest athlete in the history of women's sports. She did three wildly different things, at an incredibly high level. And that's why she's on this list. Which brings me to an important point. The first and most important thing in the Mad Dog Hall of Fame is prowess. The impact an athlete has on a sport or on society is important, but the bottom line is this: Are you a great, great athlete? To earn a spot in this company, there's got to be greatness to you. There are a lot of very, very good athletes you could put in this book—guys like Arnold Palmer—who you could include because of their social impact, but the sheer greatness is not there. And in her way, Babe had as much pure athletic prowess as any athlete, male or female, in history.

She did amazing things in three different sports. In basketball, she led her team to a National Championship, often scoring 30 points in an era when a team could win a game by scoring 20.

In track, she literally singlehandedly won the women's AAU national championship, which was also the Olympic trials in 1932. She was the only member of her team, but she scored 30 points, while the second place team, which had more than 20 members scored only 22. That afternoon she won six gold medals and set four world records. In the 1932 Olympics she won gold medals and broke her own world records in both the javelin throw and the 80-meter hurdles. She got a silver in the high jump, although she cleared the gold medal height. The judges ruled that her technique, in which she cleared the bar head first, was illegal.

And after she was done with that, she took up golf. And this wasn't some kind of John Brodie thing, just dabbling. Babe wasn't just a golfer. She was a *legendary* golfer. She won 82 tournaments over a 20-year period. Fifty years before Michelle Wie, she played against men and she competed well. She made the cut in men's tournaments. And you talk about Lance Armstrong. In 1953 Babe underwent surgery for colon cancer. She came back the next year and won the 1954 U.S. Open by 12 strokes. You could say that she was Jackie Joyner-Kersee, Annika Sorenstam, and Chamique Holdsclaw rolled into one. The reason why she isn't higher on the list is her intangibles, or lack thereof. She had plenty of tangibles, amazing things she did on the playing field. But Babe didn't have a huge impact on the world of sports. She came from an age where women's sports was a little bit of an oddity. She was really ahead of her time. Babe wasn't like Mia Hamm, getting millions of little girls out there playing sports. Come to think of it, she'd actually be an interesting role model for young girls today. She competed hard, she'd boast, and she'd talk trash. There was no false modesty with Babe Didrikson. Back then, when the public was used to demure female athletes like Maureen Connolly, people thought she was a bit crude. Today, we'd probably look at her as a breath of fresh air.

If being considered one of the all-time greats in one sport can get you into the Mad Dog Hall of Fame, how can you leave out someone who was great in three different sports? You can't. Here's the bottom line: Every woman athlete before and since has to be compared to Babe Didrikson Zaharias.

DOGBITE: EVERY PLAYER TELLS A STORY

As amazing as Didrikson was, you've got to be careful believing everything you hear about her—especially when she was doing the telling. She claimed to have got her nickname "Babe" because she hit five home runs in a single baseball game, but it probably was a childhood nickname given by her mother. She claimed to have raced freight trains to improve her speed as a youth and claimed to have been chased around a pasture by a mad bull. She lied about her age, claiming she was 19 when she won her medals, not 21, and claiming she had never played golf before when her friends recall her playing in high school. And even before a golf tournament, she'd fudge her practice round scores to dishearten her opponents.

---

4. Jesse's World

Jesse Owens was the hero of a transcendent Olympic moment.

Every now and then you've got a moment where the world of sports crosses over into the world at large. That's what happened at the 1936 Olympics. Adolph Hitler decided that he was going to make the games a showcase for his Aryan nation. Jesse Owens, an African American sprinter from the U.S., had other ideas. He went out there and won four gold medals. This son of a sharecropper and grandson of slaves did more than shock the sports world. He ruined Hitler's party.

Now, it's a great story. But once you scratch the surface of the legend, you'll find out that it wasn't quite the unalloyed victory that we might have liked. For example, Owens got his fourth gold medal when he and Ralph Metcalfe replaced two Jewish runners, Sam Stoller and Marty Glickman. Glickman would go on to become a legendary broadcaster in New York. He maintained that this was a backroom deal between U.S. Olympic Committee head Avery Brundage and the organizers, who didn't want to be humiliated further by being beaten by Jewish athletes. Of course, you can't blame Owens for any of this.

And while the German government was embarrassed by Owens's victories, remember that the German fans cheered him on. You've got to love that great story about Luz Long, the German long jumper. Owens was one jump away from fouling out in the preliminary rounds, and Long, who was one of the favorites, goes up to Owens and suggests making a mark a couple inches shy of the takeoff board, just to be safe. And when Owens won, Long was the first guy there to congratulate him. Nice moment. For the rest of his life Owens talked fondly about Long, who, sadly, was killed in WWII.

But even if you put the Olympics aside, Owens was an astonishing athlete. At the Big Ten Championships in 1935, over the course of 45 minutes Jesse set three world records and tied another. At 3:15 he ties a world record in the 100-yard dash, 9.4 seconds. At 3:25 he heads to the long-jump pit. He puts a handkerchief down where the world record is. He takes one attempt and flies 26 feet 8¼ inches, six inches past his hanky.

The world record he set on his first jump that afternoon would stand for 25 years. At 3:34, he sets a world record in the 220-yard dash. Finally, at 4:00 he shattered the world record in the 220-yard low hurdles. His time of 22.6 made him the first person to crack 23 seconds. And if you want to get technical, he also broke world records for the shorter 200-meter dash and 200-meter hurdles along the way. Pretty good afternoon.

And if Owens's times don't look incredibly impressive today, remember that he didn't have starting blocks—he would just dig little holes behind the line with a trowel. And they ran mostly on cinder tracks, which are way slower than the rubberized tracks they run on today.

Jesse Owens was, along with Joe Louis, the first black athlete in America to really have some mainstream appeal. Jack Johnson was the heavyweight champion of the world, but America wasn't really ready for him, and he wasn't about to change his lifestyle to suit small-town America. But Owens was a man of quiet dignity, a man who let his actions do the talking. In 1936 America had its own race issues—remember, this was 11 years before Jackie Robinson. Owens himself would quietly tell you that after he came home from the Olympics, he couldn't ride in the front of the bus. "I wasn't invited to shake hands with Hitler, but I wasn't invited to the White House to shake hands with the president, either." He had a ticker-tape parade in his honor, but he had to ride the freight elevator at the Waldorf Astoria.

Now, Jesse Owens didn't have much of a place to go after the Olympics. There wasn't any pro track circuit. He had to do a lot of gimmicky things—racing against horses and dogs, motorcycles. He would run before Negro League games, giving the fastest players in the game a 10-yard head

---

DOGBITE: OWENS'S SPIKES

What was Jesse Owens wearing during the Munich Olympics? The same German-made track shoes that the German team wore. These handcrafted shoes, with extra long spikes to handle the concrete track, were made by Gebrueder Dassler Schuhfabrik, the company owned by two brothers that would split into two footwear giants. Rudy would launch Puma in 1948, and his brother Adi would start Adidas.

start before beating them. "People said it was degrading for an Olympic champion to run against a horse, but what was I supposed to do?" Owens said. "I had four gold medals, but you can't eat four gold medals."

It's a shame that it took a while for Jesse Owens to get his due, but I think he deserves tremendous credit. He was the kind of guy who simply set an example. He let his feet do the talking, and in his quiet way, he was not only an astonishing athlete, but a pioneer as well.

3. The Great One

On the ice, Wayne Gretzky was everyman's superstar.

Wayne Gretzky is the greatest hockey player of all time. Now, that's going out on a limb. He holds all the records. Scoring, assists, total points. Single-season, career. Look at any list in the Hockey Encyclopedia and there's a good chance that Wayne Gretzky's name will be on the top. He won championships galore. A great scorer and even better at setting up his teammates.

Here's where you measure Gretzky's greatness. Think about who the second greatest hockey player of all time is. Yeah, some hockey purists will make an argument for Gordie Howe. Maybe Mario Lemieux. But Gretzky is in a class by himself. Gretzky is so far ahead of everybody else in the sport that it's mind-boggling.

He was also tremendous fun to watch. Gretzky is Magic Johnson on skates. He made other guys better. It was that vision thing. He saw things that other guys didn't. He had eyes in the back of his head. And he did it all with flair. Gretzky was the sort of performer that if you hated hockey, just weren't into it at all, you'd still enjoy watching him perform. You didn't have to be a hockey aficionado to appreciate Wayne Gretzky. God put him on this earth to be the face of hockey over a 20-year period.

And off the ice, Gretzky is not only a tremendously charismatic figure, he's also a tremendous guy. He doesn't have a bad bone in his body. He's the most likeable superstar we've ever had in any sport. You like him, you like his wife, you like his kids. And there's never been a moment in his playing career where Gretzky came off badly, where he did something that made you shake your head. Babe Ruth wasn't exactly a model citizen. Gretzky was. And he was accessible. The greatest hockey player of all time didn't need any security guards. Jordan and so many other stars keep you at arm's length. Gretzky doesn't. If we called Gretzky up today he would come on the *Mike and the Mad Dog* show. You've got to have an ego to be a superstar, but Gretzky keeps his in check. The other thing you like is that he's a normal-looking guy. I can look him in the eye. If he was at your gym and walking through the locker room in a towel, nobody would even turn around. It's superstardom brought down to a human scale. He's kind of everyman.

Now, there are a couple of negatives with Gretzky. First of all, we're talking about hockey, and hockey is really a distant fourth among sports in the U.S. No way around that. As I said before, if you're doing this in Canada, where hockey is king, Gretzky might very well be number one on the list. And when you look at the team part of Gretsky's résumé, there are a couple things that bother you a little. A) He played with an incredible number of Hall of Famers in Edmonton, from Messier to Coffey to Grant Fuhr, and B) Gretzky never won another championship after he was traded from Edmonton to LA, while the Oilers with Messier still managed to win a title without him.

Here's a story about Gretzky and Larry Bird. In the spring of 1988 both the Bruins and the Celtics were deep in the play-

WAYNE GRETZKY

- Upon his retirement on April 18, 1999, Gretzky held or shared 61 NHL records: 40 for the regular season, 15 for the Stanley Cup playoffs, and six for the NHL All-Star Game.
- Led the Edmonton Oilers to four Stanley Cups in five seasons
- Gretzky's nine MVP awards, including eight straight, are more than any other player in the history of American pro sports.
- The only player to score more than 200 points, Gretzky did it four times, including a record 215 points in 1985–86.
- In 1981, Gretzky scored 50 goals in 39 games, 11 fewer than previous record holders Maurice Richard and Mike Bossy.

offs and they were both playing in Boston Garden the same day, the Celtics in the afternoon, the Bruins vs. the Oilers at night. Somebody told Bird, "You can warm up the arena for Wayne Gretzky." And Bird said, "Wayne Gretzky? This is my arena. I'm Larry Bird, and Wayne Gretzky can warm up the arena for *me*." I remember at the time thinking that Bird was right. But now, thinking about it, Bird was wrong. Bird is not Wayne Gretzky. Bird is one of the all-time greats in the NBA, but he's not Wayne Gretzky. Bird can walk down the streets of Edmonton, Alberta, and Gretzky can't. Bird can walk down the streets of LA, and Gretzky can't. He's not as entertaining as Gretzky, he's not as big a star as Gretzky, he's not as good as Wayne Gretzky. So, in essence, Bird warmed up the arena for Gretzky, not the other way around.

How big was Gretzky's impact? Well, I think that Gretzky himself, single-handedly, if he were still playing today, could get a TV contract for the NHL. If Gretzky was still playing today, ESPN would not have blown off the NHL. The league wouldn't have had to become partners with NBC. No. No. No. Gretzky's got that magnetism. He brings eyeballs to the sets. And that's why he's number three in this very tough list.

DOGBITE: POWER ASSISTS

Did you know that Gretzky compiled more career assists (1,963) than anyone else had points? It's true. Three different times he tied the record of seven assists in one game. One of his record nights came against the Chicago Blackhawks on December 11, 1985. Chicago coach Bob Pulford was determined to not let Gretzky score a goal in his 25th consecutive game. Chicago shut out the Great One, but Gretzky still managed to contribute. In the highest scoring game in the stadium's 56-year history, Gretzky set up his teammates for seven of Edmonton's 12 goals on the night. Pulford was so ticked off, he refused to meet with reporters after the game. "I lost count of (points) myself. At one point, I thought I had eight," Gretzky said. "There will never be another game like that one." The Great One was wrong. Only two months later, on Valentine's Day, he'd notch seven assists against Quebec.

2. The Greatest

Muhammad Ali shook up the world . . . and not just the world of boxing.

Let's just start out with this: Muhammad Ali is one of the great boxers of all time, no doubt. Any list of the great heavyweights will have Ali among the top three or four on the list: Joe Louis, Jack Dempsey, Rocky Marciano, and Ali.

But Ali was more than just a boxer. He was an important public figure, one of those guys who transcended the world of sports, and not just by selling sneakers. He was one of the first prominent figures to speak out against the Vietnam War. It was a religious thing with him, but his bottom line was simple. "I ain't got no quarrel with them Viet Cong." And while it took four, five years, most of America eventually came around to his point of view.

And while there are some who thought that Ali was dodging the war, let's remember that the heavyweight champion of the world wasn't going to be marching with an infantry unit. Nobody was going to shoot at him. He would have done some push-ups in boot camp, taken some nice photos in uniform, appeared in some USO shows, and kept right on boxing. His hitch in the service would have been ceremonial, like Joe DiMaggio's. He had a lot more to lose by opposing the war than by just going along with it. Remember, he was convicted of draft evasion, sentenced to five years in prison, and had to take the case all the way to the Supreme Court, where he won by a unanimous decision.

As far as his greatness in the ring is concerned, what can you say? He started out his career as a phenom, with incredible speed and power, dancing around like a middleweight. And he was afraid of nothing. Remember what he did to Sonny Liston? Liston was a great brute of a guy, who everybody was scared to death of, like Tyson only worse. His snarl would have you beat before you went in the ring. And Ali threw it right back at him. "What are you looking at?" And then he backed it up when the bell rang. He was unflappable.

And during what would have been the three best years of his career in the late 1960s, Ali couldn't fight at all because they stripped him of his license. When he came back, he wasn't quite the same, physically, not quite as good. But he showed you some other things. He proved that he was a fighter in those Frazier fights. He was a tremendous warrior. In the Thrilla in Manila he beat Frazier in that incredible, epic contest in incredible heat. He had to dig deep to tap his reservoir of courage. And his command of the craft in that second half of his career was superb. He was cerebral. If he couldn't outpunch you, he'd find a way to outbox you. Big, bad George Foreman had knocked everybody out, and Ali just rope-a-doped him, let him expend all his energy bouncing Ali off the ropes, and then when Foreman had nothing left, Ali attacked and took him down in the eighth. Pure guile, one of the all-time brilliant bits of boxing strategy, just perfect.

And of course, Ali was as charismatic, flamboyant, and controversial a figure as you've ever had in sports. He took a page from professional wrestling, and just like Gorgeous George, he'd grab the microphone and tell you he was The Greatest and the King of the World. But unlike Gorgeous George, he'd have to climb into the ring and put his money where his mouth was. With his poems and his predictions he made the pre-fight weigh-in more fun than the fight sometimes. No doubt he rubbed some people the wrong way. He made them uncomfortable. My father hated him. You either loved him or loathed him, but either way you wanted to see him fight. That's why in his day, he was the most famous athlete in the world. They knew him on every continent.

Now, there was a nasty side to Ali, too. He was merciless the way he made fun of Joe Frazier, holding a stuffed monkey at a press conference, calling him a gorilla, and Frazier took it personally, still holding a grudge more than 20 years later. They've made their peace since, but Ali crossed the line there.

In the years since, partially because of the tragedy of his Parkinson's disease, that hard edge has been rounded off, and Ali has become a kind of international goodwill ambassador. He helped to negotiate the release of some prisoners held in Lebanon in the 1980s. He got to light the Olympic flame in the 1996 Olympics, and got a replacement gold medal—he threw the first one into the Ohio River after he was refused entry to a restaurant. Now, with the Parkinson's, it's weird to see Ali this way. He can't move the way he used to or talk the way he used to but he's still an amazing showman. He still has that sparkle in his eye. Muhammad Ali had so many lives, so many personalities, a guy who reinvented himself time after time, and no matter which one it was, he was always the center of attention, the guy you couldn't take your eyes off. That's why Ali is number two on my list.

DOGBITE: THE HURT IN HOUSTON

The Thrilla in Manila and the Rumble in the Jungle are Muhammad Ali's most famous fights, but for his best performance, most hard-core fight fans will tell you that you've got to go back to November 14, 1966, against the hard-punching Cleveland Williams. Before "Big Cat" Williams was dropped in the third round, after being knocked down three other times, he managed to land a total of three punches on the champ. That fight marked the debut of his trademark shuffle, and the record crowd at the Astrodome—most booing Ali—made Bob Arum one of boxing's biggest promoters.

1. The World's Greatest Athlete

Jim Thorpe made his mark on more sports than any athlete before or since.

America has never had an athlete better than Jim Thorpe. Sure it was 100 years ago, but Jim Thorpe did things that no one ever did, and no one will ever do again. Thorpe put college football on the map playing for Pop Warner at Carlisle. In one game, against Army, Thorpe had a 92-yard run, but the play was called back because of a penalty. On the very next play, he ran 97 yards for a touchdown. When they know what's coming and they still can't stop it, that's true dominance. One of those guys who knew it was coming was Dwight Eisenhower, who hurt his knee trying to stop Thorpe.

In the 1912 Olympics, Thorpe won the pentathlon, winning four of the five events. Then he came back and won the decathlon running away. He finished fourth in the open high jump and seventh in the long jump. Abel Kiviat who finished second in the pentathlon, 400 points behind Thorpe, said, "He was the greatest athlete who ever lived. There wasn't anything he couldn't do. All he had to see is someone doing something and he tried it . . . and he'd do it better."

When he came back he got a ticker-tape parade in New York City, and he was genuinely amazed. "I heard people yelling my name, and I couldn't realize how one fellow could have so many friends," he said.

After the Olympics, it came out that Thorpe had accepted some money for playing semi-pro baseball, which is something that other athletes were doing at the time, except that they were smart enough to do it under an assumed name. Thorpe was stripped of his medals—wrongfully it turned out, because the protest wasn't filed in a timely manner—and got all kinds of offers to play major league baseball. He wasn't a great baseball player, but he played in the majors for six seasons, and he got better as he went along. He hit .143 his first season, and .327 in his last. It turns out that Thorpe was also a basketball player. It wasn't well known, even to his biographers, but Thorpe barnstormed with "Jim Thorpe and his World Famous Indians" in parts of New York. Thorpe even won a national ballroom-dancing contest.

Top to bottom, Thorpe was the first superstar athlete in America. The problem is that Thorpe performed such a long time ago, before TV or even radio, very few people actually saw him perform. How many New York writers went to the Stockholm Games? Or saw him at Carnegie Mellon? So there's the tendency to brush him off, as if he doesn't count. Most people, when they're ranking the great athletes, want to begin with World War I. Maybe they'll include Ty Cobb, but they pretty much want to start with Babe Ruth and Jack Dempsey.

Last year I finally saw *Jim Thorpe: All-American*, with Burt Lancaster. Great film. Great story. I came away from it saying that this guy has to be on our list, right at the very top. He didn't have a great life off the field. He had a child who died, which took a toll on him. He got divorced. He drank. When he died, his family was so broke that his wife sent his body to a part of Pennsylvania he had never even visited, and they merged two towns and renamed them Jim Thorpe. Weird and kind of sad. But on the field, Jim Thorpe was unparalleled. When he received his medals at the Olympics, King Gustav V of Sweden told him, "You, sir, are the greatest athlete in the world." To which Thorpe responded in typical fashion, "Thanks, King." I'm with King Gustav on this one.

JIM THORPE

- At the 1912 Olympics Thorpe dominated the decathlon and pentathlon, finishing first in nine of the 15 separate track and field events that made up the two competitions.
- A first-team All-American and four-position player, he led the Carlisle Indians to a national college football championship.
- Became the first president of the American Football Association, now the NFL, in 1920
- In a semi-pro baseball game near the Texas-Oklahoma-Arkansas border, Thorpe hit homers into three different states. His first homer to left landed in Oklahoma. His second homer sailed over the right-field wall into Arkansas. His third was an inside-the-park home run in centerfield, which was in Texas.

stars. And finally, baseball is a game of big moments, and when you're talking about the greatest players of all time, you want guys who came up big in big spots, whether it's getting the big hit or recording the big out.

10. Hey, Mo

Mariano Rivera has been the secret weapon for the Yankee dynasty.

Over the last 30 years or so, there's no position in baseball that has been more important than the closer. If you want to win championships, you almost have to have that guy who can completely remove the ninth inning from the game, making it a mere formality. And that's exactly what Mariano Rivera does. The Yankee team of the mid-1990s and the turn of the millennium has been the most dominant team of the last 40 years. They won four World Series and made it to two others. For a decade the Yankees have been in playoffs every year, and every spring you start out the year looking at them as the team to beat.

The Reds didn't have a ten-year period like this. The Oakland A's didn't have this kind of dynasty. And who's next? The Toronto Blue Jays? Even if you're not a Yankee fan—as I am not—you've got to give this team their due. And keep in mind, they've won these championships during a very difficult era. Since 1994, teams have to win not four games, not seven games, not eight games, but 11 games to win the World Championship.

MARIANO RIVERA

- Won the Rolaids Relief Man of the Year Award four times, in 1999, 2001, 2004, and 2005
- Seven-time All-Star
- Holds postseason records with 34 saves, 34⅓ consecutive scoreless innings, and a 0.81 postseason ERA. He's the all-time leader for World Series saves with nine.
- Only reliever to have won both ALCS (2003) and the World Series MVP (1999) awards

During their championship run, this all-time great team has had one all-time great player. It's not Derek Jeter. It's not Bernie Williams. It's not Jorge Posada. It's Mariano Rivera, the guy who was on the mound to finish the World Series four times in five years. The huge advantage for the Yankees in this ten-year period is that they had the one guy who has consistently made it an eight-inning game. They play nine innings to beat you. You only play eight (or maybe seven and two thirds) to beat them.

Mariano's got one unhittable pitch. His cut fastball on either side of the plate is one of the great pitches in baseball history. He can throw it in the strike zone—he never walks anybody—and hitters still can't touch it. It's not just a great pitch, it's a perfect pitch. Babe Ruth would have trouble hitting it. Ted Williams would have trouble hitting it. And he's completely unflappable. He comes out there and goes about his business exactly the same way against the Red Sox in Game 7 of the ALCS as he does against the Royals in a weekend series in May.

And that changed the complexion of every game. Teams would go into a playoff game with the Yankees and think, We'd better get ahead early because Mariano's sitting there in the dugout. And having that kind of pressure takes its toll. They'd be pressing even if they scored an early run, and pressing twice as hard if they got behind by a run or two. Having a guy who's that reliable changed the way that Joe Torre could manage, both in terms of his hitting and his pitching. He knew that a one-run lead in the eighth inning was almost always a W.

Now, Mariano has had a few instances where he was less than perfect. In 1997, his first year as a closer, he gave up that home run by Sandy Alomar, Jr., that made it into the first row in right field, and the Yankees lost the game and ultimately the series. In the 2001 World Series, there was his throwing error and Luis Gonzalez got a bloop single at the end of his second inning of work. And against the Red Sox in 2004, a walk, a stolen base, and a ground single up the middle. But other than that, he was pretty much automatic.

He's got 34 postseason saves, tops all-time, more than double Dennis Eckersley's 15. And while regular season saves don't seem to matter much when it comes to things like Hall of Fame voting—look at Lee Smith and John Franco and Jeff Reardon—playoff saves are a whole different animal. The retired guys at the top of the list—Eckersley and Fingers—are in the Hall. And Mariano is the all-time leader by far, and a lead-pipe cinch for the Hall of Fame.

My radio partner, Mike Francesa, who is a huge Yankees fan, has argued that year in and year out for the last decade, Rivera has been the most valuable player in baseball, and I agree. But Rivera's never won an MVP Award or a Cy Young Award. So I guess he'll just have to settle for a bunch of World Series rings and a spot in the Mad Dog Hall of Fame.

DOGBITE: A CLOSER WALK WITH THEE

The job of most closers today is to come in and put down the hammer in the ninth, but Joe Torre has consistently asked Mariano Rivera to go longer than that in October. Of his 34 postseason saves, 12 have been of the two-inning variety. "A lot of times with these two-inning saves, it's usually the eighth inning that you're going through the middle of the batting order," says Torre. What's even more amazing is that Rivera only has 21 career two-inning saves, and more than half of them have come in the playoffs.

---

9. Ty Goes to the Runner

Cobb played hardball during the dead-ball era.

There are people—smart baseball fans—who would argue that Ty Cobb is the greatest baseball player of all-time. And there are a lot of good reasons for that. He had a .366 average, the highest all-time. He held the career hits record until Pete Rose held on long enough to break it. He held the record for stolen bases and runs scored for 60, 70 years before Lou Brock and Rickey Henderson broke them.

I can respect that reasoning, but I can't put him any higher than ninth, and here's why. Cobb was a product of the dead-ball era. His accomplishments belong to another era of baseball, where it was all about little ball, playing for that one run. Baseball was simply a different game in Cobb's day.

When Babe Ruth ushered in the era of the long ball in the early 1920s,

Cobb wasn't able to make the transition, although he was in his thirties. There's this story that he got sick of hearing about Ruth and his home runs and on a day in May 1925 against the Browns, he slid his hands down to the knob of the bat and he hit three homers in a game. And the next day he hit two more. That's all well and good, but the bottom line is that he never hit more than 12 home runs in a season.

There was this stubbornness in Cobb that didn't serve him well. In the 1950s, a writer was interviewing him and asked, "So what would you hit if you were playing today?"

"Oh, .300, maybe .310?"

"But you hit over .400 three times."

"Well, you have to remember that I'm 72 years old."

As far as Cobb's legacy beyond baseball, it isn't pretty. Ty Cobb was larger than life in the way that Joseph Stalin was larger than life. He would sit on the top step of the dugout and sharpen his spikes in full view of the other team. He would slide into second base with his spikes high, looking to bloody you up if you tried to turn the double play. And that was hardly the worst of it. He was a notorious bigot. There was some evidence that he threw a game in the 1920s, although he was never found guilty by baseball or in a court of law. I'm not going to consider that stuff too much, but you certainly can't give him extra credit for being a cantankerous SOB who was hated by everyone in baseball. Here's an example. In 1910, Cobb was fighting Napoleon Lajoie for the batting title—and a new car that would come with it. Lajoie was playing in St. Louis in a doubleheader, and in his first at-bat the out-

TY COBB

- Highest career batting average in history (.366), second all-time in runs scored (2,246) and hits (4,186)
- Won the 1911 AL MVP Award—the first one ever; won the Triple Crown in 1909, with a league-leading nine homers; reached three straight World Series (1907–09) but never won a title, as a player or a manager
- Won 12 batting titles, including nine in a row, and hit .300 or better for 23 straight seasons
- In 1936, 98 percent of voters made Cobb the first inductee of baseball's Hall of Fame.

fielder "lost the ball in the sun." Then a clean single. And from there on in the St. Louis manager Jack O'Connor told his third baseman to play deep. Lajoie got six straight bunt singles—8 for 9 on the day—but somehow Cobb still edged him by a hundredth of a point.

As unpopular as Barry Bonds is, can you see another team throwing batting practice fastballs to Albert Pujols just so he could pass him in the home run race?

The other guy you would consider from this era is Honus Wagner, and he was pretty much the opposite of Cobb in every way. National League/American League. Shortstop/Centerfielder. And while Wagner was an admirable guy who was liked by pretty much everybody, Cobb was pretty much public enemy number one. But judging from the numbers, I'd have to say that I think Cobb was a better player than Wagner. Wagner was a .327 hitter. Cobb was a .366 hitter. He wasn't likeable, but Ty Cobb sure could play baseball.

DOGBITE: NOT FAN FRIENDLY

How bad a guy was Cobb? In 1912, in New York, a fan named Claude Lueker began heckling Cobb. Cobb snapped, ran into the stands, and began beating the fan, who was handicapped after losing one hand and half of the other in a printing-press accident. The other people in the stands shouted at Cobb to stop. "He has no hands!" they shouted. "I don't care if he has no feet!" Cobb shouted back as he started kicking him in the head after he fell over.

---

8. Teddy Ballgame

Who was the game's greatest pure hitter? Try Ted Williams.

Ask my father, who goes back to 1940 but is still sharp as a tack, who was the greatest hitter he ever saw. He's going to say Ted Williams. And keep in mind that he is a Yankee fan, who idolized Joe DiMaggio. But the best hitter Tony Russo ever saw was Teddy Ballgame.

We all know about .406. A truly amazing accomplishment. But hitting for a high average was just the tip of the iceberg with Williams. He hit for power. He walked like crazy. The stats guys talk about on-base percentage. Well, Ted Williams is the career leader. There were five seasons when he had an on-base percentage of .500 or over—which means he got on base as often as he made an out.

But take a look at his career stats and then remember that he missed a good five years to the service. He missed 1943, '44, and '45, which were prime years for him, and most of '52 and '53. I think it's one thing when you miss time because you're injured, but it's another thing when you're off fighting a war. So let's do the math. Williams hit 521 home runs. If you give him 30 homers a year—and that's pretty conservative—that puts him at 671, which would have been behind only Ruth when he retired, and Aaron, and Bonds now. If you give him 170 hits for each year that he missed, and add them to the 2,654 he already had, he's at 3,504 and that puts him sixth all time, just behind Tris Speaker.

Ted Williams was born to hit. In 1969, when he's the manager of the Washington Senators (and at this point he was probably 50 or 51 years old), some fan eggs him on at Fenway Park during batting practice. "Hey Ted, let me see you hit now!" He got annoyed, said what the heck, grabbed a bat, went into the cage, and for the next ten minutes hit line drives all over Fenway Park—and he was in his fifties.

The other thing that helps you on this list is a connection with a legendary team. There aren't any Florida Marlins in

---

TED WILLIAMS

- MVP in 1946 and 1949. In 1942 and 1947 Williams won the Triple Crown.
- An 18-time All-Star and six-time batting champion, Williams hit .344 with 521 home runs.
- Williams walked more than 20 percent of the time— the highest percentage in history. His .482 career on-base percentage is the all-time best.
- From July 14, 1940, through September 26, 1950, Williams never had two consecutive games without reaching base safely (not counting pinch-hitting appearances). Only seven times in his career did he fail to reach base safely for two games running.

the Mad Dog Hall of Fame. Aside from the Yankees, the Boston Red Sox have as much lore as any team in baseball, and when it comes to Red Sox baseball, Ted Williams is the guy, bar none. The three things you think about with the Red Sox are the Curse of the Bambino, the breaking of the curse in 2004, and Ted Williams.

Williams also had a remarkable career that spanned a good portion of the golden age of baseball. He was starting his career as Lou Gehrig was ending his, and by the time he retired, Sandy Koufax was pitching. Now, that's serious longevity.

There are a couple of knocks on Williams. First off, just like Cobb, he never won a World Series. It's not as big a knock in baseball as it is in, say, basketball, but it is an issue. More to the point, he was just lousy in the one World Series he did play in, although he had a bad elbow. He hit .200, didn't have an extra-base hit, and he went oh for four in Game 7, which the Red Sox lost 4-3. In the eighth, they rallied to tie the game on Dom DiMaggio's double, and Williams popped up to second against Harry Brecheen in relief, and that was as close as the Red Sox got to winning the World Series until 2004. Williams couldn't hit Brecheen that whole series.

And that goes to the larger issues about Ted Williams. He wasn't interested in playing the outfield, he wasn't a great baserunner. Williams was a great hitter, but he wasn't a great player. And sometimes he was so uncompromising in his approach to hitting that when the Red Sox were down a run in the ninth inning, he wouldn't swing at a pitch that was three inches

---

DOGBITE: GETTING ON . . . AND ON AND ON

Who is Hall Griggs? If you're a Ted Williams fan you know the name. The Washington Senators pitcher once lost 18 straight minor league games, but he's also the man who got The Splendid Splinter to ground out on September 24, 1957. That out halted one of the most amazing streaks in baseball—Williams had reached base safely in 16 straight plate appearances. Ticked off that the streak was broken, Teddy Ballgame smacked the game-winning home run later that afternoon. And it wasn't like they were pitching around him—at one point during the streak he hit homers in four consecutive at-bats.

outside, even when his team needed a homer to win. There's a famous story about the time that he won a game with a ninth inning homer, but he was grumbling to himself as he's circling the bases because he swung at ball four. Williams was a great hitter, maybe the greatest. The thing that pushes him down the list is that he was content with stopping there.

7. St. Matty Day

The virtuous Mathewson helped to make baseball respectable.

There was a time when baseball wasn't America's national pastime. In the early part of the century it was a rough-and-tumble game played by hard-drinking tough guys, thugs really. There were gamblers hanging around. People in polite society looked at the game a little bit the way we look at pro wrestling today.

And then came Christy Mathewson. He was a gentleman, college-educated, the pride of Bucknell. He sang for the glee club, for gosh sakes. He was clean cut, articulate, and handsome. When he came to major league baseball, he became a role model, the kind of All-American guy that every parent wants his kid to grow up to be. He wrote books for kids, and the kids ate them up. And all of that gave the sport a kind of instant credibility. It's not much of an overstatement to say that he was baseball's first real star.

Mathewson and his manager, John McGraw, were kind of an odd couple. While Mathewson was refined, McGraw

CHRISTY MATHEWSON

- Pitched three shutouts in six days against the Athletics to lead the Giants to a World Series title in 1905
- His 373 wins tie him for third best in history.
- Mathewson led the league in ERA and strikeouts five times, and in wins and shutouts four times.
- Christy Mathewson was an accomplished checkers player, once beating world champion checkers player Newell Banks.

was as tough as they come, and yet McGraw realized that beneath that ve-neer of refinement, Matty was a tough son of a gun. He and his wife kind of adopted Mathewson like a son, insisting that he share their apartment. The manager actually had two sets of rules for the team, one for Matty and one for everyone else. For example, he didn't ask Mathewson to pitch on Sundays because he was a religious guy. But when Matty did get caught stepping out of line, McGraw fined Mathewson twice as much be-cause "he should have known better."

He was also a heckuva pitcher. Now, it's true that Cy Young has more wins, but you have to remember that old Denton True Young pitched a good bit of his career in the nineteenth century, when guys would throw 450 innings a year. But aside from that, Mathewson was a far better pitcher than Young. He has a .665 winning percentage; he led the league in ERA five times, while Young did it only once. Mathewson won 30 games four times, and in 1907 he went 37-11. And 373 career wins is nothing to sneeze at.

The other knock on Mathewson is that while the Giants won a bunch of pennants while he was there, they only won one World Series. In their first World Series, in 1905, he was amazing, pitching three shutouts in six days. From there on he didn't pitch badly in the World Series—look at his 1.15 ERA, four shutouts, and ten complete games—but his record was only 5-5.

A good part of Matty's legacy was created after he retired. He served in World War I and was involved in a training accident where he got exposed to mustard gas, which scarred his lungs and probably contributed to his premature death from tuberculosis in 1925. And in the 1919 World Se-ries, *The New York Times* assigned him to watch the games. As the Reds beat the White Sox, he sensed that something was amiss, and he was one of the first ones to say anything about it. And because of his unsullied rep-utation, people took him seriously, and they ultimately uncovered the conspiracy to throw the World Series. He played a big part in a crucial mo-ment. That's another reason why he's in the Mad Dog Hall of Fame.

CLOSE, BUT . . .

A lot of people are going to wonder why we have Walter Johnson and Christy Mathewson and Sandy Koufax in our Top Ten in baseball but not

Roger Clemens. Clemens is an interesting figure, a guy who's pitching incredibly well at 43, 44 years of age, a freak physically. Here's why I don't include Clemens. Number one, over a five-year period in the heart of his career with the Red Sox, Roger Clemens was 40-39. If you go through any of the pitchers that we have here in our Top Ten—Mathewson, Johnson, Koufax, and Rivera—you will not find that kind of a mid-career slump. And this wasn't like Tom Seaver, who went 11-11 one year but with a 3.20 ERA. The other thing that bothers you about Clemens is that he's been spotty in the post-season. Look at Game 3 of the 1999 ALCS against the Red Sox. Or Game 4 of the 2000 Division Series against the A's, or Game 7 of the 2003 ALCS against the Red Sox, or Game 7 NLCS against the Cardinals, or Game 2 of the 2005 World Series against the White Sox. All huge games at the time, and Clemens was lousy. Koufax, Mathewson, Walter Johnson, they win those games. A guy who's been as great as Clemens has been, you'd expect him to be a stopper, a give-me-the-ball guy. With Clemens it was always "Can't pitch him in Shea. You can't pitch him in Boston." And you never really knew if he was going to throw a one-hitter, or give up five runs in two innings. That's not what I expect from one of the Top-Ten baseball players of all time.

6. Train Man

Walter Johnson was baseball's first power pitcher

There's something that you've got to like about a power pitcher. There are plenty of guys who'll win games by nibbling at the corners, changing speeds, throwing a curveball or a screwball that breaks like crazy. But there's something about a guy who just says, Hey, you want to hit it? Here it is. And then rears back and throws it past the hitter anyway.

And that's Walter Johnson, who pitched for the Washington Senators between 1920 and 1927, in a nutshell. A pure power pitcher. He'd go out there and challenge you with his best stuff. The Big Train didn't throw at guys. It wasn't like you'd hit a bloop single and he'd put one in your ear. These were the days before batting helmets, so he was probably afraid he'd kill somebody. Ty Cobb picked up on this, so he crowded the plate and just slapped pitches on the outside corner. Johnson was a little bit like Tom Seaver, great power pitcher, a real presence on the mound, playing for a lousy team. The old saying about Washington in those days was "First in war, first in peace, last in the American League."

Now, why do I put Walter Johnson ahead of Mathewson? They were both important figures in their own way. Mathewson changed the way the game was perceived. Johnson changed the way the game was played. He was really the first strikeout pitcher, the first guy who was more about throwing smoke

---

WALTER JOHNSON

- Won 417 games, second most in history behind Cy Young
- Led American League pitchers in strikeouts 12 times and the majors seven times
- In 1916 Johnson posted a 1.89 ERA, but still lost 20 games.
- On September 30, 1927, Johnson made his final major league appearance as a pinch hitter. In the same game, Babe Ruth hit his then-record 60th home run of the season.

than fooling the hitter with a spitball or some kind of trick pitch. The Big Train played most of his career in the dead-ball era. He had only one big year after 1920, and that was in 1924, when he won 23. But that was a timing thing—he was 33 years old when the live-ball era started. He pitched in a style that would have been very effective in modern baseball. In short, you know that if you had a time machine and you could transport Walter Johnson to Yankee Stadium in 2006, he'd be making guys swing and miss.

The bigger reason is this. If you look at the balance of his career, Johnson is the best pitcher of all time. There are a bunch of pitchers in the Hall of Fame with less than 200 wins. Johnson had 417. There are a lot of pitchers who'll brag about winning 110 games. Walter Johnson had 110 shutouts. These days, 20 wins can win you a Cy Young Award. Walter Johnson won 20 or more 10 years in a row in the days before the Cy Young Award.

Here's one more interesting thing about Johnson. While we think of Mathewson as having a lot of success with the Giants, and Johnson as being a guy who just bumbled along in obscurity with a bad team, the bottom line is that each of them won one championship, with Matty's coming at the beginning of his career and Johnson's at the very end. Johnson had a second chance in 1925 against Pittsburgh. He started Game 7 and couldn't hold a 4-0 lead. He gave up 15 hits and nine runs in eight innings. Not good. So Walter Johnson is an unusual combination. He's a guy who enjoyed tremendous success in his day. On the other hand, he was very much ahead of his time, a harbinger of things to come. That is why we'll induct Walter Johnson into the Mad Dog Hall of Fame.

DOGBITE: A ONE-RUN GAMER

Talk about playing for one run. That was pretty much the story of Walter Johnson's life. In his career, Johnson lost a record 27 games by a score of 1-0 and suffered a record 65 shutout losses, 10 in 1919 alone. On the other hand, he won 38 games by a score of 1-0, including a 20-inning complete game in which he walked just one batter, and owns the major league record with an astonishing 110 shutouts.

---

5. The Mick of Time

At his best, Mantle was a huge star—and an awesome hitter.

Let me say it right here. Mickey Mantle isn't in the Top-Ten baseball players of all time based on the stat sheet. If you're talking about pure ability, pure production, there are guys you'd have to put ahead of him, guys like Stan Musial, Lou Gehrig, and Honus Wagner to name a few. But the Mad Dog Hall of Fame isn't just about numbers. It's about impact, and Mickey Mantle was baseball's first television star. In the 1950s, every time you watched the World Series, Mickey Mantle was in it.

He had a star quality to him. Big. Good looking. Blonde. And tremendous power. You didn't go to the refrigerator for a beer when Mickey Mantle was at the plate. You'd be afraid you were going to miss something. Other guys hit home runs, Mickey Mantle hit tape-measure home runs. Remember the 565-foot bomb he hit at Griffith Stadium? Or the ball off the façade in Yankee Stadium? He'd hit them left-handed. He'd hit them right-handed. Mantle was the perfect link in the chain of the Yankee dynasty, taking over for Joe DiMaggio. But where DiMaggio was the king, royalty in the outfield, Mantle was a little bit more of an everyman. Even when he was the best player in baseball, there was still a lot of aw-shucks in him.

Mantle was the ultimate peak player. At his very best in his Triple Crown year of 1956, he was as good as any player in the second half of the century. He hit .353 with 52 homers and 130 RBI. He

---

MICKEY MANTLE

- A sixteen-time All-Star and three-time MVP (1956, 1957, 1962) Mantle led the Yankees to 12 pennants and seven World Series championships.
- Won the Triple Crown in 1956, leading the American League in home runs (52), runs batted in (130), and batting average (.353)
- Established World Series records for most runs (42), home runs (18), runs batted in (40), and total bases (123)

---

didn't just lead the AL, he led the majors. And in 1961, you'll remember, Roger Maris hit 61 homers and didn't draw one intentional walk, because he had Mickey Mantle batting behind him. But that peak ended too quickly, and when he was playing out the string, he was bad, a .250 hitter with 20 home runs.

There was a human element to Mantle, too. He'd get mad when he struck out, and throw his helmet down. And he struck out a tremendous amount—1,710 times. But in a strange way, swinging and missing was part of his legacy. He'd go out with Whitey Ford and Billy Martin to the Copacabana and have one too many. Maybe they'd get into a fight. Maybe the Mick would straggle in at dawn, and try to play a day game hung over and bleary eyed. Mantle's father died young, and he figured that he would, too, so he burned the candle at both ends. At the end of his career, he was kind of a shadow of his former self, hobbling around the bases. As great as he was, there was always a little bit of a "what if?" element with Mantle. What if he had taken a little better care of himself?

Mantle also had a sense of humor, and that's something you like about him. Barry Halper, the great memorabilia collector, went to visit Mantle in the hospital when he was sick, and joked that he wanted to buy Mantle's liver. So when the doctor comes in to give him a prostate exam, Mantle asks him for the rubber gloves and he sends them along to Barry. "Here's your memento." You can't imagine Joe D doing that.

And, of course, Mantle had tremendous success. Twelve pennants, seven World Series rings. Eighteen home runs in October. Any old-time New York baseball fan will remind you that when the Yankees lost to the Dodgers in '55, Mantle didn't play the outfield in any of the last three games and got only one at-bat as a pinch hitter. That tells you something. Maybe Johnny Podres doesn't happen if Mantle plays Game 7.

At the end of his last season, Mantle needs a couple more homers to catch Jimmie Foxx for what was then second on the career home run list. They're playing Detroit, Denny McLain signals to him, "Where do you want it Mick?" And then he throws him a batting practice fastball. Mantle goes yard on it, but he's ticked off, too, and he desperately wants to hit another homer—which he did—so that his great career doesn't end this way. That's a great story because you can't decide if it's funny, or if it's sad, or if it tugs at your heartstrings a little. The truth is that it's all three, and that's what makes Mickey Mantle deserving of a spot in the Mad Dog Hall of Fame.

DOGBITE: A PIECE OF THE MICK

I'm not a huge memorabilia guy, but two of my favorite stories involve Mantle. Marty Appel, long-time Yankees PR director, told me this story about his first season with the team when he was 19. At the beginning of the year, he asked one of the bat boys, Elliot Ashley, to get him a cracked bat as a souvenir. He says sure. Months go by. No bat. Late September he asks again. And the last weekend of the season the Yanks are in Fenway. No juice. Both teams are lousy. In the first inning, Mantle's up, and he pops out to Rico Petrocelli and breaks his bat. The bat boy picks it up, and puts it aside for Appel. But Mantle took himself out of that game, he packed up, went back to New York and didn't play again that season. In March of 1969, he retired. So that broken bat was the last one that Mickey Mantle ever used. Twenty years later, Marty sells that cracked bat to memorabilia maven Barry Halper. The price? $15,000.

Here's another one. In the summer of 1970, Mantle goes to work with NBC *Game of the Week*. Halfway through the season, Mantle just packs up and asks to join the Yankees as a coach. It's Mickey Mantle, so what can they say? They put him in as first-base coach, and you've got this weird situation where Mickey and Elston Howard are splitting the time at first; Ellie's the first-base coach the first three innings and the last three innings and Mantle gets the middle three. At the end of the year, Marty asks clubhouse man Pete Sheehy for Mantle's jersey. Twenty years later, he brings the jersey to Leyland and the guy at Leyland notices some stitching on the back and determines that this jersey—the last one Mantle ever wore in a game—was also Thurman Munson's number 15 jersey he wore as a rookie the year before. That's how the Yankees did things in the days before Steinbrenner—they issued Mickey Mantle a used jersey. Leyland wants it and Marty sells it for $20,000.

CLOSE, BUT . . .

• **Barry Bonds:** Barry Bonds is the best player of his era. But the steroid thing, and I mean just the suggestion of it, is enough to remove him from the list. His numbers were downright Ruthian after 1999, but just regular

Hall of Famer stats before that. He's a polarizing figure, a little like Ted Williams. He's a great player, without a doubt, but he doesn't make it easy for you to like him, even if you're a Giants fan like me.

• **Hank Aaron:** Just the opposite of Bonds in a lot of ways. A tremendously classy guy, but he's not flamboyant. He doesn't have that bigger-than-life star quality about him. He hit the home run to break Ruth's record against Al Downing, that was huge. Outside of that, you know, in the middle of June in 1963, are you gonna go rush to buy a ticket to see Henry Aaron play? I don't think so. I know people whose fathers took them to Yankee Stadium to see Ted Williams hit. But not Aaron.

• **Lou Gehrig:** Gehrig's luckiest man alive speech, that is one of the top baseball moments—sports moments, really—of all time. The hushed crowd, 61,000, Samuel Goldwyn saw it and even though he knew nothing about baseball, he was so impressed that he made a movie out of it. And then there's the consecutive games streak, which Ripken broke. But on the negative side, he was overshadowed by Ruth during his career. He wasn't a personality. He was boring. And without Ruth or DiMaggio, his teams did not win. But he might be the 11th guy on this list.

4. K is for Koufax

For a brief shining moment, Koufax was the greatest pitcher ever.

Why do I put Sandy Koufax first among pitchers and fourth on this list? Because if I had one game to win, he's the guy I'd want to pitch it. Simple as that. At his best he was as good as any pitcher has ever been.

Now, I know that his peak wasn't that long. Koufax had five Hall of Fame years. That's it. He was good in '61. Then he had '62, '63, '64, '65, and '66. And then he was done. This is not a guy who had 10 or 12 Hall of Fame–type years. This is not Walter Johnson or Tom Seaver or Roger Clemens, who pitched very well for close to 20 years. And I know that

SANDY KOUFAX

- Led the Dodgers to three World Series titles with a 0.95 ERA in his four career World Series
- Three-time Cy Young Award winner (1963, 1965, 1966) and two-time World Series MVP (1963, 1965). Led the league in ERA five consecutive years. He compiled 2,396 strikeouts in 2,324 innings, including a then-record 382 strikeouts in 1965.
- Threw a perfect game against the Cubs on September 9, 1965. For four straight years, he pitched at least one no-hitter.
- At 36, he became the youngest player voted into the Hall of Fame.

Don Mattingly had five Hall of Fame years, too, and he's not in the baseball Hall of Fame, much less the Mad Dog Hall of Fame. But Don Mattingly didn't have five years that were better than Babe Ruth or Ted Williams. That's what Sandy Koufax did.

If you want to understand the greatness of Sandy Koufax, go to your Baseball Encyclopedia and look at those years. Look for the bold type, which signifies that he led the league in that category. Hits allowed. Strikeouts. ERA. Count up the bold face entries. There are 22 of them. He led the league in ERA five years running. Fewest hits allowed five times. Strikeouts four times. Shutouts three times. Wins three times. Winning percentage twice. Complete games twice. Won the Triple Crown in 1963, 1965, and 1966. Then go to Cy Young. Koufax has as many bold face stats over those few years as Young did in his whole career. You can go through the whole book and you won't find a pitcher who had five years like that. That's why you want to give the ball to Sandy Koufax in the seventh game.

To look at it another way, think about some of the best seasons any pitcher has ever had. In the last 30 years, two years that you're going to think about are Guidry at 25-3 in '78 and Gooden at 24-4 in '85. Completely dominant. Unanimous Cy Young Awards. Twenty games over .500, ERAs are under two. Tons of strikeouts. But the next year the clock struck midnight and they were back to being merely good pitchers. Koufax sustained that level of total dominance for five years.

That is the legacy of Sandy Koufax. It took Koufax a long while to find his control, to harness that great lefty stuff, that Lord Charles curve ball.

And then he came down with arthritis in his elbow. He pitched well, but he was pitching in pain, and he just decided he couldn't do it anymore. He didn't want to risk permanent injury and retired at age 31. If he had been able to pitch for ten years at his level instead of five, he'd be at least number two on this list.

The other thing you like about Koufax is that he did have a bigger-than-life aspect to him. He was a man of principle, and a real hero in the Jewish community. He wouldn't pitch in the World Series against the Twins because the game fell on Yom Kippur. It wasn't because he was that religious, but he just thought that it wasn't the right thing to do. That made him a legendary figure.

Mike, my radio partner, tells this story all the time, about how automatic Koufax was. He remembers that if you were at a ballgame in the early 1960s and saw that number 32 was pitching for the Dodgers, you looked up at the scoreboard and just expected zeros. If the team that he was pitching against got two runs in the second inning you couldn't believe it. Wow! They got two off Koufax. Look at that! You were shocked. It was news. Koufax has an aura about him that nobody else really has in the history of baseball. As Willie Stargell said, "Trying to hit like Sandy Koufax was like trying to drink coffee with a fork."

Then go look at his performances in the big spots, like the World Series. You could look at his 4-3 record and wonder. But then look at his ERA. 0.95. And then look at the games he lost. In 1959 he went seven innings, gave up one earned run, lost the game 1-0. In 1965 against the Twins, in what might be his worst World Series start, he struck out nine in six innings and left trailing 2-1, with only one of those runs earned. In 1966, again, one earned run in six innings and got tagged with the loss when Willie Davis made three errors and Jim Palmer pitched a shutout.

Koufax never gave up more than two earned runs in a postseason start. And for those of you who don't remember what he did against Minnesota at the end of the 1965 World Series, I will give you the composite line. Eighteen innings, no earned runs, seven hits, four walks, 20 strikeouts. Two consecutive shutouts. The second on two days rest. That is certainly the greatest postseason pitching performance of modern times.

Here's one of my favorite Koufax stories from that great Jane Leavy biography. In '66, the Dodgers, Giants, and Pirates are in a great pennant race. LA is in Philadelphia the last weekend of the season and the Giants are playing the Pirates. The Dodgers were struggling a little—they had a lead and lost it. The Dodgers end the season in Philadelphia. The Giants did a good job against the Pirates and knocked them out. The Dodgers are rained out in Philly on Saturday, so they had to play a double-header on Sunday. And on two days rest, Koufax goes out there and takes the ball against Jim Bunning. This is his last year, his last regular season, so his elbow is killing him. Nobody knows about it, but he's hurting. Koufax did an amazing job of gutting the game out. After the game, Doug Harvey, one the great umpires in the history of the sport, told Koufax privately, "Sandy, it was an absolute privilege to umpire your game today." That's Sandy Koufax—it was an absolute privilege to watch him pitch.

DOGBITE: THREE-FINGER KOUFAX?

We all know about Sandy Koufax's elbow problems, but what about his finger? In 1962, Koufax was in danger of losing more than a few games—he could very well have lost his finger. The 26-year-old pitcher had injured his left hand while batting against San Francisco. He continued to pitch with the injury and somehow managed the first of his four no-hitters. A lack of circulation in the artery of his palm turned the finger purple and gangrene set in. The diagnosis was Raynaud's phenomenon. If the condition worsened, Koufax was looking at the end of his promising career. "The doctor didn't tell me until after the crisis had passed," Koufax relayed later that season. "He told me if the clot hadn't been dissolved, it might have been necessary to have the finger amputated."

3. Where Have You Gone, Joe DiMaggio?

The Yankee Clipper was the epitome of class . . . and winning.

What do you need to know about Joe DiMaggio? He played 13 years, and he played in 10 World Series. And won nine of them. In that way, he's kind of baseball's answer to Bill Russell, basketball's ultimate winner.

But he had even more going for him than Russell. He was an amazing hitter. We all know about 56 games. But try this on for size. He hit 361 home runs and only struck out 369 times. Think about that. Most of today's sluggers will strike out that much in three years, or even two and some change. And he hit those home runs despite playing in Yankee Stadium when the left- and left-center-field dimensions were absolutely cavernous.

And to a lot of big fans, he's the ultimate Yankee. He didn't have the power of Ruth or Mantle, but he played with such panache, such grace. He was the consummate hitter. He's a career .325 hitter with power. And I don't even really need to say it, but his 56-game hitting streak is one of the singular feats in the history of baseball.

DiMaggio's really the most important link in that chain of great Yankees that stretches from Ruth to Mantle. Remember that the Yankees had a letdown at the end of Ruth's career, from 1933 to 1935. Gehrig couldn't carry the team alone. And in comes DiMaggio. All of a sudden here's this guy from San Francisco, and they put him out in left field. Now Gehrig's got someone else to lean on, and in DiMaggio's first four years, they win four World Series. The 1936

> **JOE DIMAGGIO**
>
> - Led the Yankees to 10 World Series, winning nine of them
> - The 13-time All-Star won three MVP awards (1939, 1941, and 1947).
> - Won the batting championship in 1939 and 1940 and the home run championship in 1937 and 1948

Yankees still had a strong connection to the Babe Ruth teams of the roaring twenties, with Gehrig and Lazzeri and Bill Dickey. By 1951 a lot of the guys would go on to play until the early 1960s—Mantle, Berra, and Ford, most notably. And you even had Billy Martin, who would be a connection to the next great Yankee team of the late 1970s.

There are things about Joe D that you don't like. He was aloof with his teammates, although he did take a liking to Billy Martin, who became Little Dago to his Big Dago. It drove you crazy that he screwed up Mantle in the 1951 World Series. He went after that fly ball, and Mantle had to put on the brakes and hurt his leg because Joe D refused to be embarrassed. The great Joe D wasn't going to be called off by some rookie right fielder.

Still, there's no doubt that DiMaggio was a larger-than-life figure. He played at a time when you could still do that, when fans got most of their news from the newspaper, and the beat writers still made the players out to be heroes. If you saw Joe DiMaggio play, it was either in person, or on a newsreel. Television wasn't a factor. Tony Russo, that man again, and his father used to go to Yankee Stadium to see Joe D play. It's easy to forget it now, but he meant so much to Italian-Americans then.

Joe DiMaggio also married Marilyn Monroe. It wasn't a great marriage, but it was a great story, two huge stars like that. And after she died, he sent fresh roses to be placed on her grave twice a week for 20 years and only stopped when people started stealing them.

When Paul Simon wanted to sum up the way America had changed in a couple of lines, here's what he wrote: "Where have you gone, Joe DiMaggio, a nation turns its lonely eyes to you." Said the hero of Hem-

---

DOGBITE: A STREAK ENDS, A STREAK BEGINS

We all know about Joe DiMaggio's 56-game hitting streak in 1941. Did you know what he did after a couple of great plays by Cleveland third baseman Ken Keltner—a diving backhanded stab in the first, another lunging backhanded pickup in the seventh—ended the streak? He started another one. He started a 17-game hitting streak the very next day. Think about that. In the history of the Milwaukee Brewers, they've had only three players who had a streak of 20 games or more. DiMaggio got a hit in 73 out of 74 games that summer. Amazing.

ingway's *The Old Man and the Sea,* "I think the great DiMaggio would be proud of me today." That is what you call transcending the game, and that's why the great Yankee Clipper makes the Mad Dog Hall of Fame. On and off the field he was a star. No, he was more than that. He was a legend.

2. The Five-Tool Player

In the field, at the plate, and on the base paths,
Willie Mays was the most complete player in history.

Baseball scouts have five tools when they judge a prospect: Hit for average, hit for power, run, catch, and throw. If you want to rate a guy on a scale of one to ten in each of those categories, with ten being as good as anyone ever, there's only one player in baseball history who would get nines or better all the way across. That's Willie Mays. Let's take him category by category and see how he stacks up.

Baserunning. He's a ten. He wasn't the base stealer that guys like Ty Cobb, Rickey Henderson, and Lou Brock were. But that was really a function of the era in which he played. If Mays had the green light the whole season the way that Rickey Henderson did in the 1980s, I don't think there's any doubt he could have stolen 100 or more bases. And he was a smart baserunner. I've had old-timers tell me about the time when he was on third base in the ninth inning of a game, and he intentionally got caught in a rundown, knowing that with the element of surprise he could beat the ball to the plate, elude the tag, and score the winning run. You've got to give him a ten as a baserunner.

Catching the ball. He's right in the center of any argument about the greatest center fielders of all time. Some guys will lean toward DiMaggio, others will bring up Tris Speaker or Richie Ashburn. But here's the bottom line: Mays hit 660 home runs, and the thing he's best remembered for is The Catch against Vic Wertz in the 1954 World Series. It's the single most memorable defensive play in the history of baseball. And it was on the biggest stage of all. When they ask Mays about it now, he says, "I don't rank 'em, I just catch 'em." What he was really trying to say is that he was kind of sick of telling people that he made other catches every bit as good, and having them argue with him. Another ten.

Throwing. Every real baseball aficionado knows that the best part of The Catch was The Throw. He didn't just stand there admiring the ball. Mays spun around 180 degrees like a shotputter and hurled the ball back to the infield. Now, there may be a couple of right fielders—Roberto Clemente, Vladimir Guerrero—who had arms that were maybe a little stronger than Willie's. But when you roll it all into one—quick release, strength, and accuracy—and add in the fact that he was making tough throws from center, I think you've got to give Willie another ten here.

Hitting for power. Just look at the all-time home run list. You've got Aaron, who hit more homers than Willie, but never hit as many in a single season. You've got Barry Bonds, and you've got to take the steroid factor into account. And you've got Ruth. Ruth was a better power hitter, but the gap's not as big as you might think. They were hitting a lot more home runs back in the early 1930s than they were in the 1960s. And while Ruth had that friendly short porch in right field in Yankee Stadium, Willie played in Candlestick Park, which was windy and cold and big, and a really tough place to hit a ball out of. I think that Willie merits at least a 9.5, and if you gave him a 10, I couldn't really argue.

Hitting for average. What's the career benchmark of a great high-average hitter? Getting 3,000 hits. Well, Willie ended up with 3,283, which is more than Wade Boggs and Tony Gwynn and Rod Carew. And he ended up with a .302 career average. And remember, he played a big portion of his career in the 1960s, when guys could win a batting title by hitting .315. No, he's not a Tony Gwynn, much less Joe DiMaggio or Ty Cobb, but he's in the top 25 of all time. I've got to give him a nine in this category.

All of this made Willie a great player. But it was his style that made him an enduring figure. He had an enthusiasm for the game that was infectious, his hat flying off when he made a diving catch, playing stickball with the kids in the street on his off day. He became a star on both coasts. Probably the biggest negative is the fact that Willie only won that one championship. You'd like to see more than one ring. And in 71 World Series at-bats, not a single home run, and only one homer in 18 NLCS at-bats. But when you want to sum up Willie Mays in one sentence, here's the bottom line. He was more fun to watch than any player in history. That's why he's number two in the Mad Dog Hall of Fame.

DOGBITE: SIMPLY A THROW BACK

The Catch is Willie Mays' most famous play, but it might not even be his best. How about this play during the famous '51 NL pennant race? On August 15 at the Polo Grounds, the Giants were still more than ten games out of first, and were locked in a pitcher's duel with the Dodgers. The score was tied 1-1 going into the eighth. Carl Furillo hit a fly ball deep to right-center. Billy Cox, representing the go-ahead run, tagged up at third, thinking he would have to beat right-fielder Don Mueller's average arm. Mays came racing over from center, caught the 330-foot drive, wheeled around, and uncorked a perfect throw to catcher Wes Westrum. Writer Roger Angell describes it this way: "Willie spins completely around and lets loose the peg before he can see home plate." Cox never even saw the throw and was shocked to see Westrum just waiting there with the ball. Westrum would hit the game-winning homer in the bottom of the inning. After the 3-1 loss, Brooklyn manager Charlie Dressen shook his head and said, "Let's see him do it again." If Mays doesn't make that catch and that perfect throw, maybe Thomson never hits The Shot Heard Round the World.

1. We Got You, Babe

Babe Ruth is two Hall of Famers rolled into one larger-than-life package.

Babe Ruth is the top baseball player of all time. Okay, there, I said it. But that's really just the tip of the iceberg. It's like saying Shaquille O'Neal is tall. Ruth at number one on this list is one of the few no-brainers in this book. In my opinion, he's one of the Top Ten public figures of the twentieth century. Not sports figures. Public figures. Who else is on that list? FDR. JFK. Einstein. Freud. Martin Luther King Jr. Hemingway. Jonas Salk. Babe Ruth. I mean, who else you got? You want to put John Wayne on that list? I can live with that. But he's not bigger than Babe Ruth.

Go to a second-grade class anywhere in America today and ask the kids about Woodrow Wilson. No clue. Ask them about Samuel Goldwyn. No clue. Ask them about Henry Ford. No clue. Ask them about Franklin Roosevelt, and they'll think he was Teddy Roosevelt's brother. But they all know who Babe Ruth was. Maybe that's a commentary on today's youth, but it's the truth.

Even though he played 70, 80 years ago, Ruth's legacy is lasting. People have pretty much forgotten about Bill Tilden and Bobby Jones. But not Ruth. When a Babe Ruth uniform comes up at auction it goes for $500,000. You think FDR's pen goes for that much? David Wells is such a huge Babe Ruth fan, he goes to the mound wearing a Babe Ruth Yankee cap and the umpire tells him he has to take it off. Do you see Manny Ramirez trying to wear a Tris Speaker hat in a game? Remember the TV show *Dragnet*? Jack Webb's badge number was 714 in honor of Babe Ruth. The great sports columnist Jimmy Cannon hit it right on the head when he called Ruth's legacy "a national heirloom." The stories get handed down, from father to son, from generation to generation.

You want to talk lasting impact, how about this? Babe Ruth *saved . . . the . . . game.* In 1920 baseball was in a bad way. The Black Sox had just thrown the World Series. Ray Chapman was killed by a pitch. The game of baseball, which hadn't really established itself as the national pastime, was struggling, and Ruth was a larger-than-life character. He was making more than Herbert Hoover, and when a reporter asked him about it, he said, "I had a better year than he did." Here's another Herbert Hoover story. A little boy asked the president for three autographs. "Why three?" the president asked. He wanted to keep one and trade the other two for a Babe Ruth autograph.

And he's lived on in a way, even more in the minds of Red Sox fans than he has with Yankees fans. I'm talking about the Curse. Until 2004 you had Red Sox fans putting flowers on his grave, trying to dredge up the piano he dumped in the pond, just trying to make peace with the guy so the Red Sox wouldn't have to wait another 85 years to win a World Series. (I guess it worked, but that's another story.)

You've heard the baseball arguments. Babe Ruth hit more homers than whole teams. Well, in 1921 Ruth hit 59 home runs. Care to guess how many his old team, the Red Sox hit that year? Seventeen. He hit three times as many homers as another team, with a few left over. That's dominance. And he wasn't just a one-dimensional slugger, a guy like Mark McGwire, with a David Wells beer gut. His career average was .342. That's better than Tony Gwynn, Rod Carew, or

---

BABE RUTH

- Ruth won seven World Series, three with the Red Sox (1915–16, 1918) and four with the Yankees (1923, 1927–28, 1932), hitting .382 with 10 homers and 23 RBIs. Ruth pitched the longest complete game victory in World Series history, going 14 innings to defeat the Brooklyn Dodgers in 1916.
- In 490 at-bats as a pitcher, Ruth hit .304 with a .504 slugging percentage. He scored 75 runs, had 34 doubles, 11 triples, 15 home runs, and drove in 73 runs.
- Won 12 home run titles
- The last team Babe Ruth beat as a pitcher? The Boston Red Sox, on October 1, 1933
- Of players with at least 200 at-bats, Ruth has the second worst stolen base percentage in history (123-for-240, 51.3 percent, better only than Lou Gehrig (102-for-203, 50.2 percent).

Wade Boggs, not to mention DiMaggio and Stan Musial. And people forget what a phenomenal pitcher Ruth was. In 1916 he led the league with a 1.75 ERA. And Walter Johnson was pitching then. That year, he went

23-12 and came back in 1917 and went 24-13. His career winning percentage is .671. That's higher than Sandy Koufax. That's higher than Christy Mathewson. Ruth ranks sixth among retired players who pitched in the twentieth century. Go look it up. And while you're at it, have a look at the Red Sox record book. You'll see four names all over the pitching categories. Roger Clemens. Lefty Grove. Pedro Martinez. And Babe Ruth. If he had continued pitching, he would have been a lead-pipe cinch Hall of Famer. And remember this: Babe Ruth was 3-0 in the World Series for the Red Sox, with a 0.87 ERA, and the team won every postseason game that he started and every series that he played in. He set the scoreless innings streak in the World Series, which lasted for 30 years until Whitey Ford broke it.

Let's add it up. The greatest hitter of all time. An All-Star-caliber pitcher. A giant, colorful, larger-than-life player. And the guy who saved baseball in its darkest hour. What does that add up to? The greatest baseball player of all time, and number one in the Mad Dog Hall of Fame.

DOGBITE: RUTH'S 715TH HOMER

No one disputes that Hank Aaron broke Babe Ruth's career home run mark. But whether he did it on the right day is debatable.

The origins of the controversy go back to a game in 1918. With the Fenway Park scoreboard showing a score of 0-0 in the bottom of the tenth inning, Ruth hit a walk-off shot into the bleachers. But in the box score he was awarded a triple. What? At the time, the rules stipulated that when the winning run crossed the plate the game was over, and thus the hitter didn't get credit for the homer. What was known as the "sudden death" rule was abolished in 1920.

What does all this mean? In 1969 the baseball records committee decided that Ruth should be given credit for this homer and his home run total should be 715 not 714. However, the committee's decision wasn't final, and commissioner Bowie Kuhn decided the record should not be altered.

One man who's legacy is affected by the decision is knuckleballer Charlie Hough. If Ruth's total had been adjusted, he, not Al Downing, would have earned the distinction as the pitcher who gave up the record-breaking home run to Hank Aaron in 1974.